The Race to Save
the World's Rarest Bird

The Discovery and Death of the Po'ouli

Alvin Powell

STACKPOLE
BOOKS

0 11557 03448 6

Published by
STACKPOLE BOOKS
5067 Ritter Road
Mechanicsburg, PA 17055
www.stackpolebooks.com

Printed in the United States of America

10 9 8 7 6 5 4 3 2 1

First edition

Library of Congress Cataloging-in-Publication Data

Powell, Alvin, 1961–
    The race to save the world's rarest bird : the discovery and death of the
po'ouli / by Alvin Powell. — 1st ed.
        p. cm.
    ISBN-13: 978-0-8117-3448-6
    ISBN-10: 0-8117-3448-X
    1. Po'ouli. I. Title.

QL696.P246P69 2008
639.9'78883—dc22

                                                                2007044003

CONTENTS

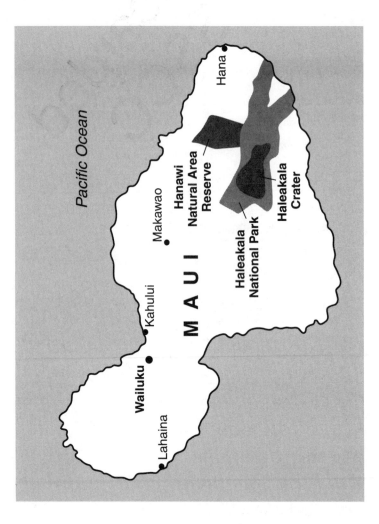

INTRODUCTION

I REMEMBER READING A SHORT ARTICLE SEVERAL YEARS AGO about the extinction of a Spanish mountain goat, the Pyrenean ibex, described in a more recent article as "one of Europe's most striking wild animals." The original story, which must have been written in 2000, told of a thirteen-year-old female named Celia that had become her species' sole survivor a year earlier upon the last male's death.

Celia died, of all the rotten luck, when a tree fell on her. Besides her unusual demise, however, it was the length of the article that caught my attention.

The piece, which I viewed online, was no more than a couple paragraphs. It was the sort you'd find buried deep in the A section of a newspaper with other not-very-important international news, or as filler somewhere even deeper in the paper.

There's something wrong with this, I thought. A species' extinction marks the end of an era in the earth's history. Celia's death marked the end of the millions of years of evolution it took to create her kind. It marked the end of millions more years during which her kind had interacted with the creatures and plants surrounding it. With a single tree fall, those years are over. Surely we humans must acknowledge the passing with something more than just a couple paragraphs.

Over the years since, I've seen other, similar articles, some longer, some not. Having worked in the news business, I realize that news is almost entirely relative. On a busy news day, stories that might otherwise lead the paper get bumped down and then off the front page.

But it seems to me that as the planet's dominant species, and the one responsible for many of the extinctions taking place today, we ought to at least make sure people know that we snuffed another one out. If we can't save them, it's the least we can do.

I became acquainted with the po'ouli's story several years ago, while taking a class on rainforest conservation and ecology. I was looking for a paper topic and chanced upon a short news article on the bird's plight during the 2002 translocation. I was struck by the poignancy of the situation: the last three individuals held the key to the species' survival, but they sat in separate home ranges, unwilling to stray far enough that they would meet.

I wrote a paper on the bird for that class and, along the way, became introduced to the extraordinarily difficult conservation situation throughout the Hawaiian Islands. The islands are home to an exquisite suite of species that evolved in long isolation and are found no place else. But through large swaths of the islands, they've been almost entirely replaced by invaders brought by humans.

Over the years, I kept an eye on the po'ouli's story, and when I found a similarly short article that the last known bird had died, I decided to do something about it. Perhaps for my readers, the po'ouli's story will serve as it did for me—as a doorway into the lives of these birds, the lives of those who cared about them, and the conservation challenges still facing Hawaii and, more generally, the rest of the world.

As Hawaiian names can be unfamiliar to some readers, here's a quick pronunciation guide to a handful that appear repeatedly in the book. The bird's name is pronounced "poh-oh-OO-lee." The bird's home forest, in the state's Hanawi Natural Area Reserve, is pronounced "hah-nah-VEE." Similarly, the i'iwi, a striking black and red honeycreeper, which thankfully is still common on the islands, is pronounced "ee-EE-vi."

There exist myriad variations on the spelling of the bird's name, some of which appear in direct quotations of others' work. I've also seen it spelled poouli, po'o uli, poo-uli, and possibly a few more ways. "Po'ouli" appears in most government and pubic documents, so I've gone with that.

It has been said before that no species should go extinct quietly. I couldn't agree more. This, then, is my effort to make some noise for the po'ouli and draw attention to the forest birds still hanging on in Hawaii's misty mountain trees.

Alvin Powell
Cambridge, Massachusetts
September 3, 2007

ACKNOWLEDGMENTS

I WOULD LIKE TO THANK THE MANY PEOPLE WHO HELPED ME TELL the bird's story. Countless people opened their hearts to me and shared their thoughts and feelings about what for some was a difficult time.

I am grateful for the help of the nearly sixty people who agreed to talk with me about this bird, but I would like to specifically thank a few: Karen Rosa, for enduring my multiple requests for documents with good humor; and Kirsty Swinnerton, Eric VanderWerf, Dave Leonard, and Tony Chen, for shepherding me around the forest. Without their help, I would surely be there still.

Thanks also to Thane Pratt, Sheila Conant, and Carter Atkinson, for providing expert advice on the manuscript; Tonnie Casey, Jim Jacobi, Alan Lieberman, and Cameron Kepler, who all went above and beyond the call in sharing their stories, enduring multiple inquiries, suggesting other sources, and digging up old field notes to ensure that I was getting it right; the staff at the American Museum of Natural History, for providing me access to their po'ouli specimen and Dean Amadon's letters; those at the Bernice P. Bishop Museum, for giving me access to the specimens there; and the staff at the San Diego Zoo, for help during my visit.

I'd specifically like to thank my wife, Jennifer, who not only picked up the load at home while I vanished to scribble down notes, write drafts, and jet off to do interviews, but also provided editing advice. I thank Terry Murphy, who made time in her life to edit even as I was furiously writing and my manuscript deadline was looming. My sister Laura Lynne Powell also deserves applause for the advice and encouragement she provided from the very beginning.

1

ELEVEN WEEKS

IT WAS AN UNLIKELY DAY TO CATCH THE WORLD'S RAREST BIRD.

September 9, 2004, dawned with typically rotten weather in Hawaii's Hanawi Natural Area Reserve. Maui's sunny beaches and clear Pacific water had built the island's reputation as a tropical paradise, but the rainforest perched on the flank of Maui's towering Haleakala volcano was a world away from the tourists below.

Always cool and sometimes downright cold, the rainforest—as it usually did—lived up to its name that morning.

Sheets of gray clouds blew uphill from the Hana coast, bringing a fine rain that hissed in undulating waves against the corrugated metal roof of the shack known as State Camp. A T-shaped building roughly twelve by twenty feet, State Camp was far from luxurious. The building's interior had been painted white but was otherwise unfinished. The crosspieces joining the bare studs acted as impromptu shelving, and from nails driven into the woodwork, all around hung the gear of daily living in the forest: pots and pans, lanterns, plastic bottles, and various containers.

The accommodations may have been basic, but State Camp, with its green exterior and shiny metal roof, was the only man-made structure for miles. After a long, wet day on the forest's narrow trails, its dry confines were a welcome sight to the biologists working there.

Surrounding the shack stood one of the last remnant native Hawaiian rainforests. Among the best preserved in the state, the forest is an environmental jewel, home to a host of rare and unique plant, insect, and bird species. Many are found nowhere outside the Hawaiian Islands, and even within the islands, they are limited to protected tracts like Hanawi.

Twisted trunks of ohia trees provide the forest's foundation. The boughs hold aloft green canopies of oblong leaves, dotted with the ohia's bright red flowers. The punk rocker of the plant world, the ohia's spiky blossoms yield a nutritious nectar that provides sustenance for a suite of forest birds.

In many places, the trees' limbs are covered with thick, brown moss, a natural sponge saturated by the frequent rains. Even after the rains, the moss's moisture drips onto the growth below. Layer after layer of luxurious leaves fill the space between the forest's canopy and its volcanic soil.

Trees and undergrowth press close on three sides of State Camp, built small to disturb the forest as little as possible. On the fourth side is a clearing. A few dozen yards long and half as wide—a mere postage stamp viewed from the sky—the tiny clearing provides just enough space to land the bush choppers that, when the weather allows, ferry people and supplies in and out.

Warm in their sleeping bags that morning were six members of the Maui Forest Bird Recovery Project field crew. A mix of seasonal help and full-time staff, they shared a passion for the natural world that had led them to one of the most difficult yet dramatic natural environments on earth. They had returned to the forest the day before after a three-day turnaround from their last trip.

Their quarry that day, as it had been so many other days in the forest, was a poʻouli. A small brown and gray forest bird sporting a black mask—a unique feature among Hawaiian birds—the poʻouli was one of just three left in existence and had already eluded them on three previous capture trips.

For several years, the poʻouli had held the title of the world's rarest bird. The last three known individuals lived nearby, all within Hanawi but in separate home ranges from which they refused to budge. After years of sometimes acrimonious debate on the best course to take with the bird, officials had finally decided to capture all three in an effort to get them to breed in captivity.

Captive breeding was their last hope to rescue the species. They had already tried everything else.

Capture efforts had begun more than a year and a half earlier, in February 2003. But time and time again, the field crews came back empty-handed. As the months ticked by, hope was turning to desperation.

No one knew how old the three remaining birds were, but it had been years since they were young. They had been banded as adults in 1997 and 1998, making them at least seven or eight. The last known poʻouli breeding was in 1995; if these birds were born earlier, this would make the youngest of them nine years old. Though it wasn't unheard of for small birds to live into their teens, it was pretty unusual.

The biologists were racing against time.

They were led by Kirsty Swinnerton, who cut her teeth as a field biologist working with rare birds on the Indian Ocean island of Mauritius for fourteen years. Swinnerton had come to Maui to work with the po'ouli. "Who wouldn't want to work with the world's rarest bird?" she later asked. She got her wish and had been thrown into efforts to catch one almost immediately.

Hearing the rain that morning, the crew was likely slow getting moving, relishing their warm, dry clothes and in no rush to get wet again. Hanawi's rain comes in various forms, and the field crew had learned to work through most of them. A fine, damp mist as the clouds roll uphill was almost always with them. A light rain, sometimes steady, sometimes off and on, was never far away. Drenching deluges were common as well, and the field crew got used to working while wet, using waterproof notebooks and encasing paper maps and the like in plastic bags. If it rained hard enough, though, the birds hunkered down and stayed silent, making them difficult to see and impossible to hear. Better then to wait for the rain to pass.

The field crew talked about plans for the day, sipping coffee or tea and hoping the weather would break. Then they packed food, maps, radios, and binoculars into their daypacks. They donned the green-and-brown-camouflaged raincoats and pants that passed for their work uniforms, smeared with mud and damp from the day before. They pulled on their calf-high rubber boots and camouflaged rain hats and headed out.

The trail to Home Range 2—the haunt of the bird they were hunting—began on the other side of the landing pad. Almost invisible, obscured by low growth, the trail was marked by plastic flags tied to tree branches along the route. They walked the first few yards through knee-high ferns and other low-growing plants, then passed single file into the silent, dripping forest.

Despite the morning's rain, there was some reason for optimism. The weather in the preceding weeks had been unusually clear, and the field crew had gotten several good glimpses of the bird they were after. They had a good idea about the likeliest places to erect the long, fine nets they would use to snare their prey.

That afternoon, the clouds broke and the sun shone through, lighting up the gray forest with a hundred shades of green and brown, punctuated by the brilliant red ohia blossoms. The moisture on the mosses and leaves glistened in the sun, giving the forest a silvery, magical appearance. Way below, the Hana coast and blue Pacific were visible through gaps in the clouds, reminding the workers that they were perched high up the steep side of an ancient volcano.

The field crew waited a bit after the clouds broke, just to be sure Hanawi wasn't toying with them, and then set to work. They unfurled the tools of their trade: light nets twenty to thirty feet long and five feet high, so sheer they were nearly invisible to birds flying through the forest. Called mist nets, they were erected on long aluminum poles in areas where the field crew thought the po'ouli might fly.

Each crew member oversaw a circuit of five nets and tended them constantly. They hiked from one to the next, checking for a struggling bird in the net's folds at each stop and ensuring that no net was unattended for more than twenty or thirty minutes.

It was the least likely net that caught the po'ouli. It was a long way from the bird's last sighting and in a spot where the sun shone through, making the net easier to see. Lisa Baril, a seasonal worker who wasn't qualified to handle an endangered bird, was tending the net. She radioed Swinnerton and John Vetter, a project veteran stationed nearby, that, after nineteen months of exhausting, soaking effort, they had a po'ouli.

Vetter set out immediately, traveling quickly to the spot where Baril waited. He untangled the po'ouli, put it in a soft cloth bag that immobilized the bird, and hastened back to the station.

Vetter and Swinnerton carefully removed the bird from the bag and examined it. The first thing they noticed was that it had only one eye. That surprised Swinnerton, because the bird had been observed repeatedly since its banding years earlier. No one had noticed the injury. Though at one time severe, it appeared to have healed well.

Swinnerton was questioned later about how such an important change in such an important bird could have gone unnoticed. She explained that biologists have to take observations in the field however they get them. Though long, sustained looks at a bird do happen, observations are sometimes the barest glimpses, at odd angles. She wrote:

When we see po'ouli in the field, we don't usually get a good head view and observations are usually in the distance and in the shadows of a tree (and usually only for a few seconds). I had a fairly close observation recently, but from underneath, so I mostly saw her legs and bottom!! Having said that, now recalling an observation I had on the trip before last, which I remember was from the right side, I remember thinking it didn't look quite right (but was intent on getting a net up to catch her rather than scrutinising her physiology). . . . I mostly noticed the lack of a glint from the eye rather than the missing eye, and then she was gone!

Swinnerton and Vetter brought the bird back to State Camp. By then it was too late to get a helicopter in, so they transferred it to a small cage outside, protected from the weather by a tent. The cage was equipped with cloth sides to prevent the bird from injuring itself should it fly about in panic and a video camera so the crew could monitor it from the shack.

The po'ouli quickly allayed fears that it would be a difficult guest. Though some wild birds are panicky and fly against the sides of their cages when captured, the po'ouli appeared calm and began eating within minutes.

The po'ouli would be going to the Maui Bird Conservation Center in Olinda the next morning. A collection of low buildings partway up Haleakala's northern slope, the center stood on a narrow, twisting road lined with towering eucalyptus trees. The road wound steeply uphill from the small town of Makawao, itself uphill from Kahului, Maui's largest city and the site of the island's airport.

The Maui Bird Conservation Center is one of two captive-breeding facilities in Hawaii run by the San Diego Zoological Society. Staff at the Maui Bird Conservation Center and the Keauhou Bird Conservation Center on the Big Island had successfully bred a variety of endangered Hawaiian birds in a collaborative program with the state and federal governments and private landowners.

The center's staff needed to know they would have a visitor the next day. Swinnerton called on the satellite phone but got the center's answering machine.

She tried a different number, ringing a small on-site apartment where a full-time staffer and the center's interns stayed.

Mary Schwartz, who had headed the facility for four years and had been waiting for more than a year and a half for a po'ouli to be caught, picked up.

"I was just totally shocked," Schwartz says. "It just took me completely by surprise. It was like, 'Oh my gosh, okay, we have to get ready. They're coming in the morning.'"

Schwartz and the Maui Bird Conservation Center's four or five staffers swung into action. Their extensive experience breeding endangered birds, they knew, was about to be tested.

"My feeling was, 'Well, now we're going to war,'" Schwartz's boss, Alan Lieberman, says. "Not with somebody, but now we're going to put all our training into action."

The center staff began prepping the aviary and a "howdy cage," a small cage used to introduce new birds. They also made sure they had the right food on hand. The po'ouli ate snails as a large part of its diet, but it also ate insects and native berries. In the coming weeks, center staff would serve twenty-five different food items to the bird, prepared in different ways. Insects, both live and partially crushed, were on the menu.

"We were ready," Lieberman says. "We were set up for quite a while. We built a special cage for it. We had snails brought in from the field. One of the first questions is how well a bird acclimates to nonwild food."

Lieberman admitted later he had hoped they wouldn't catch the bird. He recognized the bind conservation authorities were in and cared deeply about the fate of Hawaiian bird species—after all, he'd worked with eight endangered birds during his years on Hawaii. But he also believed that the prospects for success of this endeavor were poor.

Lieberman's employer, the San Diego Zoo, laid out its position two years earlier in a letter to officials at the U.S. Fish and Wildlife Service (FWS) and the Hawaii Department of Forestry and Wildlife. Though the zoo supported efforts to stop the po'ouli's extinction, they didn't think captive breeding was the best way to do it and instead supported stepped-up efforts to improve its rainforest home.

"Although we may not agree that 'hard captivity' is the best biological strategy for the recovery of this species, we recognize that there is no 'good' option for the po'ouli at this point," San Diego Zoo Executive Director Douglas Myers wrote. "We will respect the agencies' decision and agree to bring the birds into captivity."

Though they had success breeding other Hawaiian bird species, several hurdles faced the Maui Bird Conservation Center crew. First was the uniqueness of the poʻouli. It was the only known snail eater among native bird species and was so unrelated to other Hawaiian birds that it occupied its own genus on the Hawaiian honeycreeper family tree.

Second, despite three decades of fieldwork, there were still critical gaps in scientists' understanding of the bird's basic biology. Nobody knew how long poʻouli lived, how they selected their mates, or how they raised their young. In fact, poʻouli had been observed nesting only once, in the 1980s, when four eggs laid in two successive nests had yielded only one fledged bird.

More critically, there were questions about the sexes of the three remaining birds.

Tests run in 1998 on feathers extracted from the birds indicated that there were one male and two females. In 2002, birds thought to be male and female were captured again and feathers taken for sexing. This time, however, results came back as both male.

When queried about the inconsistent results, the testing company explained that the bird's rarity made it difficult to be certain, since the normal procedure is to check results against known male and female samples of that species. For the poʻouli, there were no known samples.

For all these reasons, Lieberman, Schwartz, and the Maui Bird Conservation Center crew knew they had their work cut out for them. Still, they had to get ready—one of the world's last three poʻoulis would be there in a few hours.

The next morning, Swinnerton packed up the bird, putting its carrier into a larger, noise-proof box. She glanced anxiously at the cloud cover, listening for the sound of a helicopter. The weather was already closing in when the helicopter arrived, and Swinnerton hurriedly loaded her charge onboard and climbed in herself.

They skimmed the treetops as they flew along Haleakala's flank, which rose thousands of feet to the volcano's crater on their left and dropped thousands more to the ocean on their right. Riven by numerous gullies from the constant runoff, the forest below looked like green corduroy as they flew over.

They reached clear skies, and a few minutes later, Swinnerton directed the chopper to a landing on the lawn near the Maui Forest Bird Recovery Project in Olinda, just up the road from the Maui Bird Conservation Center.

Mary Schwartz was waiting. Swinnerton handed her the carrier, and a few minutes later, Schwartz and the bird were at the center. She set the bird in the howdy cage and quickly left to watch it on video. What Schwartz saw was a small bird, about the size of a sparrow, with a light grayish brown belly and darker brown back and wings. Its head was brown except for a black mask of feathers that extended to a point behind its eyes.

The po'ouli appeared calm. It observed the world around it with a cocked head, peering out of its good eye.

It's impossible to know what the bird was thinking or feeling, but its treatment over the past twenty-four hours and dramatically different surroundings hadn't hurt its appetite. It began eating almost from the start, devouring mealworms, waxworms, and olapa berries. It made such a stir in the food pan that Lieberman said the resulting "hully-gully" made it tough to tell what it was eating and what it was just moving about.

Though the center staff was getting its first extended look at the po'ouli, the bird was no stranger. Field workers had followed its movements for years, and the fate of all three remaining birds had been the subject of lengthy discussion. Schwartz and the other members of the Maui Bird Conservation Center knew they were observing a tough, old bird in the aviary that day, a survivor on whose shoulders rested the fate of its species.

While the staff at the facility focused on the bird, Lieberman had been dealing with the administrative side of the venture. Within hours of hearing that it had been captured, he had e-mailed state and federal wildlife officials involved with the po'ouli conservation effort: Scott Fretz, Jolie Wanger, and Paul Conry at the Hawaii Department of Land and Natural Resources, and Eric VanderWerf, Gina Schultz, Marilet Zablan, Jay Nelson, and Barbara Maxfield at the U.S. FWS. He also e-mailed Christina Simmons and Ted Molter in the San Diego Zoo's public relations department to prepare them for media calls and notified staff at the Keauhou Bird Conservation Center.

Lieberman began to play defense, issuing a blanket denial of requests for press access to the center and turning down a suggestion that they get video of the bird for television distribution.

"The staff at MBCC will be harried enough, so please make all enquiries about 'howzit goin' to me," Lieberman wrote. "I really don't want the staff over there to be answering the phone all day when I would prefer they be monitoring the bird."

In a press release issued the day after the bird's capture, Lieberman characterized the job that lay ahead: "Establishing a breeding pair of po'ouli may be the most challenging task we've ever attempted. We have successfully bred several Hawaiian bird species, including the 'alala, puaiohi, and palila, and even reintroduced them into the wild, but to start off with only three birds, all of which are at least six years old, just increases the difficulties."

Several steps lay ahead in making the po'ouli a permanent member of the Maui Bird Conservation Center. Its initial howdy cage, lined with cloth to prevent injury, was intended to get it past the critical first few days in captivity as it adjusted to new sights, sounds, and surroundings. Once the bird adjusted, it would be moved to a new howdy cage without the cloth padding, and eventually to a larger aviary where it would be free to make short flights.

It had to clear quarantine first, however. The thirty-day isolation period ensured that it didn't carry diseases from the wild that could harm the center's other avian inhabitants.

The staff weighed the bird daily—weight loss is often the first sign of trouble—and fed it twice a day. They put ohia branches in its cage to give it natural cover and a chance to forage in the bark. When they noticed it wasn't visiting the water dish, they fed it insects in a shallow dish of water and misted the ohia foliage provided in the cage.

For the next several weeks, the bird did well, acting calm and eating heartily. An initial physical examination was "unremarkable," noting that the bird's weight was between twenty-five and twenty-seven grams. It completed its thirty-day quarantine period without incident. Blood was drawn for sexing on September 20, and the bird was moved to a regular wire howdy cage during the first week of October.

Despite his early fears, Lieberman acknowledged that the bird's initial transition to captivity went about as well as he could have hoped. "As far as acclimating a wild bird, it was as easy acclimating as I've ever seen."

The biggest problem, according to reports filed by center staff, was that it was tough to find the tiny native snails the bird naturally ate. That difficulty was overcome, however, because it happily ate waxworms, wild collected insects, and ohelo berries.

On October 2, Lieberman contributed a passage to the San Diego Zoo's weblog, an online diary of activities at the zoo for those interested in goings-on there. Despite the smooth initial sailing, he reminded readers, with only one bird captured, the future of the species was still far from secure. "Our hopes are for a long life for this bird, and Godspeed to the field biologists who are anxiously preparing to capture the other two poʻoulis. The future of the species depends on the dedication and expertise of all players in this conservation drama."

As October wore on, another change occurred at the center. After four years at the helm, Schwartz was leaving. Her successor, Rich Switzer, overlapped with her for a week or so, and then Switzer took over the center's direction for good.

Though he was new to the job, Switzer was not a new face. He had worked on and off for several years at the center's sister facility, the Keauhou Bird Conservation Center. There Switzer had added to his experience with small passerine birds like the poʻouli, with which he had initially worked in conservation projects on Mauritius.

Switzer's transition turned out to be rockier than that of most people starting a new job, however. By the end of the week, there were signs that something was wrong with the world's rarest bird.

While the captive poʻouli was settling in at the Maui Bird Conservation Center, Swinnerton's field team began breaking down their gear in Hanawi. Because the birds lived in separate home ranges, the equipment used to capture the first had to be moved to the next bird's range.

When that work was done, the crew came out of the forest for a break. But with one bird in captivity, the break would be short. The push was on to bring in another poʻouli so that breeding could begin. Swinnerton planned two trips for October that would keep the crew in the field for nineteen days.

They were moving full steam ahead to capture the remaining birds, but within a few weeks, they would be wondering whether they were chasing ghosts.

For months, Swinnerton had been concerned about the bird in Home Range 3. Crews had tried to catch that bird first, sighting it regularly but failing to net it. Partway into the capture effort, however, the sightings ceased, forcing the crew to shift their efforts to the po'ouli from Home Range 2, which they had eventually caught.

The capture effort being planned now was aimed at the third bird, which lived in Home Range 1. But as they prepared to leave, Swinnerton told Lieberman that the Home Range 3 bird hadn't been seen for ten months and seemed to have disappeared. She wrote Lieberman on October 1:

> We have continued to look for the male in HR-3. We lost sight of this bird in December 2003 and it has not been seen since. Since December, we have carried out three 10-day capture trips in March and April, two 10-day rat density monitoring trips and about 12 days of predator control at this site. On the most recent trip into HR-3, a team of six staff searched intensively for two days throughout and adjacent to the grid, with no sightings. The HR-2 bird (the one just caught) also disappeared previously for two years and was only re-sighted again early in 2003, so they can disappear for long periods but currently, we are unsure where this bird is.

In the coming weeks, Swinnerton also found Home Range 1 empty, prompting the crew to put down its nets and begin to search intensively for the po'ouli that had lived there.

"We had the same problem [as in HR-3]," Swinnerton says. "We set up our net lanes and we were netting, netting, netting, but not seeing that bird. It was unusual because that bird was very well known. Eventually, we gave up netting and just set out to try to find her."

For the eight or nine years since they were banded, all three birds had been reliably sighted in their home ranges. It was becoming increasingly likely that the bird at the Maui Bird Conservation Center wasn't one of three, but the very last po'ouli.

"The surprising thing about all of those three po'ouli is that you found them exactly were they were supposed to be," Swinnerton says. "Anybody who knew what they were doing, every time you went into the home range, you pretty much could find it. So the unusual thing was that we couldn't find them."

With discouraging news coming in from the field, the situation at the Maui Bird Conservation Center was taking its own turn for the worse.

By the last week in October, the po'ouli had been doing well in captivity for more than a month and a half. Center staff were eager to move the bird into larger quarters and prepped a twelve-by-four-foot aviary. Before moving the bird in, they stocked the cage with plenty of ohia branches. The branches not only mimicked the bird's natural environment, they also cut down flying room so that the bird couldn't build up a head of steam and crash into the aviary's sides.

The move had another purpose besides allowing the po'ouli to stretch its wings. With field crews searching intensively for the other po'oulis, the move also freed the quarantine room for any new bird that arrived.

After just a day in its new surroundings, though, staff noticed the bird struggling when flying up from the ground. Alarmed, they weighed it. It had lost three grams—almost 10 percent of its body weight—an indication that something was wrong.

They immediately moved it back to its smaller howdy cage and provided a heat lamp nearby to keep the bird warm. Over the next week, the bird was less alert, sitting near the heat lamp with its feathers fluffed up.

Not sure what the problem was, Switzer consulted with San Diego Zoo veterinarians and began to give the bird fluids and a broad-spectrum antibiotic. He also gave it antifungal medicine to guard against aspergillosis, a common fungal disease that is usually fought off by a healthy bird's immune system but can take hold when a bird gets old or sick. The staff took a blood sample and shipped it to San Diego for analysis.

By November 12, Lieberman was concerned enough to alert officials at the Hawaii Department of Forestry and Wildlife and the U.S. FWS. He said that after sixty-three days in captivity, the bird was not "its usual perky self" and described the medical regimen they had begun.

Lieberman said later that as small birds have such quick metabolisms, they typically don't linger long with an illness. He knew the situation with the po'ouli could quickly go from bad to worse. "Birds get sick and recover or get sick and die, especially small birds."

2

NO MORE MIRACLES

BETH BICKNESE WAS HOME WHEN THE PHONE RANG.

It was Sunday, November 14, 2004, and at the other end of the line was her boss, Pat Morris, head veterinarian for the San Diego Zoo. Bicknese already knew what he was calling to tell her: she would fly to Hawaii that week to care for the po'ouli. Lieberman had e-mailed her the news that morning. The world's rarest bird, possibly the very last of its kind, was sick, and it fell to her to try to cure it.

Lieberman was completely comfortable with Bicknese's skills, describing her as one of the best avian veterinarians in the world. She had been a San Diego Zoo vet for eight years, with another two years of residency there in the early 1990s tacked on for good measure. With some four thousand animals under the zoo's care, Bicknese had enormous experience. She had worked with animals of all kinds, including the zoo's fourteen hundred to fifteen hundred birds, with a wide range of conservation value.

Bicknese had become used to dealing with animals that were stars in their own right—rare, endangered, and popular—such as the California condor and the panda. The San Diego Zoo had long been involved not just in public education, but also with conservation of animals from the wild.

Zoo veterinarians regularly worked at the tip of conservation's spear, tending sick creatures whose fellows are dwindling in the wild and whose genetic code holds critical diversity for the population's future health. But when a veterinarian tends to a sick animal, Bicknese says, they have to put all that out of their mind and concentrate on the task at hand. The panda, the condor, the po'ouli all must cease to be the hope of future generations. They become instead a sick individual like the family dog, no less cherished because thousands like it exist in homes around the country.

"We try to be professional here and not focus on 'it's a panda,' 'it's a condor,' and instead focus on the animal," Bicknese says. "Working here at the San Diego Zoo was good training for working on the po'ouli. You focus on the animal and [do] not get frazzled by the fact that this animal, as an individual, matters a whole bunch."

Bicknese admits that was a harder task than usual with the po'ouli. She had worked with many rare animals, but nothing approaching the scarcity of the po'ouli.

"A little thought sneaks into your head: 'Are they going to catch the other two? Is this the last one? Could I be touching the last one in captivity?'" she says. "I couldn't allow myself to think about this too much. I had to focus on my job and get everything in line. I tried to stick to the details at hand."

But the details were not encouraging.

Bicknese knew that the bird was ill and quite likely very old. Though nobody knew how long po'ouli lived, this bird was at least eight years old, roughly equivalent to a sixty-year-old human and susceptible to organ malfunctions, cancers, and other problems that crop up with age.

"The smaller the bird, the shorter they tend to live," Bicknese says. "They burn out pretty quickly."

The next day, the bird's blood tests came back. The news couldn't have been worse. The po'ouli had malaria.

Malaria is known worldwide as a scourge of humans living in tropical areas, killing an estimated one million people each year. The avian form was even more devastating to Hawaiian birds. The disease was a relatively recent introduction to Hawaii, and native birds had no natural resistance. It proved overwhelmingly fatal. The disease had driven native birds high up on Hawaii's volcanoes, to the areas where the temperatures were so cool that malaria-carrying mosquitoes couldn't breed.

The following day brought another surprise. The results from the sexing tests conducted on the po'ouli came back: the San Diego Zoo's genetics department had "unequivocal results." Their bird—thought for years to be a girl—was a boy.

The sex of the bird, though a critical factor in efforts to breed it, had ceased to be of immediate concern, however. Its physical health trumped all other matters.

Over the next two days, Bicknese gathered all the information she could. She spoke with Morris about the people and government agencies involved and the species recovery efforts so far. In between, she packed and made arrangements for her children's care, staying up late the night before her flight and getting up early to catch a plane out of Carlsbad.

Bicknese got out of the house late and was greeted with a traffic-slowing fog. She got to the airport to find that the parking area near the terminal was closed because of construction, forcing her to park farther away and hurry across the airport. She boarded just before the attendants closed the doors.

Adrenaline still pumping from her mad dash through the airport, she settled in her seat. Though she often sleeps on plane flights, Bicknese stayed awake this time, preparing for her task at the other end. She laid out her materials, reviewing the bird's history and thinking about the logical course of action. Addressing the malaria would be her first item of business, so she focused her attention on that, calculating and recalculating dosages of the antimalaria drugs chloroquine and primaquine based on the tiny bird's weight.

Both drugs were needed, because the malaria parasite lives in both the bloodstream and the liver. The most immediate threat was the parasite in the blood, which they'd attack with chloroquine first. Later they would dose the bird with primaquine to get rid of any remaining parasites.

"It was kind of like a big cram session," Bicknese says. "I wanted to make sure I had it all right. I reread the plan for captive breeding so I understood the whole situation. I just wished I had more space to spread out."

Staff from the Maui Bird Conservation Center were waiting for Bicknese at the Kahului Airport and immediately took her uphill to the center.

Rich Switzer breathed a sigh of relief when he saw her. Though he was experienced in handling captive birds and knew how to administer first aid, he was not a veterinarian. Despite that, he had been overseeing the sick po'ouli's care for weeks. Even though he had been in constant contact with Lieberman and the San Diego Zoo veterinarians, the situation was extraordinarily tense and beginning to wear on him.

The malaria diagnosis a few days earlier had been bad news to the center's staff, but Switzer also felt encouraged that they finally knew what was wrong and could begin to treat it. "I was so relieved to have a good vet here," he says. "The vets in San Diego were very helpful and responsive, but when it comes to the crunch, they're still two and a half thousand miles away."

On arrival, Bicknese immediately set to work. First she and Switzer went over their notes, planning and prepping for the initial examination. Given the bird's importance, they didn't want to take any chances. They warmed up an avian intensive care unit—a small clear plastic container within which they could control temperature, humidity, and oxygen levels. Bicknese also prepared emergency drugs, measuring the proper doses and laying them out just in case they were needed.

Besides the weight loss and malaria, blood tests showed that the bird was slightly anemic. It also had raised levels of one liver enzyme and uric acid. The uric acid reading gave Bicknese pause. Though it could just be due to the metabolism of insects in the po'ouli's diet, it also could be a sign of impaired kidney function, especially in an older bird.

With its deadly track record, however, malaria was the top priority. After an initial examination, Bicknese decided to begin chloroquine treatments, which would hammer the malaria parasite with an injection every six hours for the first day.

When they walked in the aviary, Bicknese was immediately encouraged.

"From my initial peek at him, I felt a little bit better. He cocked his head and had a peek at us with his good eye. He knew we were there but was not overly stressed by our presence. He looked reasonable at that time."

They set about their business, giving the bird fluids to guard against dehydration and its first shot of chloroquine. Bicknese gave it a body score of three out of nine: thin, but not emaciated. She used a transilluminator, the light doctors use to examine human eyes, to check internal organs. Bicknese saw to her relief that the liver was of normal size and no unusual masses were inside the body cavity.

A few hours later, they returned to give the bird its second chloroquine treatment, then they grabbed a few hours' shut-eye before waking at 4 A.M. to give the third shot.

"It's cold up there, at elevation," Bicknese says. "It was a little surrealistic waking up, thinking, 'I'm waking up to go treat a po'ouli.'"

When they got to the aviary early that morning, the bird didn't look quite so perky. It was sitting huddled by the heat lamp, letting them know it was feeling crummy. But by later that day, the bird already seemed to be responding and had gained a little weight.

Lieberman, meanwhile, was dealing with the question of where the bird got malaria. It was a difficult situation. The bird, possibly the last of its kind, was diagnosed with a known killer of Hawaiian birds while in his facility.

Eric VanderWerf, Hawaiian bird recovery coordinator for the U.S. Fish and Wildlife Service, asked Lieberman the tough question in an e-mail:

I would suspect that po'ouli have poor immunity to malaria because they, like many endangered forest birds, are found only at high elevations. Assuming the test results are accurate, this raises important questions about where the po'ouli contracted malaria. It may have been bitten in the wild, but in that case the bird should have exhibited symptoms much earlier. The alternative is that the bird was somehow bitten in captivity. What do you think the chances are this occurred?

In response, Lieberman defended the facility's record, saying this was the first time in eleven years of dealing with twelve species of Hawaiian forest birds that any had come down with malaria. He also said that a third possibility had been raised by the zoo's chief veterinarian: the poʻouli may have the chronic form of malaria, a second stage of the disease that begins after a bird survives the initial infection. If that was the case, the bird may have been living with it for a while.

The idea that the poʻouli had been living with malaria was intriguing. It would mean that the bird over the years had been bitten by a malaria-infected mosquito and developed at least some resistance, and that its system was handling the disease, keeping it in check well enough to live with it. It would be a hopeful development and a sign that nature and evolution were helping Hawaiian birds build a new resistance to one of the worst diseases of native birdlife throughout the island chain.

Carter Atkinson, a U.S. Geological Survey avian malaria expert, agreed with the idea that it could be chronic malaria. If the bird had contracted the disease just before or after capture, its illness would have been obvious as it struggled through the intense fevers of the disease's acute phase. The fact that the bird appeared healthy until recently indicated to him that the malaria infection must be an older one, contracted in the forest well before capture.

Resistant or not, malaria or not, something was still ailing the poʻouli. After gaining weight the first day after Bicknese arrived, it lost it again the day after, and a bit more the next, Saturday, November 20.

Despite the weight loss, Bicknese and the facility staff were encouraged by the bird's demeanor. The poʻouli seemed to have plenty of energy and flitted around its cage to avoid Switzer's grasp. The exertion, which would drain a seriously ill bird, causing it to pant with an open beak, didn't seem to overly tire the poʻouli. The bird was feisty enough after being caught to chomp hard on Bicknese's fingers. It hurt, but it was a good sign.

Though concerns remained about the weight loss, Bicknese thought it was likely due to the added handling, which can make a bird more wary and cause it to fly down to the food dish less frequently. With the antimalarials started and the bird's demeanor okay, they decided Bicknese could fly home after she had instructed Switzer in the next phase of the bird's treatment.

When she left, Switzer would again take charge of the bird's care, administering the second malaria drug, primaquine. He would use the gavage procedure, sending medicine through a small tube inserted down the bird's throat.

"We felt that if malaria was the problem, the only way to get him to turn the corner at this point was to make sure he took his medicine," Bicknese says.

Switzer had experience with gavage, but he wanted to try it with Bicknese there before tackling the sick bird on his own. A native puaiohi, or small Kauai thrush, had injured a wing and was left behind after the previous release of captive-bred birds into the wild. With no other option, Switzer and Bicknese practiced the gavage procedure on the puaiohi, reflecting later that only the extreme rarity of the po'ouli made it acceptable to practice on a bird whose population was just three hundred to five hundred.

"Any other day of the week, that bird [the puaiohi] we'd consider a gravely endangered animal. And here we're using him to practice gavaging," Bicknese says. "The bird was fine, and I think it was subsequently released. But we were just shaking our heads. It all puts it in perspective."

Bicknese flew back to California on Saturday the twentieth, leaving the po'ouli in Switzer's hands. She kept tabs on the situation through e-mail and frequent telephone conversations. Within a few days, however, the bird began to go downhill quickly, eventually losing nearly a third of its body weight.

With such a tiny bird, Bicknese says, they had been walking a knife edge between too little intervention and too much. Unlike a larger-bodied bird, small birds like the po'ouli can be overtaxed by too much care, even the proper care. "It's just hard. On birds that size, there's a big balance between giving supportive care and going too far and taxing it and pushing it over the edge."

With the bird's weight loss critical, they decided they had to risk yet another intervention: using gavage to feed the bird a liquid diet in hopes of boosting its strength.

On November 25, Thanksgiving Day, Switzer began to gavage a liquid diet into the po'ouli. Both he and Bicknese realized, however, that the bird might never recover.

"I remember being in my kitchen, talking with Rich multiple times that day. It was a sunny day out. I looked out the window, thinking, 'This is it,'" Bicknese recalls. "I said, 'Oh, enjoy your turkey later,' but whatever niceties I was giving, I knew it was a bad case and it was probably going to get worse."

By this point, Switzer was exhausted. For three weeks, he had been surviving on four hours' sleep a night, and for the last three nights, he had been checking on the bird every ninety minutes. Though the center's staff helped with the bird's care during the day, Switzer, who lived on the site, took care of the overnight duties.

He had also been neglecting his other responsibilities to focus on the po'ouli. The center that Switzer now managed also housed breeding programs for endangered Hawaiian geese, Hawaiian crows, and two other kinds of forest birds. But Switzer had no choice. Not only had he started a new job, but he had also taken on the biggest challenge of his career: the future of a species was in his hands. "I really wasn't focusing on managing the facility," he says. "Although I was trying to do that as well, the number-one thing was this bird."

As he made his late-night and early-morning checks, handled the bird's medication, and now managed its feeding, Switzer began to wonder where the heck everyone was. The po'ouli recovery program had a long history of involvement by a wide variety of players and officials from the state and federal governments. But beyond Lieberman, the far-off staff of the San Diego Zoo, and the Maui Forest Bird Recovery Project crew, who stopped by with snails when they returned from the forest, Switzer was alone.

"I really felt, well, where's everybody else?" Switzer says. "Where are all these folks in Hawaii who had so much input in planning to bring this bird into captivity? I had nothing to do with the decision-making process. I was literally there holding the protocols and just following what had already been created for me."

By the day after Thanksgiving, Friday, November 26, the bird's weight had not improved despite the force-feeding. It got weaker as the day went on, sitting back on its haunches and unable to perch. Switzer put the bird in the avian incubator to warm it up and turned on the oxygen. He rolled up a small towel and formed it into a ring, putting it around the bird to support it.

At the 10 P.M. check, the bird's condition hadn't improved. When Switzer went in at 11:30 P.M., he found it lifeless, still supported by the towel he had wrapped around it earlier in the day.

"It sounds silly, but when I found the bird dead, I actually felt happy for it because it no longer had to endure the sickness, the hands-on prodding," Switzer says. "I remember saying to Alan a couple of days previously, 'This bird is so sick that if it was my own bird, I'd find a vet who could end its misery.'"

But that was just part of a complex swirl of emotions Switzer was experiencing. Even as a child, he had been fascinated by endangered species, visiting a local zoo to see such animals there. He had dedicated his professional life to improving their chances on an increasingly hostile earth and came to Hawaii to work with some of the most endangered birds on the planet. So though he was relieved for the bird as an individual, he also understood what he may have just witnessed.

"I can actually remember feeling very sad . . . tremendously overwhelmed by the fact this was potentially extinction that had just occurred," Switzer says.

Switzer again followed protocols. He put the bird in a plastic bag in the refrigerator, preserving tissues so that samples could be taken to provide as much information as possible from this po'ouli. Once that was done, he went to bed, falling into an exhausted sleep, the first undisturbed rest he'd had in weeks.

3

The Hana Rainforest Project

THEY ALMOST DIDN'T FIND IT AT ALL.

The poʻouli was discovered in the summer of 1973 in mountainous rainforest so steep and dense and tangled and wet that it had essentially kept people out for fifteen hundred years.

Native Hawaiians settled on the coast below and regularly visited the Haleakala volcano crater, which lies four thousand feet above the poʻouli's rainforest home. If they ventured there, they left no record of what they found. And if they saw the poʻouli, they gave it no name, at least none that existed in the Hawaiian language in 1973. Though hunters may have occasionally penetrated the forest, there had never been a scientific survey of the area.

But 1973 was a watershed year for environmental protection in the United States. President Richard Nixon signed into action one of the most significant environmental laws in U.S. history: the Endangered Species Act.

The law was just the latest indication that the country was getting its environmental act together. In 1970, the Environmental Protection Agency was created in response to public demand for cleaner air, land, and water. In 1972, Congress passed both the Marine Mammal Protection Act and the law that, after amending in 1977, would become the Clean Water Act.

It was an era of environmental awareness, and a University of Hawaii undergraduate named John Kjargaard wanted to be part of it.

The story of the po'ouli's discovery began a year earlier and farther down the mountain, in the forests of Haleakala's Waihoi Valley. One of several large valleys carved into Haleakala's sides, the Waihoi Valley is the remnant of an ancient lava flow and subsequent erosion that created a steep-sided, flat-bottomed valley.

At the time, very little was known about the Waihoi Valley, though hunters occasionally penetrated the open forests of ohia and olapa. Its lower reaches contained patches of taro and banana, evidence that it had been used by native Hawaiians in the distant past. Feral cattle from more recent centuries had entered the valley's southeastern corner. Their activities had brought in exotic shrubs and grasses. The plants had taken hold in patches opened by their grazing, sprouted from seeds carried in their fur and dung, by the wind, and by birds.

Taking advantage of a National Science Foundation program created to encourage student environmental initiatives, Kjargaard secured a $16,000 grant and organized an expedition to the valley in the summer of 1972. The valley is low enough on the mountain that it is accessible from the narrow, twisting Hana Highway, which winds along Maui's coast. That was the way expedition members came in, but on at least one important occasion it was not the way out.

One of the reasons the area remained unexplored is that it is so wet. The valley sits on Haleakala's eastern flank, exposed to the trade winds that drive the Hawaiian rain machine. The winds pick up moisture as they blow across two thousand miles of Pacific Ocean. When they hit the Hawaiian Islands' volcanic mountains, they're forced to rise, cooling as they do. Cool air holds less water than warm, so the cooling wrings the moisture from the air as it blows uphill, bringing rain, rain, and more rain to the slopes below.

The rain machine creates some of the highest rainfall amounts on the planet. A few islands away, Kauai's Mount Waialeale is one of the world's wettest spots, with 460 inches of rain annually, an amount rivaled only by Lloro, Colombia, and Mawsynram, India.

When the students went into the Waihoi Valley that summer, the area was virtually unknown to science. The students wanted to draw a scientific picture of the area. They measured rainfall, surveyed vegetation, insects, and mammals—mainly introduced rats—and documented sightings of several native Hawaiian birds.

As the summer wore on, however, several members of the crew became restless. Finally Kjargaard, another University of Hawaii undergraduate named Tonnie Casey, and Richard H. Davis, whom Kjargaard refers to as a "mountain man," hatched a plan to hike to Haleakala's crater, through the roughly fifteen miles of unexplored rainforest above. What they found would set the stage for the po'ouli's discovery a year later.

Davis set off first with his daughter Marilyn, leaving the expedition's base camp at two thousand feet. An experienced woodsman, Davis hacked his way through the undergrowth, heading for the steep slopes at the head of the valley, marking the trail with short strips of blue plastic tied to trees along the way.

Kjargaard and Casey followed three days later. Able to travel faster along trails Davis had already cut, they quickly caught up to the pair ahead.

From the air, this section of Haleakala looks like a uniform green carpet. The nubby tops of ohia trees undulate over countless ridges running down the mountainside. No clearings. No roads. No trails. No power lines. No sign of humans at all. Just trees and streams and clouds.

From the ground, the view is quite different. The green blanket seen from the air is held up by a riot of roots and branches and trunks. Below and between the trunks grow smaller shrubs, head-high and impenetrable. The ground layer is a carpet of calf- and thigh-high ferns and other undergrowth, always wet, always dripping, shielding the ground and lending uncertainty to each step.

Trail cutting requires endurance, a feel for the land, and a sharp machete. As the cutter moves ahead, he or she slashes the smaller growth and moves over, under, and around larger obstacles such as trees and gullies too steep to cross. The cutter ties small strips of plastic tape to branches as a guide to those who follow. The flags are desperately needed. The trail that results is intentionally low-impact through a rare and fragile environment. Except for the most regularly traveled, they are barely passable even when freshly cut. Without the tape, a hiker would quickly be lost.

Traveling such trails is a whole-body experience. The trail twists and turns and constantly climbs up and down, not just along Haleakala's slope, but in and out of numerous gullies carved by the region's many streams. As the hiker walks this torturous path, he or she simultaneously negotiates an obstacle course of fallen logs, calf-high chunks of lava, and drooping tree branches. In a hundred yards, a hiker can step over a log, duck under a branch, step into a water-filled ditch, bend left, bend right, climb up a hill, and then start the process all over again.

Traveling such trails requires not just stamina and strength, but determination as well. And it's even harder when you're lost. Kjargaard recalls:

> We got lost because there are magnetic anomalies throughout the whole area. Following a compass leads you in a circle, in the fog and rain. It was very difficult terrain to move in because of its hills and swamps. The swamps are the kind of things that look okay and the next minute you're up to your armpits.
>
> Everything you owned was wet. The sleeping bags were damp, all your clothes were wet. You had one pair of shorts and a T-shirt that were just damp to go into the tent with. Every morning, you had sopping wet, mud-covered clothing, and you put on everything wet. You had no compass to go by, and you were cutting as you went. The vegetation was so dense you couldn't get through with your packs without cutting with machetes.

At one point, the group worked its way over a ridge that wasn't marked on the maps, and after descending for a distance, they realized they were going not up into Haleakala's crater, but down into the neighboring Kipahulu Valley. Discouraged, they had to turn around and fight their way back up.

Twelve days after Davis left the Waihoi Valley camp, the four reached the crater, home to a national park, a visitors center, and perhaps most welcome, a road down.

"We knew we'd make it. We knew we'd get somewhere eventually," Kjargaard says. "We were pretty used to being in really tough conditions. Besides, we were in our twenties and didn't know any better."

Despite the rigors of the trip, the group saw firsthand the pristine high-altitude Hana rainforest. By the third day, they had climbed the valley's back wall and reached fifty-four hundred feet. Casey noted that the trees were far more dense and there was a dramatic increase in native birdlife. By the trip's end, they would report sighting the rare 'akepa, which had been seen once a few years earlier but before that had been absent for twenty-one years.

At the time, they were just happy to be out of the forest and had no thoughts of a follow-up project. But when the report on the Waihoi Valley Project's work was written, the government organizers of the grant program were thrilled at what the students had found. They asked them to present their results at an American Association for the Advancement of Science meeting in Washington, D.C.

Though the program was not intended to fund ongoing research, the organizers encouraged them to apply for funding to continue work the next summer. Their new goal would be the Hana rainforest.

The scientific goals of 1973's Hana Rainforest Project were similar to that of the Waihoi Valley Project: conduct a scientific survey of the area and catalog plants, animals, insects, soils, and anything else that came to mind.

Kjargaard assembled an eight-person crew, five of whom had been on the previous summer's Waihoi Valley trip. All were students of some type, graduate or undergraduate, and all had connections to the University of Hawaii except one. Alvin Yoshinaga grew up in Hawaii but was working on a master's thesis in botany from the University of Wisconsin.

In addition to Kjargaard and Yoshinaga, other crew members were Tonnie Casey; Betsy Harrison, who with Yoshinaga would study the area's plants; Grant Merritt, the photographer; Jim Jacobi, studying mammals; undergraduate Heather Fortner, studying soils; and Charley Whittle, another undergraduate, who would study the rainforest's insects.

These students, none of whom had an advanced degree, were to provide the scientific community with its first snapshot of one of the most endangered biological communities on earth, a remnant Hawaiian rainforest.

Though the scientific aims for the 1973 Hana Rainforest Project were similar to those of the earlier expedition, the facts of life on the ground were very different. After scouting the area and consulting with the National Park Service, Kjargaard decided to put the group's base camp in scrub vegetation on the edge of treeline, above the rainforest proper at roughly seven thousand feet, five thousand feet higher than the Waihoi Valley's camp.

The high altitude meant that in addition to the rain and rough terrain, group members had to worry about temperatures cold enough for frost some mornings. If they got wet, hypothermia was a possibility, a threat they hadn't had to deal with in Waihoi.

And getting wet was pretty much guaranteed. Though 1973 was a dry year on Maui, it was still wet in the rainforest. One extraordinary day saw seventeen inches of rain, and on another occasion forty to fifty inches fell in just over two days.

When asked what they remember most about their weeks perched on Haleakala's shoulder, Hana Rainforest Project members almost invariably first mention the rain: drenching deluges and penetrating gray fog that kept everything dripping even when the rain wasn't hammering down.

"It was miserable," says Jim Jacobi, a U.S. Geological Survey biologist who in 1973 was a graduate student surveying mammals—mainly invasive rats, pigs, and goats—for the project. "It rained all the time. Rain ran down your raincoat, soaked your pants, and ran down into your boots. Your boots would literally fill up."

Though he had a raincoat and rubber boots, Jacobi didn't bring rainpants and was constantly wet. In a desperate water-proofing effort, he one day painted a pair of blue jeans with melted candle wax. "It worked until I walked and it cracked," he says.

Heather Fortner, the group's soil scientist, spent time study-ing the area's alpine bogs. One day she took soil samples from the bottom of Lake Waieleele. Donning a mask and snorkel, and wearing a rope around her waist for safety, she swam while Tonnie Casey—who'd joined Kjargaard for a second summer—stood onshore, holding the rope's other end. It was pouring rain, and as Fortner looked back at Casey through the mask's drip-ping glass, she wondered which of them was wetter.

Long days in wet weather made dry clothes valuable. Though the layers they wore kept them warm enough during the day, they always kept dry clothes in a plastic bag in their tent to wear to sleep. They'd shuck their sopping duds outside when they returned and slide gratefully into dry clothes and a warm sleeping bag.

Of course, that left cold, wet clothes waiting when the sun rose. Getting dressed in the morning was universally hated. "Nothing is worse than putting on cold, wet pants after crawl-ing out of a sleeping bag," Jacobi says. But if it meant having something dry to get into at the end of the day, they gritted their teeth and put their clothes on.

For shelter, they rigged a large plastic sheet over the small tents they shared to help keep them dry and give them a small dry area to work in. But the wind above treeline kept them constantly on the lookout for loose ropes and blowdowns.

According to Grant Merritt, the group's photographer, "It howled up there, easily forty knots," Merritt says. He was washing dishes in an aluminum tub one night when a gust blew his tent off the ground, straight up into the plastic tarp. Another night, the rain and wind blew the whole contraption down on the sleepers, causing a yelling, soaking mass of students, wet clothes, and flapping plastic.

Some days it was merely foggy, though that came with its own challenges. The fog was a bit drier, but not much. Its tiny water droplets settled everywhere, keeping things wet. Driven by the wind, fog could roll uphill and envelop an area with startling quickness.

One day, in whiteout conditions, Merritt got off the trail and became disoriented. He knew there was a valley ahead. If he could find it, he could follow it to base camp. He began bushwacking through the forest, trying to stay at roughly the same elevation as he made his way around the hill.

After a while he heard voices, very close, but still couldn't see anything. He soon realized the voices belonged to other project members who were on the main trail, to which he had been walking parallel.

"I wasn't panicked, but I was kind of concerned," Merritt says. "I contoured three-quarters of a mile, twenty feet downhill of the real trail. That's how thick the fog could get."

The rain, the altitude, and the tropics sometimes combined for strange experiences. As Merritt hiked back to base camp one clear afternoon, the sun was setting in front of him over Haleakala's crater while a breeze kicked up behind and blew a cool mist up the slope. One side of his body was becoming numb from the cold while the other side was sweating. "It was really strange," Merritt said.

The weather not only made travel on the ground an adventure, but also played havoc with Kjargaard's efforts to supply the camp by air. He budgeted as much as he could for helicopters, but the weather frequently socked them in, sometimes for days, delaying scheduled pickups and drops. "Sometimes they had to airdrop through the clouds because it was just a solid blanket," Kjargaard says.

During their initial setup, project members established a staging area in a parking lot just off the road to Haleakala's summit. The weather refused to cooperate, however, socking in the base camp's drop-off point and forcing them to send the helicopter home. They kept a round-the-clock vigil over their supplies, waiting for the weather to clear. The last of the gear was flown in after more than a week of delays.

The mountain wasn't always shrouded in fog, and when it cleared, the views could be breathtaking. The Maui coast was visible through breaks in the trees, as was the vast Pacific. The big island of Hawaii lay just across the Alenuihaha Channel, the massive humps of Mauna Kea and Mauna Loa visible from Haleakala.

"There were a couple of days with just perfect views along the ridgetop, through an opening in the trees or from the crater," says Alvin Yoshinaga, then a graduate student working as one of the project's two botanists. "I wondered how many people had been here before. Probably not many."

The interplay of cloud and sky and wind sometimes provided a visual feast of dramatic beauty. One day, as Merritt walked down to Lake Waianapanapa with the sun at his back, the lower slopes were shrouded in clouds, as they often were even when it was clear above. Looking down, he could see his shadow cast onto the clouds below, completely encircled by a rainbow.

Even taking care of nature's necessities could be rewarding if the sky cleared. Merritt says the view from the latrine, called a lua in Hawaiian, was the best he'd ever seen. "It was the most awesome view you could imagine. You could see all the way down the Keanae Coast to Molokai. It had to be the best lua I've ever sat in."

Even when the weather was dicey, the trip to the lua could be spiced up with a sighting of native Hawaiian birds that frequented the area. "You're sitting there in the rain and fog and have a couple of 'amakihi, 'apapane come by. I had an i'iwi come and sit. It was right close by. I couldn't see it, but I could hear it."

Though helicopters were the easiest way in and out of the site, funds were limited, and they were a luxury reserved for ferrying supplies. People had to walk.

Base camp was in a circular clearing the crew came to call Frisbee Meadow, partly because of its shape and partly because of the games they played there. The hike in or out of Frisbee Meadow took eight hours. Project members would drive to the top of Haleakala and hike down, usually by the Sliding Sands Trail. A desolate and beautiful path through Haleakala's crater, Sliding Sands starts at a breath-grabbing ten thousand feet and heads downhill. It carves a light-colored scar across the volcano's dark, sandy crater as hikers' feet stir tan dust through the dark upper sands.

Thousands of visitors come to Haleakala National Park each year to see the enormous crater, magnificent and awe-inspiring, doubly so at sunrise or sunset. The crater's dark floor and sides are patched with lighter colors. Smaller cinder cones march into the distance even as the bright line of the Sliding Sands Trail fades into the scenery.

Team members often took a different way out of Frisbee Meadow, hiking up the switchback Halemauu Trail to avoid Sliding Sands' exhausting climb and unsteady footing. It took determination to get in and out of Frisbee Meadow, but they made the trip whenever necessary, guiding in visitors or making a run for fresh food. They always returned with heavy packs.

They even occasionally made the journey at night, which had its own rewards: "It was a moonscape, beautiful, spooky, and scary," Merritt says of a nighttime excursion to pick up visitors and groceries. "You know you're the only people for miles. Everything looks different at night."

The terrain that Hana Rainforest Project members were working on was different from that of the previous summer as well. Unlike the flat volcanic flows that made up the bed of the Waihoi Valley, the Hana Rainforest stood on the steep slopes of Haleakala's shoulders. Virtually every trip by team members—even to fetch water—was uphill or down.

Though their youth likely made them more brazen than they'd be today, they did take precautions. Each carried a radio and checked in regularly. They often traveled in pairs for safety, but they also traveled alone when necessary, a risk given the treacherous terrain. "It's amazing what we did. . . . It's amazing we didn't lose anyone or get anyone hurt," Jacobi says.

Despite the hazardous conditions, there were no real medical emergencies. The worst accident may have been when part of a tree fell on Whittle's head, causing him to bite through his lip. He charged into camp, finding Yoshinaga on cooking duty.

Yoshinaga stopped stirring that night's spaghetti sauce and grabbed a jug of ethyl alcohol to clean out the wound. Unfortunately for hungry project members, the ethyl alcohol jug looked a lot like the water jug. After treating Whittle, Yoshinaga poured alcohol into the sauce, starting a fire on the camp stove, which they put out. The major casualty of the incident turned out to be supper.

Climbing up and down the Hana Rainforest's hills burned lots of calories, so supper was not to be missed.

As with everything else, Kjargaard economized on the food, opting for quantity over quality. Among other things, he bought freeze-dried vegetables in bulk. The result, he said, was that though the menu had several different items on it, they all had virtually the same cooking instructions: "Add two cups of water, cook until done."

The crew jazzed up the dishes with different spices, adding meat to some, sauce to others. Still, the food became something of a running joke, earning descriptive monikers like Slippery Glip and Sloppy Glop, which still elicit chuckles from project members.

Some team members slept in the field to tend their projects, but those who got back to camp at night saved their energy for work. Despite their youth and enthusiasm, they had precious few sing-alongs around the campfire. After a long day in the field, most had climbed into their sleeping bags within an hour of supper to read a bit and get some sleep. According to Merritt, "It pretty much was a dawn-to-dusk project. Read for a while, write in a journal, maybe an hour after dusk."

It wasn't all work, though. Frisbee Meadow got its name because team members often threw a Frisbee around. After a while, they began to add features to the game, gathering in a circle, getting a couple of Frisbees going, and tossing dirt clumps stirred up by the area's wild pigs at the disks and each other. They dubbed it "clod Frisbee."

Despite the hardships, the crew members all were excited to be experiencing firsthand a chunk of Hawaii as it was before the Polynesians arrived and began to convert the forests they found into agricultural land.

Over the course of that summer, the students understood that they had stumbled into a uniquely Hawaiian wonderland, brimming with native species not seen in decades, if ever.

Newspaper reports after the expedition's conclusion said they had discovered twenty-four new species of insects and found various species of plants rare elsewhere. They'd seen thousands of greenswords, a less showy relative of the glittering silversword, which lived in the deserts atop Haleakala. They found fifteen-foot-tall specimens of a native lobelia that reaches just six feet on Maui's Puu Kukui, a remnant peak of what was once Haleakala's twin, which created Maui's lower western half.

They also saw many rare birds, native Hawaiian species that had disappeared from lowland forests and settlements. They observed at least four species that were classified as endangered by the federal government at the time: the small, yellowish 'akepa, last seen in 1953; the long-billed nukupu'u, last seen in 1967; the crested honeycreeper, the largest of Maui's honeycreepers, seen only once since 1950; and the endangered Maui parrotbill, first seen in the twentieth century in 1950.

But they'd also bitten off a little more than they could chew. Jacobi later said that their goal of a complete survey of the area was far too ambitious for a single summer's work, particularly by young, inexperienced scientists.

By August, despite the groundbreaking discoveries, several team members realized they would have to come back in the fall to continue gathering data. And after they discovered a new bird species, they'd have company.

4

THE
MYSTERY BIRD

JOHN KJARGAARD WAS RESTLESS. IT WAS STILL EARLY IN THAT summer of 1973. The Hana Rainforest Project had been under way for a month or so. Much of the project members' activity was directed south of their camp, focusing on national park land and the area below two high-altitude lakes, Waianapanapa and Waieleele.

But there was more rainforest closer to camp, right below the ridge where their tents were pitched. It was just as unexplored and appeared equally pristine. Kjargaard grabbed his machete and headed downhill, crossing into the state Hana Forest Reserve, hacking and flagging as he went.

The first day, he dropped about a thousand feet in elevation, noticing much larger ohia trees than they'd seen before, as well as other interesting vegetation. Then he turned south and began to cut along the same elevation, stopping when he reached a large stream.

A few days later, he returned, pushing the trail along the same contour and then turning back uphill, creating a loop that project members could follow.

Intrigued by Kjargaard's reports, the project's two botanists, Betsy Harrison and Alvin Yoshinaga, began to explore. On July 26, Harrison let Yoshinaga go ahead on the way back to camp. She was alone on the new trail, at sixty-four hundred feet between the East and West Hanawi Streams, toiling uphill.

It was late afternoon when a small flock of Maui creepers came by. The creepers are a native Hawaiian species common enough not to be listed as threatened or endangered by the federal government. They were calling with short *chik* sounds and flitting from branch to branch.

With them was a rare nukupu'u, Hawaii's bizarre evolutionary answer to the mainland's woodpeckers. With a long, curved upper bill and short lower bill, it pries up bark and hammers open insect burrows in search of food. Unlike the mainland woodpeckers, however, the nukupu'u hammers with its mouth wide open, striking the wood with its short, stiff lower bill and using its wiry upper bill to probe out the insects.

Harrison was immediately excited about the nukupu'u, but with it and the creepers were three small, brownish birds, flitting along not making much noise. "It's like they just materialized," Harrison says. They were about five and a half inches long, somewhat smaller than a human hand. They had light buff-colored bellies, with darker brown backs and wings. And unlike any known native Hawaiian bird, the black feathers on their faces formed masks.

She stood and watched the birds for a while. Then, realizing she was seeing something unusual, she used flagging tape to tie a blue bow onto a nearby native hydrangea before hiking slowly back up, stopping, looking, and listening. "I still had six hundred feet in elevation [to climb]," she says, "an hour straight uphill."

It was late by the time Harrison got back to camp. Though she excitedly told the others about the nukupuʻu and the strange new birds, they would have to wait to search for them until the next day.

Jim Jacobi and Tonnie Casey, the group's ornithologist, were puzzled by Harrison's description of the new bird. It sounded like a common chickadee, and with introduced species being a scourge on the islands, it was possible.

But still . . . these forests were amazingly pristine, brimming with not just Hawaiian species, but entire communities of species with ecological relationships among plants and insects and birds still intact. It was a strange place for a chickadee.

The next day, with Casey occupied with nesting Maui creepers, Jacobi headed downhill on his own. As Harrison had, he first heard a flock of creepers nearby. Instead of looking for them, he began to call them in, making *chik, chik, chik* sounds. Unafraid, the birds came closer to investigate. With them was one of Harrison's "chickadees."

"I thought, 'That's not a creeper. What is it?'" Jacobi says. "It was so close I couldn't even use my binoculars. I said, 'What in the world is that?'"

Jacobi realized he was seeing something new, or at the very least, unusual, so he immediately sketched the bird in his field notebook and described it in words as best he could. "I got some very good looks at it. It had a brown body, and it was like nothing I'd ever seen before. I had gotten to know Hawaiian birds and knew what to expect. It was nothing like anything else."

He watched as the bird hopped along the branches, prying up bark and moss, looking for insects to eat. He lost all sense of time. "It could have been seconds or minutes," he says. The bird flew off once but, apparently unafraid, returned when Jacobi whistled.

"I all but ran back to camp with my pack on. I said, 'There's something down there, really something different.'"

Jacobi's first thought was that an alien species had penetrated the impenetrable forest. He shared his drawing and his thoughts with Casey and Kjargaard. Casey, who had some experience drawing birds, made a sketch based on Jacobi's and Harrison's descriptions. After that, Jacobi and Casey began to spend a lot of time trying to figure out what it was.

As the bird's description didn't match any known Hawaiian species, its identity became the subject of lively discussions in camp, which one project member said typically went: "Oh, it's gotta be a sparrow." "No, it's no sparrow." Team members dubbed it the "mystery bird."

Two days after Jacobi saw it, on July 29, Casey became the third member of the project to spot the bird. The creepers she had been observing abandoned their nest, freeing her to explore this intriguing new development.

Casey and Jacobi began to spend more of their time observing the bird. Over the coming weeks, they found several more—four or five pairs—and got to know their mystery bird better.

"They come very close. They are very, very inquisitive. They probably came within eight feet of me," Casey says. "They had no fear."

The birds appeared to be insect eaters, slow-working and methodical, that spent their time in the lower, leafy portion of the forest, among the shrubs and middle trunks of the trees.

"It seemed to know exactly what it was doing," Jacobi told the author of a 1975 article on the discovery. "As a matter of fact, whenever we later observed these birds, they paid very little attention to us. They seemed to know we were there but apparently felt no threat and went about their feeding."

Casey came to know just where to find the birds. They were pretty high on Haleakala's slopes, between fifty-three hundred and sixty-eight hundred feet in forest dominated by forty-five-foot-high ohia trees. They were quieter than other Hawaiian birds and seemed to enjoy other birds' company, as they were almost always found with Maui creepers, Maui parrotbills, or the greenish 'amakihi.

"Hawaiian birds are very vocal," Jacobi says. "I kept waiting for a song, but I just got *chik*s out of it."

With the other project members occupied with their own tasks, Casey and Jacobi began to pursue the mystery bird's identity. They talked to experts on Hawaiian birds. One, Andrew Berger, author of *Hawaiian Birdlife* (University of Hawaii Press, 1981), dismissed the sighting, explaining it away as a non-native species, an all-too-common problem on Hawaii.

In mid-August, they contacted Dean Amadon, Lamont curator of ornithology at the American Museum of Natural History in New York, who had written a definitive work on Hawaiian honeycreepers in 1950. As students contacting a prominent expert in the field, Jacobi was prepared for a brush-off, but he was pleasantly surprised: "He didn't say, 'Oh, who are you? I don't have time for this.' He was extremely interested immediately."

They soon discovered, though, that their enthusiasm, notes, and drawings weren't enough. Experts needed to see a specimen in order to really evaluate it.

The two reluctantly realized that they'd have to kill a couple of these unusual, unique, and trusting birds in order to get the world to recognize what they had found. It pained them, but the recognition would open the way for additional scientific study and allow protection under state and federal endangered species laws.

"It was a real tough step," Jacobi says.

State biologist David Woodside was in the office of Michio Takata, Hawaii's director of Fish and Game, when he first heard of the new bird. There with him was Casey, who was seeking a permit to collect specimens. Takata had called Woodside in to ask him whether he'd heard of Casey's new bird. He hadn't.

"Takata said he can't give a permit for a bird that they don't know," Woodside explains, "so he told me to go and collect one for them."

By early September, Casey, Jacobi, and Woodside had made plans to head back to Frisbee Meadow with the hope of securing three specimens. They planned to send two to Dean Amadon in New York, either preserved in alcohol or as prepared skins.

When the trio arrived at Frisbee Meadow, they weren't alone. Several members of the Hana Rainforest Project, which had officially ended August 10, were still there, gathering information.

On September 15, the three headed downhill to the area where the birds had been seen, Woodside toting a shotgun.

"We went back and forth and back and forth and finally found one bird. It was close enough in and—it sends shivers up my spine, but we shot it and got it," Jacobi says.

Two days later, on September 17, they got a second bird and hiked its body out right away. Woodside then shot a third bird, which was supposed to be the specimen preserved in alcohol, but they lost it.

"I hit it, I guess." Woodside says. "It flew up to a higher branch. I shot again. I must have hit it, because it fluttered down into the gulch in the brush. We hunted for it for an hour, but it was getting dark, so we lost that one."

After preparing the two birds they had retrieved, Casey shipped a specimen to New York.

Though Amadon hadn't brushed the students off, he was not convinced they had a new species. A new bird in Hawaii, with its long history of losing species to extinction, not gaining them, would indeed be an extraordinary find. The last new bird discovery in Hawaii—a subspecies—had come in 1923.

Hawaii also had a long history of accumulating species introduced by humans. A bird familiar elsewhere would seem strange and unique when discovered in a new Hawaiian setting.

Amadon expressed his skepticism privately to colleagues. In a note attached to the letter from Casey telling him they had secured two specimens, which he sent to fellow ornithologists Les Short and Walter Bock, Amadon wrote, "Evidently they still think they have a new species." Later, in a note in the margins of an October 9 letter from Casey that described how fat the bird seemed, Amadon had circled the word "fat" and written, "Hope it's not a bobolink!"

But by November 2, the specimen Casey sent had done the trick, transforming skepticism to enthusiasm. It had arrived in New York the day before. After examining it, Amadon's doubt evaporated, replaced by a growing sense of excitement. This new bird was different enough from other Hawaiian birds that if it proved to be native, it was not only a new species, but also a new genus, the next higher category in the scientific ordering of life.

"The bird is remarkable—if a Hawaiian endemic, then probably a new genus as well as a species," Amadon wrote Casey. "The only remote possibility is that it could be a crazy introduction—e.g. an African 'nuthatch-weaver,' but I am almost certain that is not the case and will be completely certain before the day is out."

Amadon remarked about only one physical characteristic of the bird: its tail. "The tail of the bird is so short that I thought maybe it had been ripped out and growing in again. But the second bird in the photo looks equally short tailed???"

Casey wrote back that all the birds they'd seen in the field had extremely short tails.

Amadon called the find astonishing and said the bird was most likely a member of the islands' most spectacular family: the honeycreepers. He wrote:

The discovery is quite startling from two points of view. First, the fact that this could be an undiscovered species of bird seems incredible at this late date, particularly since so many earlier ones became extinct in Hawaii for various reasons. And secondly, biologically it is a new genus. The so-called honeycreeper family is an extreme example of adaptive radiation on an island—comparable with the famous Darwin finches in the Galapagos.

Other authorities agreed with Amadon's sense that the mystery bird represented a whole new genus. Despite his initial skepticism that the students had found an unknown bird, Berger, though saying it might not be a honeycreeper, agreed that it must be a new genus, calling it "a most strange bird."

As the analysis of the two specimens went on through the fall, Casey, Jacobi, and Amadon had trouble keeping the lid on the discovery. In October, Casey wrote to Amadon, "We have had some trouble with leaks in the publicity end." She went on to detail how the National Science Foundation's (NSF) public information office had called, demanding descriptive information and saying that because NSF funded the Hana Rainforest Project, it had the right to the information.

The news finally broke for good in December. An article in the *Honolulu Star-Bulletin* trumpeted "New Species of Bird Found on Haleakala." The *New York Times* reported on January 6, 1974, that the NSF believed the as-yet-unnamed bird was the first new bird genus and species found worldwide in ten years. "The discovery is an exciting event for birdwatchers because 'most birdwatchers assume everything has already been discovered,'" the *Times* article quoted one prominent ornithologist as saying.

Once the public announcement was made, a scientific description had to be prepared. Casey's relationship with Berger, who had been her adviser on the project, had become strained. Berger wanted Amadon, rather than the students, to describe the bird. In a January 14, 1974, letter to Amadon, he pushed this idea, dismissively describing Kjargaard, who wanted project members to describe all new species, as "not even a biologist."

But Amadon stayed firmly in Casey and Jacobi's corner. He responded a few days later that the students had asked him to describe or codescribe the bird. Though he had "roughed out a new description" with them, he wrote, "It is their discovery and I felt that it would mean a lot more to them to describe it than it would to me."

Berger also wanted the bird to have an English common name, which Casey and Jacobi resisted. Instead, they consulted a Hawaiian language expert, Mary Kawena Pukui, who suggested the name poʻo uli, meaning "black-faced" in Hawaiian. For the scientific name, they settled on *Melamprosops,* or "black forehead," for the genus and *phaeosoma,* or "brown body," for the species name.

In recognition of Amadon's help, they decided early on that one of the two specimens would go to the American Museum of Natural History, while the other would stay in Hawaii, at the Bernice P. Bishop Museum in Honolulu, the islands' largest natural history museum.

Casey and Jacobi toiled through the winter to write the scientific paper describing the bird. Published August 2, 1974, in the *Occasional Papers of the Bernice P. Bishop Museum,* the description was the poʻouli's official introduction to the scientific world. It also would permanently link the authors' names with that of the small, brown Hawaiian bird.

5

HAWAII

YEARS BEFORE HE FIRST SAW A POʻOULI, JIM JACOBI HAD FALLEN in love with nature on Oahu, where he grew up. He wandered the cool forests of towering eucalyptus, feeling a connection with the life around him as he walked their shaded paths.

That feeling guided his academic and professional life. He studied the natural world in college and after he graduated, when he joined the Hana Rainforest Project in the summer of 1973. He eventually worked for the federal government as a biologist in various agencies, including the National Biological Service and the U.S. Geological Survey.

It is ironic that a lifetime of working to understand and protect Hawaii's native environment started as it did. Though the forests he wandered gave him an appreciation of nature, they consisted chiefly of introduced plants, including the eucalyptus tree, and were an example of one of Hawaii's biggest natural problems: the islands' takeover by non-native species.

Almost from the moment humans arrived on the islands, they brought plants, animals, and insects that gained a foothold and spread, displacing native Hawaiian plants, animals, and insects along the way. In the limited confines of Hawaii's main islands, as the human population grew, so did the problem. Agriculture consumed more land, until native Hawaiian species could be found virtually nowhere on the islands' lowlands.

The problem accelerated with the arrival of Europeans, who brought along a whole new suite of plants, animals, and insects, which continued the assault on those that had adapted to the islands' environment over eons of isolation. Today, Jacobi says, most people—Hawaiians and tourists alike—don't realize how little of the natural world around them is Hawaiian.

"The most recognized native plant in Hawaii is koa, but we know it by its wood," he says. "People don't know the tree, don't know the leaves. There are no native plants at low altitudes, so there's no connection to what's native here. Residents and tourists alike don't recognize the distinction."

The reality in Hawaii is that the astonishingly diverse collection of species that evolved during the islands' long isolation is in retreat, up the slopes of the volcanic mountains that formed the islands. The islands remain, but humanity's comings and goings ensure that they are no longer isolated.

The history of humankind on the Hawaiian Islands is a relative blink of an eye in their long history. For millions upon millions of years, the islands have resided in one of the world's most remote locations in the middle of the Pacific Ocean.

But today's Hawaiian Islands are just the latest there. They were created by a volcanic hot spot in the Pacific Plate that, for millions of years, has allowed molten rock to flow up from beneath the earth's crust. Solidifying as it hits the cold ocean water, the lava builds some of the world's largest mountains, the tops of which become islands when they break the surface thousands of feet above.

The hot spot is stationary, but the islands ride on top of the Pacific Plate, which is moving slowly northwest to its destruction in a deep ocean trench near the Aleutian Islands. The combination has produced a conveyor belt of island creation and destruction. Its work is written in an arc of islands and underwater seamounts stretching from the hot spot, currently located under the Big Island (Hawaii), all the way to the Aleutian Trench.

Each of the eight main Hawaiian Islands was created by the same hot spot in its turn. Tiny Niihau is the oldest, with lava dated to 5.5 million years ago. Then come Kauai, Oahu, Molokai, Lanai, Kahoolawe, Maui, and Hawaii, which is still erupting.

Maui, the po'ouli's home, is the second-youngest of the islands and still considered volcanically active. Its oldest lava dates between 1 million and 1.75 million years ago.

Beyond Niihau stretches a chain of smaller islands, known as the Northwestern Hawaiian Islands. Formed by the same Hawaiian hot spot and dragged slowly away by the movement of the Pacific crust, the chain stretches fifteen hundred miles, past Midway, to the Kure atoll.

Beyond Kure lie six more mountains, all submerged seamounts. And curving to the north of them lies the Emperor Seamount chain, twenty-five undersea mountains created by the Hawaiian hot spot 80 million years ago, heading in a line toward the Aleutian Trench.

The process of creation continues today. As Hawaii rides the Pacific Plate ever so slowly northwest, a new Hawaiian island is rising from the ocean floor. Dubbed Loihi, the new seamount is nineteen miles from Hawaii. Despite the distance, some scientists believe its flows may merge with the active flows of Hawaii's

Kilauea volcano and become an extension of the Big Island before it breaks the surface.

As the islands move slowly away from the building volcanic forces beneath the seafloor, they erode and shrink until they disappear below the surface. Although Maui is just the second-youngest island, some scientists believe that its Haleakala volcano, standing ten thousand feet above sea level, was once three thousand feet higher.

In many cases, the place where an island once stood is marked by a shallow lagoon, surrounded by land built up on its coral reef. These reefs, whose growth has kept up with the island's shrinking, can reach incredible depths. The coral reef at Midway, for example, has been measured at more than twelve hundred feet thick. Eventually, as these reef islands, called atolls, move north into cooler water, even the coral ceases to grow, and the atoll too sinks below the waves.

In between an island's creation and destruction, it becomes a platform for life and a laboratory for evolution. But first life has to get there.

The Hawaiian Islands are among the most remote on earth, two thousand miles from the nearest continent. Gleaming and steaming above the waves, new islands provided an incredible challenge for life from distant islands and faraway continents to colonize.

Like the forces that pushed the islands out of the earth to begin with, the colonization of the Hawaiian Islands happened slowly, over enormous stretches of time. When the Emperor Seamounts were young islands, as long as 70 to 80 million years ago, they may have looked similar to the Hawaiian Islands before human contact. Much of that life perished, however, when the last one, today called the Koko volcano, sank into the sea, leaving its low, ring-shaped atoll. There were no other high islands to take its place, nowhere for creatures and plants adapted to life on a mountainous volcano to go, until Kure appeared above the sea 28 million years ago.

Though just a low atoll today, Kure was once a high island, like Maui or Hawaii. Plants, insects, and animals that made it to Kure and became established could have jumped to the island that is now Midway when it first poked its head above the surface, and then to Pearl, Lisianski, Laysan, French Frigate Shoals, Necker, Nihoa, Nihau, Kauai, and the rest of the current main islands. Yet not all the species on the islands would have established themselves first on Kure and then jumped methodically to new islands. Some, perhaps even most, would have made landfall on whichever island chance and the prevailing winds and currents directed them to. They easily could have arrived on an island in the middle or at the other end and spread up and down the chain.

They had time to spread, because colonization of the Hawaiian Islands was a million-in-one event every time it happened. Not only is Hawaii remote, but it is out of the path of the enormous currents flowing east and west, north and south. That makes the chances even less that life-holding debris might wash up on the islands' shores.

And just reaching an island wasn't enough. A life form had to land in a place where it could survive, falling onto fertile soil with the right growing conditions or winding up near other members of its species so it could bear young. A bedraggled bird finally flying ashore or a sun-baked bug gratefully walking off a beached log after a long journey would need others of its kind and the proper habitat to start a colony.

Timing of these excursions is everything. Arrive too early in an island's life cycle, and the colonists land on bare lava. But give the wind and weather enough time, and soil can form. Some plants, like the ohia lehua tree, are lava specialists. Even today ohia is the first tree to colonize a lava flow.

Insects are thought to have been the most frequent colonizers of Hawaii, but even they averaged just one successful colonization every 70,000 years. Flowering plants were slightly less successful, with a colonization once every 105,000 years. Mammals were the least successful. The only existing native Hawaiian mammal—not including marine mammals—is a bat, a subspecies of the hoary bat found in North and South America.

One consequence of the difficulty of colonizing Hawaii is that chance played a role in the makeup of Hawaii's natural communities. So when Polynesian settlers first grounded their canoes on the islands, several pieces were missing from Hawaii's version of the puzzle of life.

There were no native frogs, toads, salamanders, or any other kind of amphibian, most likely because their soft bodies couldn't withstand drying from the sun and the salt on a long voyage to reach the islands. There were no snakes, lizards, or freshwater turtles either. In fact, if not for the sea turtles visiting Hawaiian waters, there would have been no reptiles at all on the islands.

With plants, the missing puzzle pieces were also evident. Bamboo, widespread elsewhere in the Pacific, didn't make it to Hawaii.

Sandalwood made it. Aromatic sandalwood fueled a furious trade in its lumber in the decades after Captain Cook arrived in the islands in 1778. Koa is an important native species in today's remnant native Hawaiian forests. Ohia lehua was a crucial arrival. Able to colonize bare lava flows, ohia remains the dominant tree in many Hawaiian forests today.

But ohia's arrival in Hawaii still presents a bit of a mystery for scientists. Its tiny seeds are easily dispersed by wind, but the tree is common on Pacific Islands to the southwest, in the opposite direction of the prevailing trade winds. Some speculate that high-altitude winds blowing north may have gotten it there.

In many ways, ohia is the perfect tree for Hawaii. Even on smooth, hard lava flows, called pahoehoe, the tree can establish itself in cracks that collect the moisture needed for germination. On 'a'a lava, which has a rough surface with more cracks and spaces for seeds and water to collect, ohia trees can root and grow even more quickly.

Studies have shown that winds as light as four miles per hour can keep an ohia seed aloft. A report published in 1992 said that the density of the "seed rain" from an ohia forest bordering a lava flow lessens quickly the farther it blows from the trees. Still, the study indicated that enough seeds were cast by the trees to exploit available cracks in a nearby lava flow for hundreds of yards, sufficient for good-size populations to become established quickly over large areas.

Just the thing for a bare island seeking life.

Ohia isn't the only species that likely arrived on Hawaii by air rather than sea. Studies have illustrated that insects—even those without wings—can be blown aloft and travel considerable distances before precipitating out like a living rain. Birds are another source of colonization by air, as seeds, insects, and even snails can be tangled in feathers and stuck to feet. Seeds can also be deposited through bird droppings.

In the 1950s and 1960s, researchers from the Bishop Museum in Honolulu used boats and planes to suspend nets over open Pacific waters and see what they'd catch. Their nets revealed numerous flying and floating insects and spiders, found in roughly the same proportion as in the Hawaiian Islands' native communities.

Thus a slow-motion army of seeds, spiders, snails, and other creatures made its way to Hawaii. Many individuals set out, but few arrived. And once they did, they were left undisturbed until the next arrival thousands of years later. Over time, the creatures that landed and managed to gain a foothold evolved in isolation.

In some cases, the results were spectacular; in others, the differences were more modest. The Hawaiian hoary bat, for example, changed just enough to be considered a subspecies of the hoary bat found in North and South America.

Snails, on the other hand, went wild. Scientists believe that the 770 species of native Hawaiian snails descended from just 29 different founder species, an average of 26 new species from each founder. It may have helped that some species are hermaphroditic, and a single snail could have fertilized itself and bred. With so many species of snails found nowhere else, the Hawaiian Islands may have had more snails relative to its size than any other place on earth. Much of that diversity has faded, however, as three-quarters of the islands' native snails are now thought to be extinct.

The relative immobility of land snails highlights an important mechanism for the evolution of new species within an isolated island chain like Hawaii. Once a type of creature reaches the island group, individuals that travel to different islands can form new species as the populations evolve separately.

Snails from the Succineidae family eventually evolved into 40 different Hawaiian species. Whereas similar snails in other parts of the world tend to prefer the borders of ponds, lakes, and other aquatic habitats, salt or fresh, Hawaiian species exploit a wide variety of habitats, both on the ground and in trees, including the wet rainforests of Hanawi, where they were a favored food of the po'ouli.

Insects were also prolific in creating new species from old. The islands' 5,377 insect species are thought to be descended from 434 founder species, and 1,014 native flowering plants from 291 new arrivals.

Through a combination of immigration and evolution, new species helped fill in the gaps in Hawaii's natural world. The islands had no large grazing animals, so over time, flightless geese became important herbivores. They had a shortage of insect pollinators, so birds with fantastically long beaks, curved to match the corollas of flowers, developed. No creatures lived in the dark lava tubes, so blind wolf spiders evolved from sighted ones, becoming a walking contradiction: no-eyed big-eyed spiders. Over time, beaks grew longer and legs shorter. Thorns disappeared. Birds that no longer needed to fly lost the ability to do so.

And from the small finchlike ancestor of the po'ouli, a diverse group of birds called the Hawaiian honeycreepers eventually evolved, in one of the world's most spectacular cases of adaptive radiation.

6

THE
HONEYCREEPERS

A MIGRATION GONE WRONG MAY HAVE BROUGHT THE PO'OULI'S ancestors to Hawaii.

Scientists believe those finchlike founders made landfall sometime between 3.5 million and 5 million years ago, possibly sailing in on trade winds blowing steadily toward Hawaii from the northwest.

Though the exact circumstances of their arrival are unknown, millions of years before humans left Africa in their own spread around the globe, a small flock of four- or five-inch-long birds, normally at home in forests, flew into the vast Pacific, soaring over the crests of waves instead of leafy tree tops.

Though seabirds and migratory waterbirds made the Hawaiian Islands a regular stopover, for forest birds not adapted to life at sea, the flight to Hawaii would have been difficult.

Nobody knows whether some of the flock tired and fell into the sea, never to rise again. But at least some birds kept together and stayed aloft, eventually making a grateful landfall. They would have perched on unfamiliar branches, perhaps of the ohia tree, native to another part of the world, and surveyed their new surroundings.

The event seeded a very different Hawaiian Islands with the ancestors of the po'ouli. At that time, the two largest islands, Hawaii and Maui, hadn't appeared yet, nor had Lanai, Molokai, or Kahoolawe.

Over time, the ancestral birds adapted to their environment, thriving and evolving, dividing into new species again and again. Eventually, those wind-borne finches became fifty-five new kinds of birds called Hawaiian honeycreepers, found nowhere else on earth.

The group's diversity would one day astound ornithologists, who referred to the honeycreepers as "the most remarkable evolutionary event among island birds" and as "a brilliant and unequalled natural experiment in evolution and biogeography."

The group contains a remarkable array of colors, from the po'ouli's more drab browns and blacks to the dazzling red and black i'iwi; the descriptively named black mamo, with a long, curved sickle bill; and the yellow of the nukupu'u.

Scientists who have explored the roots of the Hawaiian honeycreeper family tree believe that the ancestors of all this dazzling variety were likely seed eaters, arriving where food was plentiful enough to sustain them and allow them to multiply.

The ancestral honeycreepers likely began to first diversify in eating habits, still resembling their forebears except in the size and shape of their beaks. Some began to take advantage of the nectar of native plants and trees, developing special tongues adapted for sipping nectar. Those birds' bills eventually became long and curved, some extraordinarily so, matching the shape of native flowers. Others evolved long upper bills, similar to those of parrots, for crushing and tearing wood in search of insect larvae. Still others began to use their tongues to pick insects from the plants on which they foraged.

The poʻouli is an unlikely bird among this unlikely family of birds. Thane Pratt, a federal biologist who worked with Hawaii's endangered birds for many years, describes seeing the poʻouli on his first trip into the forests of Hanawi in the 1980s:

> That was marvelous. It's a very striking Hawaiian honeycreeper. There's a lot of plumage variation among the species, but none of them are brown. None of them have that raccoon mask that the poʻouli has. None of them has that incredibly short tail. It's a very weird bird all around. It's surely one of the great ornithological mysteries of the islands. Compared with other Hawaiian honeycreepers, it's very, very peculiar.

Their coloration makes them very hard to find, perhaps because they're foraging in the undergrowth. According to Pratt, "You can go spend a whole day on a home range and not see one at all. They're doing something. They're going down into the undergrowth where you can't see them. They're very silent birds. Most of the birds on the islands are quite noisy," which makes it difficult to locate and study the poʻouli.

The poʻouli seemed so different from other honeycreepers that some questioned whether they were honeycreepers at all. Dean Amadon puzzled over its proper place in the array of Hawaiian birds. He finally came down in favor of its inclusion as a Hawaiian honeycreeper, writing late in 1973 to Andrew Berger that the bird must be a honeycreeper, even though quite different from the others, asking at one point, "What else could it be?"

Not everyone was convinced, however. H. Douglas Pratt, who wrote a book on Hawaiian honeycreepers in 2005, was initially skeptical. He wrote in 1992 that the poʻouli was so different from other honeycreepers in two traits shared by most—a distinctive odor he described as smelling like "old canvas tents," which the poʻouli lacks, and certain characteristics of their tongues—that it should not be considered a honeycreeper until proven to be one. He pointed out that the poʻouli differed in other ways as well: in its coloration, especially its black mask; its susceptibility to being called in by particular sounds; and its unusual and very quiet vocalizations. Pratt wrote:

> The Poo-uli does not look, smell, act, or sound like a Hawaiian honeycreeper, and its tongue lacks a derived state that clusters all drepanidine genera except *Paroreomyza*. . . . At present, the only unequivocal statement that can be made about the affinities of the Poo-uli is that it is a nine-primaried oscine of uncertain affinities. . . . Speculation as to its actual relationships would, at present, be baseless.

Almost a decade later, DNA analysis finally confirmed the poʻouliʼs membership among the Hawaiian honeycreepers. An examination of mitochondrial DNA extracted from the two specimens collected in 1973 showed that the poʻouli was a honeycreeper, but it also confirmed Prattʼs sense that it wasnʼt a typical honeycreeper: "This troubling (and troubled) little bird is a Hawaiian honeycreeper, albeit an extremely distinctive one," the studyʼs authors wrote. The poʻouli, they explained, likely diverged from other honeycreepers early enough in their shared history that the defining characteristics described by Pratt hadnʼt yet evolved. They continued:

The Po'ouli has had a long independent evolutionary history. This long period of independent evolution can perhaps explain some of *Melamprosops'* unique phenotypic characteristics. Such . . . distinctiveness also increases the Po'ouli's conservation value, in that the species represents a significant fraction of the genetic diversity of the drepanidines [the family that includes the honeycreepers]. . . . The Po'ouli's unique evolutionary history convinces us that serious efforts should be undertaken to avoid its impending extinction.

Extinction, unfortunately, was a phenomenon that threatened not just the po'ouli. Species after species that had evolved in isolation on the Hawaiian Islands succumbed to invasive plants, animals, snails, and insects introduced to the islands by humans. Hawaiian honeycreepers, extraordinary and beautiful in their diversity, were hit hard.

One-third of the known honeycreeper species were extinct before Europeans stumbled on Hawaii. That was just the start, however, of what one author described as "an avian holocaust in Hawaii." Fourteen of the thirty-six species known since Captain Cook's 1778 arrival at the islands are also gone, six more are likely extinct, and eight of those known to be still around are listed as endangered by the U.S. government. Of the remaining eight, two have had population crashes in recent years, leaving only six of the fifty-five known honeycreeper species neither extinct nor in imminent danger of extinction.

Extinctions began to mount in the late 1800s. The Oahu nukupu'u was last seen in the 1860s. The year 1892 was a brutal one, with the last of three species—the ula-'ai-'hawane, lesser koa-finch, and Oahu akialoa—recorded. Two years later, in 1894, the last Maui Nui akialoa was observed, followed a year later by both the last greater koa-finch and Kona grosbeak. The year 1898 saw the last Hawaii mamo, followed by the last Kauai nukupu'u in 1899. In 1901, the last greater amakihi was reported, followed, in 1907, by the last black mamo.

There was an eleven-year respite, but then in 1918, the last Lanai hookbill was recorded, followed by the last Laysan honeycreeper in 1923. In 1940, the last lesser akialoa was observed. Twenty-three years later, in 1963, the last kakawahie was seen.

Despite modern conservation techniques, the roll call has continued in recent decades, with the last Oahu alauahio in 1985, the last 'o'u in 1989, and the last known po'ouli in 2004.

Many of those working in conservation on the islands have their own lists of lasts they've experienced or witnessed: a last sighting, a last song, a last nesting. In addition to those birds thought to be extinct, there are others whose numbers have dwindled to the point where a sighting is cause for excitement, or where the lack of a sighting increases the conviction that they may be gone. Jacobi says:

> I've actually seen and listened to the 'o'o on Kauai, and it was the last one, as it turned out to be, and the po'ouli and the 'alala. I have been woken up in the morning by the 'alala when I was camping out in the Kona forest back in the seventies. The kama'o. It's those kinds of things that really strike me . . . the day I first saw a po'ouli. I can show people pictures and tell them what it was like, but they're never going to see them.

The recovery efforts aimed at the po'ouli weren't the only ones going on in Hawaii over the last three decades. In fact, state and federal biologists, as well as private conservation partners such as The Peregrine Fund and the San Diego Zoo, are forced to constantly juggle recovery efforts of several species at once. They perform an intricate balancing act between conservation needs and available resources, adjusting to accommodate budgetary realities, staffing constraints, and developments in the field.

Captive-breeding efforts, initially run by the state of Hawaii, then by The Peregrine Fund, and now by the San Diego Zoo, have been aimed at a number of species. The state began its first captive-breeding program decades ago. Those efforts were aimed at the native Hawaiian goose, called the nene, which was down to between 30 and 50 birds in the 1950s. The nene program has seen its ups and downs, but as of 2001, 2,450 captive-reared nene had been released on Maui, Kauai, and Hawaii.

The state turned the captive-rearing program over to The Peregrine Fund in 1993. By 2001, the program had reared 153 chicks of Hawaiian songbirds, releasing some into the wild in an attempt to restore populations. Hawaiian honeycreepers involved in the program include Hawaii amakihi, i'iwi, palila, akohekohe, Hawaii creeper, Maui parrotbill, and apapane.

The road hasn't always been, and still is not, a smooth one. Conservationists, scientists, members of the public—particularly Hawaii's hunting community—and government officials sometimes don't see eye to eye on the conservation of these endangered birds. To some people, the Hawaiian honeycreepers are jewels of evolution, exemplars of what is possible given genetic raw materials, isolation, and time; to others, they're just birds.

One notable clashing over Hawaii's native birdlife came in the late 1970s over the conservation of an endangered striking yellow and white honeycreeper called the palila. Dependent on the seeds and flowers of the native mamane tree for food, the once-widespread palila is largely limited to the western and southwestern slope of Hawaii's Mauna Kea volcano, though some small populations are located on the eastern and southern slopes.

By the late 1970s, the palila had been reduced to a remnant of its original range, vulnerable to fire, storm, or blight. It was down to sixteen hundred individuals, a specialist under siege, much as the poʻouli must have been upon its discovery earlier in the decade.

The mamane on which the palila depended was also under siege, being browsed by introduced cattle, goats, feral sheep, and mouflon sheep maintained for public hunting. The state drafted a master plan for the area in 1977, and in 1978, it was sued by environmentalists, including the Sierra Club and the Hawaii Audubon Society. The environmentalists argued that the state failed to comply with provisions to fence out feral animals from a portion of the forest and also failed to comply with the Endangered Species Act.

The court's ruling, issued a year later in 1979, went in favor of the palila. The court found the state in violation of the Endangered Species Act because it was actively maintaining feral sheep and goats in the mamane forests, and ordered them removed.

The palila case set a precedent that sent lawmakers and government bureaucrats scrambling. It was the first case in which the Endangered Species Act—specifically the federal government's designation of critical habitat on Mauna Kea for the palila—forced state action on nonfederal land. Some say the case prompted a weakening of the act through redefinition of the word "harm," reducing the priority of conservation.

Today sheep are not eradicated, but their numbers are low enough that the mamane are regenerating. Though the palila prefer older trees, about one-third of mamane trees on Mauna Kea have sprouted in the last twenty years and are more than six feet tall, with the largest of them possibly starting to benefit the birds. Unlike the case of the poʻouli, protection of the forest alone seems to be making the difference for the palila, whose numbers were estimated at roughly four thousand in 2001.

The story of another honeycreeper, the 'o'u, illustrates the danger of letting the palila, the po'ouli, or any other endangered species dwindle to a single population. Concentrated in one spot, even if a population's numbers are healthy, it is vulnerable to disease or another natural catastrophe—such as a hurricane.

Once one of the most common honeycreepers, the 'o'u, a chunky green bird with a thick beak, was found on six different islands. Over the decades of the twentieth century, however, it disappeared first from Oahu, then Maui, Molokai, and Lanai. The last 'o'u was seen on Hawaii in 1987 and on Kauai in 1989.

"I've had quite a number of experiences with the 'o'u. I was dangling from a tree halfway through the canopy having some 'o'u come right by me," Jacobi says. "The 'o'u for all intents is extinct now."

Scientists believe that any remnant 'o'u left on Kauai were likely finished off in 1992, when Hurricane Iniki, a category four monster, roared through the Hawaiian Islands. With winds of 140 miles per hour, the eye of the storm passed directly over Kauai. Iniki destroyed fourteen hundred houses, caused $1.8 billion in damage, and killed six people.

7

THE PO'OULI'S
DECLINE

It was April 1986, springtime in Hawaii, thirteen years after the po'ouli's discovery. A team of biologists was doing something no scientist—and perhaps no human—had ever done before: watching po'oulis nest.

They didn't realize it, but they were also about to witness something else no one had seen before: a po'ouli's natural death.

It would be the only time scientists saw something that apparently was occurring all too frequently. Since the bird's discovery, its numbers had declined steadily. The lifeblood of a species that had existed for millions of years was slowly but relentlessly draining away.

Scientists hoped that by watching the birds raise young, they would discover a clue that would help reverse the decline. Failing that, though, they grimly understood that their role was to document behavior the world might never see again.

By 1986, much of the damage had been done. Scientists estimated that po'ouli numbers—not particularly abundant at its discovery—fell 90 percent between 1975 and 1985. From initial estimates of several hundred, the bird had already disappeared from the area in the forest where it had been discovered, and just a few handfuls were hanging on in the newly created Hanawi Natural Area Reserve on Haleakala's slopes. Though no estimates exist from 1986, a two-week survey in 1988 found just five individuals.

Pigs, rats, and bureaucratic dithering would take another eighteen years to kill the last po'ouli, essentially finishing the job begun by the Polynesians fifteen hundred years earlier when they began clearing lowland forests to plant taro, bananas, breadfruit, and sugarcane.

Nobody knows how many po'oulis there were when the bird's population peaked. But fossil finds indicate that the bird was not uncommon and its range spread far beyond this narrow patch of rain forest to the drier forests beyond.

But those details were far from the minds of three researchers in the po'ouli's home forest in early March 1986. After working transects in the area where the first po'oulis were found, Cameron Kepler, Betsy Gagné, and Allen Allison decided to try their luck across the East Hanawi stream, in what looked like good po'ouli habitat.

The stream flows through a steep gulch not far down the mountainside, so the three crossed at the top and worked their way downslope for three hours, traveling less than a mile before reaching six thousand feet.

They were still near the stream after lunch when they heard it: *chik*.

"It stopped us dead," Kepler says. "It stopped us in our tracks because in those days, '86, it was rare."

They began to search for the bird that made the noise, and about forty minutes later, they had their first sighting. But the po'ouli wasn't just flitting from tree to tree looking for a meal. The bird was on a mission, repeatedly picking up moss and other nesting material in its beak and flying to another tree, disappearing in the foliage.

After watching for more than an hour, the three knew they were seeing something special, something never seen before: a po'ouli was building a nest.

Facing a three-hour hike, they reluctantly began to head back at 3 P.M., wondering whether they'd be able to locate the nest tree again in the sea of ohia. Then, Kepler recalls, "We stopped and said, 'This is silly, we have a po'ouli carrying nest material.' We didn't have a tent, we didn't have anything, but it didn't look like it was going to rain. We voted right then and there."

The three radioed base camp and told the others that they'd decided to stay, then went back downhill to watch the bird.

"We had it down to one tree," Kepler says. "There were what looked like a couple of nests in the tree, but we never saw the bird go to the nest. We lost it every time it got to the tree."

They saw the po'ouli six times before packing it in for the night. The last four times they saw it, the bird was silent, making them realize how lucky they were to have heard it in the first place.

With evening approaching, they walked back uphill, looking for a level spot to lie down for what would be an uncomfortable night in the rainforest. They didn't have any sleeping gear and carried precious little food. But they did have an unparalleled opportunity. That was enough.

They settled on what Kepler describes as a "mossy, semi-comfortable place on top of some tree branches. It was kind of grim." They pooled their food, mainly lunch leftovers from that day plus a few just-in-case items. Between the three of them, they had half a bag of gorp, six jerky sticks, some prunes and figs, eight small candy bars, an apple, a few sips of Gatorade, and some Tang. "That was it. That was our dinner, our breakfast, and our lunch for the next day. We savored every bit."

The night was cold. Not wanting to lie down, the three traded stories until 11 P.M. Eventually they gave up and tried to get comfortable, huddling together on the slope.

"Every hour or so, we'd go 'one, two, three, switch,' and we'd switch to our other side because our hips were hurting. It was cold. We had our raingear on. It was really, really cold," Kepler says.

By 4 A.M., they gave up, rising and doing calisthenics to warm up. When it got light, they headed back downhill to the nest tree, counting themselves lucky that it hadn't rained.

Help was on the way. The three were part of a larger team assessing ecological factors and pig damage in Hanawi. Two others came down from the base camp that morning and stayed behind when Kepler, Gagné, and Allison headed back in the early afternoon. It was a three-hour hike that Kepler remembers as slow and painful.

"Everybody was totally zonked because we hadn't had much food and we were basically up for [two days]." Kepler says.

In the coming weeks, researchers took advantage of the rare opportunity. A. Marie Ecton, a federal biologist who had joined Kepler on Maui, led the field effort, logging many nights in the dripping forest. Researchers eventually spotted a second bird that looked much like the first. Unlike some bird species with distinct differences in plumage between males and females, po'ouli males and females look very much alike.

The nest, about six inches across and made of bare twigs with moss filling the spaces, was about twenty-five feet up the ohia tree, well below top of the forest canopy. It had been so hard to spot because the birds regularly used the dense ground cover of ferns and shrubs below to camouflage its location. When leaving, they would drop almost vertically to the top of the low vegetation and fly along it before rising to land on the branches of another tree.

The team visited the site ten times in the ensuing weeks, staying between one and five days before summoning the helicopter to get them out. They kept their distance, not wanting to disturb the birds, using binoculars and spotting scopes from beneath a tarp across a small stream about 120 feet away. Ecton recalls how difficult the observations were, sitting quietly for long hours to avoid disturbing the birds, eye glued to the scope so as not to miss an observation.

The rushing water from the cold mountain stream sometimes drowned out the po'ouli's low calls, but it was the weather that most frustrated the team. The birds were putting the finishing touches on the nest when they were first seen on March 5. The very next day, dense fog completely blocked the scientists' view. Regular downpours soaked researchers in the coming weeks and made observation trying at best.

Despite the rain, Ecton and other researchers camped out near the po'ouli nest and watched the birds court. The male fed the female, sang, and displayed. He chased her, circled her, flicking his wings, and sang some more. Focused on creating a small family, he was oblivious to the doom that would overtake his species in a few short years.

It took several weeks, but the researchers' patience was eventually rewarded. On March 25, they saw some unusual activity. The female hopped onto the nest rim and directed her attention inside. On April Fool's Day, researchers saw the chick for the first time. A few days later, they watched it begging for food. Though they believed the nest originally contained two eggs, they were happy to see at least one chick emerge.

Their joy was short-lived, however. A week later, on April 8, the skies opened. By this time, researchers understood that foul weather in the forests of Hanawi was not only possible, it was likely. But the ferocity of this storm took researchers by surprise.

It rained nearly twelve inches over the next six days, testing the endurance of human and bird alike. It was raining so hard that water flowed down the mountain in a sheet, as if the entire slope had become a shallow river.

Though most of the time they had to hike out of the forest to the treeline for a helicopter pickup, Ecton says it was as if they were caught in a flash flood, so they called the chopper to pick them up directly at their camp. "That's the one and only time we bailed in a field situation. It was not letting up. It was a continuous downpour. We knew we had to get out of there."

The field crew went to an open spot on the sloped forest. In an extraordinary feat for which Ecton is still grateful, the chopper pilot, who could barely see, brought the craft in, touching a skid to the slope so they could scramble inside.

"He couldn't see me and I couldn't see him. He landed with one skid touching the slope," Ecton recalls. "Then he went down to the ocean and flew to the airport from there. It was really scary."

By the end, it was apparent the weather had won. The soaking rain, cool winds, and the parents' reduced ability to find food had created a lethal combination. The chick had died.

The adult po'oulis regrouped, however. They began building a second nest, even closer to the researchers, laying two eggs inside. This nest, too, had a nestling die. But it also saw success, and a few weeks later researchers watched a young po'ouli take its first flight, bringing new hope in its short excursions into nearby trees.

The months of observations proved invaluable, providing the first details of po'ouli courtship and parenting, critical information in an effort to save a species on the brink of extinction. Perhaps the most important clue gleaned during that damp, chilly spring of 1986, however, was in the struggles of two po'ouli to raise a family amid a rainforest deluge.

The birds raised just one chick from four eggs, even though there was no outright catastrophe such as a rat, cat, or mongoose attacking the nest, destroying eggs, and devouring young. Death instead came on the trade winds and in the relentless showers. Though the male po'ouli feeds the female and the chicks, extended periods of rain and wind reduce his ability to forage. Foul weather also forces a hungry po'ouli mother, which forages herself for brief periods, to choose between staying on the nest and leaving it to find food thereby risking death of eggs and young. With the mother gone, rain and wind can quickly chill both chicks and eggs, threatening them with hypothermia.

The worst stretches of weather may have had an even greater effect on the parents' ability to care for their young. But some storms were so severe that they brought a curtain of rain through which the researchers couldn't see the nest at all.

That soggy field team's observations took on new meaning when coupled with fossil evidence reported just a few years earlier showing that po'oulis were once plentiful on the other, drier side of Haleakala. That got researchers thinking that though they discovered the po'ouli in the rainforest, maybe this bird wasn't supposed to be there at all. If the po'ouli were naturally a dry forest bird, it might make sense that it would struggle to raise young during a rainforest spring.

Because the po'ouli was discovered so recently, in 1973, researchers don't have the benefit of previous scientific studies, oral history accounts of ancient Hawaiians, or the writings of early Western naturalists to help them tell the po'ouli's story. Scientists don't have enough evidence to say how the po'ouli wound up in Hanawi. They don't know whether the rainforest was once part of the bird's range or whether it was forced there by a variety of factors. They can't say that the po'ouli was eliminated from this place at this time and for that reason. They don't have the certainty that forms the basis of scientific papers and talks at conferences. They do know, however, that Hawaii's tale of woe applies to the po'ouli as it does to the birds with which it once shared the forests.

They know the bird was relentlessly hemmed in and set upon by a variety of enemies. They know its forests were probably burned to clear land for bananas, breadfruit, and sugarcane. They know it was hounded by disease, most likely into the most inhospitable corners of its former range. They know it has been forced to make a final stand on Haleakala's rainy slopes against tree-climbing rats, carnivorous snails competing for its food, and forest-destroying pigs.

And they can be pretty sure that the po'ouli's decline began with the coming of humans to Hawaii.

For many years, it was thought that the bulk of the destruction of Hawaiian birdlife came after Cook arrived in 1778. But in the early 1980s, published reports about fossil finds of bird bones revolutionized our view of Hawaiian birdlife and its extinction. The reports greatly increased modern understanding of the toll that the islands' earliest human inhabitants had on its birds.

Fossils showed that forty-four species of birds were destroyed before Cook came ashore. Human hunting and predation by the rats that accompanied the Polynesians were doubtless a major scourge. Gone by Cook's time were a host of flightless birds that, unaccustomed to large ground predators, must have seemed easy prey.

Habitat change likely also took its toll, reducing the birds' range and perhaps leading to some extinctions as the new settlers cut and burned trees across the islands to make room for the plantations that covered much of the lowlands by the time Cook arrived.

This first round of forest clearing may have been the initial step pushing the po'ouli backward and up Haleakala's slopes. It may have been the first step on a path that eventually led to a cage at the Maui Bird Conservation Center for the last of the species, which died surrounded not by other birds and its forest home, but by wire mesh and scientists and veterinarians trying to undo the damage done by generations of humans before them.

But the destruction of the lowland forests by the Polynesians was just the first wave pushing the po'ouli backward, forcing it to retreat into its last stronghold in Hanawi.

Quite possibly the most destructive act in all of Hawaii's natural history occurred in 1826, when sailors from the *Wellington* rinsed out a water barrel filled in Mexico before refilling it from a fresh Maui stream. The sailors returned to the ship and continued on their voyage, oblivious to what they had left behind.

In the water they dumped from that barrel were the larvae of *Culex quinquefasciatus,* also known as the southern house mosquito, one of the world's thirty-five hundred mosquito species.

Mosquitoes and disease have gone hand in hand for as long as humans have felt the itchy bite, cursed, slapped, and begun scratching. In addition to the blessings of a tropical climate, beautiful beaches, lush vegetation, and unique wildlife, Hawaii also had the comfort of being mosquito-free.

Until 1826, that is.

It didn't take long after the watering party left for the mosquitoes to spread. Mosquitoes breed in water, both fresh and brackish, which is not hard to find on Maui. Females lay hundreds of eggs that hatch, pupate, and grow into adults in just days. That first crop of mosquitoes exploded across Maui, and from there to the other main islands. An early account tells the story:

> Dr Judd was called upon to treat a hitherto unknown kind of itch, inflicted by a new kind of *nalo* (fly) described as 'singing in the ear.' The itch had first been reported in early 1827 by Hawaiians who lived near pools of standing water and along streams back of Lahaina (Maui). To the Reverend William Richards, their descriptions of the flies suggested a pestiferous insect, from which heretofore the Islands were fortunately free. Inspection confirmed his fears. The mosquito had arrived!

The southern house mosquito, though happy to bite humans, horses, and other animals, prefers birds. And Hawaiian birds, like the islands' human inhabitants, had no experience with either this new *nalo* or the diseases it spread.

Hawaiian birds provided easy meals for mosquitoes at night. One study in 1959 compared the sleeping posture of native Hawaiian birds with that of birds introduced from continents where mosquitoes are plentiful. Those introduced birds slept with their faces buried in their back feathers, crouched down over their feet with their breast feathers fluffed to cover as much as possible.

Hawaiian birds, on the other hand, didn't take these protective measures, leaving the fleshy corner between the beak and eye as well as the legs and feet exposed to mosquito bites. Researchers counted the numbers of mosquitoes on the sleeping birds, finding five to ten times as many on the unprotected Hawaiian birds as on the introduced species.

Once bitten by the mosquitoes spreading across the islands, the Hawaiian birds' immune systems were similarly unprepared for what they were about to face. Unlike birds on the continents, whose ancestors for generation after generation had to deal with mosquitoes and fight off the diseases they carry, Hawaiian birds had no inborn immunities for mosquito-borne ills.

It took just a few decades for two diseases to match the destruction of Hawaiian birdlife previously wrought over hundreds of years by Polynesian hunting and forest burning.

When smallpox first reached the Americas, it found a human population whose bodies had never faced anything like it before. In the absence of natural defenses, the disease tore through the continents, playing a major role in the destruction of Native American civilizations. It killed nearly half of the Aztecs, weakening the Aztec empire, making it more easily conquered by the Spanish.

Farther south, in the Incan empire, the disease spread from Central America ahead of the Spanish, killing a large part of the population, including Emperor Huayna Capac and his son, throwing the empire into turmoil and contributing to the Spanish conquest.

Bird pox took much the same toll when it reached Hawaii's defenseless bird community. Exactly how it arrived in the islands is unknown. Some believe it was present in the seabirds and waterfowl that visited Hawaii for millennia and that when the mosquito arrived, it provided a way for the virus to cross into Hawaii's native forest birds. Others think it arrived with domestic fowl such as chickens, while still others attribute its arrival to the influx of nonnative songbirds, brought in and released by settlers when Hawaiian birds began to disappear from the lowlands. Recent research shows that there may actually be several strains of avian pox virus among Hawaiian birds.

Regardless of how it got there, bird pox's impact was devastating.

Mosquitoes and other biting bugs picked up the virus and flew off to bite native forest birds, in which it found a defenseless host. The avian pox virus exploded, causing grotesque, tumorlike lesions at the spots where the mosquitoes were most likely to feed: the rim of the eye, the corner of the beak, the legs, and the toes.

Even in birds exposed to the virus for millennia, the disease can be dangerous. It has two forms. The "dry" form, which occurs on the skin, causes wartlike lesions that will often dry up and fall off. The "wet" form of the disease affects the internal organs and, though less visible, is more deadly.

In Hawaiian birds, both forms were equally lethal. A pox lesion on the corner of a Hawaiian bird's eye could grow so large as to blind the bird. Pox lesions on the birds' feet prevented them from grasping branches and roosting. Lesions at the corner of the mouth could grow so large that the bird couldn't eat.

By the late 1800s, the disease was widespread, and its effect on Hawaii's birds extreme. R. C. L. Perkins in 1903 described wild birds so incapacitated by the large pustules on their head, legs, and feet that they refused to move and could be picked up by hand. As one researcher, Richard Warner, summed up the situation in that era: "Severe infestations by bird pox . . . were so numerous and extreme that large numbers of diseased and badly debilitated birds could be observed in the field."

In the late 1950s and early 1960s, Warner conducted a series of experiments on the susceptibility of Hawaii's native birds to disease to understand why they seemed to be limited exclusively to high-altitude forests. It had been widely assumed until then that the destruction of lowland forests was the cause of this retreat to high ground. But Warner had noticed that though much of the lowland forest was gone and many native plants had been replaced by non-Hawaiian species, some lowland forests still remained and some native birds appeared happy to feed on the new plants. The 'o'u, which normally fed on the fruits of the ieie vine, had been seen feeding on guava and mulberries, for example. Even more suspicious was that native bird populations were absent from the segments of original lowland forest that remained.

Warner's suspicion was that disease, not habitat destruction, was the major factor influencing which forest birds lived where. And he set out to prove it.

In 1958, he caught finches on the small island of Laysan, in the northwestern Hawaiian Islands, hundreds of miles away. Protected by distance and open water, Laysan remained mosquito and bird pox free. Warner believed the birds of Laysan would be good examples to show what happened on the main islands when bird pox first began to spread. He brought the captured birds to Honolulu, where he let the birds settle in for a while, and then opened wide the windows and let in the mosquitoes.

Within two weeks, the birds developed swelling on the feet, wing joints, and in the space between the beak and eye. The swellings grew larger and then erupted as granular lesions that resembled tumors, finally becoming infected. After one month, every bird had at least one lesion, and several had three or four, at the corners of the mouth and on the forehead, eyelids, and feet. The birds gradually weakened and died.

Warner's report on the research includes a picture of him holding a finch with a bird pox tumor on its eye roughly the size of his thumbnail and almost half the size of the bird's head.

Mosquitoes can spread many kinds of diseases, and the one that came second likely provided the knockout punch for both the po'ouli and other native birds.

In 1902, an observer of Hawaiian birds, H. W. Henshaw, wrote about their puzzling tendency to drop dead from no apparent cause. He attributed it to the birds' lack of hardiness and susceptibility to temperature change.

> I am not aware that birds of the Hawaiian Islands are more subject to fatal diseases than those of other lands. Dead birds are, however, found rather frequently in the woods on the island of Hawaii, especially the iiwi and akakani [apapane]. There is no doubt that sudden and marked changes of temperature affect Hawaiian birds unfavorably, especially the two species just mentioned and, after heavy and prolonged storms, many individuals of both species are driven into sheltered valleys and even along the sea-shore far from their woodland haunts. Under such circumstances scores of the above named species are picked up dead or dying, and the mortality among other birds is, perhaps, unusually great.

Warner, in examining the impact of disease on Hawaiian birds, had an alternative explanation: malaria. "I am convinced that the mass mortality of birds driven into the lowland areas by winter storms or other causes and exhibiting no bird pox lesions can be directly attributed to massive infections of one or more species of plasmodium, the organism causing avian malaria," he wrote in 1968. He went on to say that the native birds' stormy-weather habit of flying from higher-altitude haunts down the mountain to calmer air may have turned out to be lethal. "What had been in primeval times a retreat from inclement weather had become, with the advent of the *Culex* mosquito, a death trap for native birds."

Like bird pox, malaria is spread by mosquitoes, though there's some uncertainty about when it was introduced to the islands. Unlike bird pox, malaria is not caused by a virus, but rather by a parasite. The parasite enters the bloodstream, where it multiplies and completes its life cycle. In the process, it infects red blood cells, often destroying them, making the blood thin and watery and causing severe anemia. Birds afflicted by malaria are typically emaciated and listless, have difficulty breathing, and have weakness in one or both legs.

In humans, malaria remains one of the world's most deadly diseases, killing about one million people each year. In Africa alone, a child dies of malaria every thirty seconds, according to the World Health Organization. In Hawaiian birds, Warner demonstrated that the disease is no less deadly.

Starting in 1959, he conducted a series of experiments similar to those on bird pox, again using Laysan finches. He brought trapped birds to Lihue, on Kauai, one of the smaller of the main Hawaiian islands. After a settling-in period, Warner exposed them to the island's mosquitoes in an outdoor cage.

It took only five nights for the first bird to die. On day twelve, five more birds had died. After sixteen nights, just over two weeks of exposure to Kauai's night air and mosquitoes that hadn't been there before 1826, all thirteen birds in the group were dead. An examination of the birds' blood showed massive infections of avian malaria.

Warner repeated the experiments on three kinds of native birds from the main Hawaiian islands, as well as introduced Japanese white-eye and house finches. Similar experiments produced similar results. After nine days, all the Hawaiian birds were exhibiting symptoms of malaria, panting and shivering.

"The lesser Amakihi that had first shown signs of debility on 11 August was now in the final stages of the disease," Warner wrote. "One Amakihi was panting heavily and in apparent extreme discomfort. The remaining birds were listless, with occasional bouts of shivering and panting."

Blood tests showed that all the native birds had severe malaria. The introduced Japanese white-eye and house finches included in the experiment also developed malaria, but unlike the Hawaiian birds, had just mild cases, illustrating their ability to fight off the parasite.

These dramatic results left Warner—and many others—wondering just how deadly malaria was to the native birds. He got a partial answer after limiting five birds' exposure to mosquitoes to just three nights, and then bringing them inside to mosquito-proof cages. When he ended the experiment after seventeen days, three of the five birds were dead and the other two were sick with malaria.

The rest of the answer was provided more recently in a series of experiments summed up by Sue Jarvi in 2001. Using modern laboratory techniques, researchers infected a group of birds with the number of malaria parasites found in a single mosquito bite. Jarvi described mortality in the experiments as extraordinarily high. A single mosquito bite killed 90 percent of the i'iwi and 75 percent of the Maui 'alauahio in the experiment. Two other native bird species showed more resistance, but a single bite still killed 63 percent of the apapane and 65 percent of the Hawaii amakihi receiving that small dose.

What emerged from those experiments was a clear understanding that disease has been the determining factor in where the native birds can be found in Hawaii. And it is by following the mosquitoes, deadly carriers of malaria and pox, that we can understand where Hawaiian birds can and cannot live.

Warner realized that and thus took his work out of the laboratory and onto the slopes of Hawaii's volcanoes, near Hilo on the island of Hawaii and on Maui's Haleakala. His surveys and bird counts confirmed that the abundance of native birds rose the higher one climbed. He noticed a particularly dramatic increase above eighteen hundred feet. This elevation coincided with the upper range of what he called the "Culex belt," above which it was too cool for the mosquito to breed in large numbers. Warner's work finally demonstrated that it was disease, not the loss of lowland forests, that has limited native Hawaiian birds to higher elevations.

> It is my conclusion, in view of the recent evidence, that the principal reason that the more ubiquitous drepanids remain strictly in regions above 600m is to be found in their continued susceptibility to introduced diseases, principally avian malaria and bird pox. Any protracted visit to the lowland mosquito belt would mean immediate death from infections of Plasmodium. Even if some survived the malaria, onset of bird pox would complete the extermination.

Nearly twenty years later, another group of researchers repeated Warner's experiments, getting similar results. Charles van Riper III, Sandra van Riper, M. Lee Goff, and Marshall Laird enriched the picture drawn by Warner. They showed that mosquitoes, though in low numbers, are indeed present even at high altitudes, and that drier forests harbored fewer mosquitoes, allowing native birds to exist at lower elevations. Their most hopeful finding, however, was that native birds on the main islands had begun to develop some natural resistance to the disease, though for most a diagnosis of malaria still constituted a death sentence.

They also found, not surprisingly, that the abundance of different Hawaiian bird species today is directly proportional to their resistance to malaria. The brilliant red, sickle-billed i'iwi, for example, which was widespread in 1903 and has undergone the largest population decline, was the most susceptible to malaria of the native birds tested save the Laysan finch. The yellow-feathered common amikihi, the most resistant of the native birds, is still found in fairly high numbers and, as of the writing of van Riper's team, had reinvaded areas from which it had once been extirpated.

Habitat destruction and disease further pushed native birds up Hawaii's mountains, into remnant rainforests high on the slopes of former volcanoes. Unfortunately for these birds, however, the invasion didn't stop there.

The mammals were coming.

8

RATS, EXTINCTION, AND THE BATTLE OF MIDWAY

WHEN THE POLYNESIAN COLONISTS STEPPED OFF THEIR CANOES after their long sea voyage from the Marquesas, they were the first land mammals the islands had ever seen. A close second—or perhaps third, after the pigs intentionally brought by the Polynesians—was the rat.

When rats first came ashore, leaping from the Polynesian canoes where they had stowed aboard, they found islands full of birds and plants that had no idea what was about to hit them. On continents where rats, pigs, and a host of other predators are common, predator and prey have evolved together, with the prey animals developing defensive traits and behaviors that safeguard them against being killed and eaten.

Nature has an efficient way of ensuring that those characteristics are passed on to the next generation. Those individuals in whom the traits aren't strong, or that lack them entirely, are more likely to be eaten and less likely to breed and pass their genes along.

Buried in antiquity, there is little evidence of the impact of the Polynesian rat. But it seems a safe bet that it followed the pattern Hawaii saw again fifteen hundred years later, when the black rat was introduced.

The rat, in many ways, is the perfect invader. It is tough, agile, adaptable, and fertile. Polynesian rats can have four litters of six young each year. As often happens with introduced species moving into a land that lacks natural predators, Polynesian rats probably exploded in numbers after arriving in Hawaii.

The fossil evidence of native Hawaiian birds found in the 1970s showed that among the species of land birds extinct before Cook's arrival were several species of flightless geese, two species of flightless ibises, and seven flightless rails.

It is likely no coincidence that most of the islands' flightless birds were among the first to go. Ground-dwelling and nesting birds with no clue how to defend themselves or their nests against these new predators—both human and rodent—would have had little chance of survival.

The stunning speed with which a rat infestation can destroy a bird population was illustrated on the two islands of the Midway atoll in the 1940s.

By 1943, Midway was home to the last population of the Laysan rail, a flightless bird with red eyes, green bill, and green legs. The rail had been exterminated on its native island of Laysan years earlier, when the manager of a guano-mining operation there released rabbits, hoping to start a rabbit-meat cannery.

The rabbits rapidly multiplied and stripped the island of vegetation, creating a sandy desert devoid of shelter for either the rail or the insects it lived on. The Laysan rail disappeared from the island on which it arose.

Though eliminated from Laysan, several rails had been transplanted years earlier to the two islands of Midway, which were free of both rats and rabbits. The rails had multiplied there and were doing well, and it appeared that humans had preserved a unique character among the world's birdlife, as the Laysan rail quickly endeared itself to those who encountered it. Paul Baldwin wrote in a 1945 *Audubon Magazine* article:

> Unquestionably, its humorous behavior provided one of the chief interests at Laysan. The rails would come into any man-made shelter and run over the occupants' shoes, peering intently and snapping up flies that buzzed about. Unable to fly, they flapped their diminutive wings in balancing and jumping. . . . No wonder this little elf never failed to captivate the hearts of those who watched it.

When black rats were inadvertently introduced onto Midway in 1943, the rails' decline was breathtaking in its swiftness and heartbreaking in its finality. The rats first were seen in February or March on Sand Island and soon on Eastern Island as well. In June 1944, little more than a year after the first rat was sighted, researcher E. L. Caum reported four or five rails on Eastern Island, making the last recorded sighting of the Laysan rail.

Whereas the rabbits on Laysan destroyed the rail's habitat, likely starving it to death, the rats killed and ate young and adult rails alike, slurped eggs, and devoured the insect prey on which the birds depended.

The story of the Laysan rail on Midway is just one stanza of a monotonous dirge sung on island after island across the Pacific after rats made their way ashore. One writer, A. R. McCullogh in 1921 gave voice to that sad song, describing the destruction on Lord Howe Island in the Southwest Pacific, infested by rats in 1918 when a ship wrecked off its shores:

> But two short years ago the forests of Lord Howe Island were joyous with the notes of myriads of birds, large and small and of many kinds. . . . Today, however, the ravages of rats, the worst enemy of mankind, which have been accidentally introduced, have made the note of a bird rare, and the sight of one, save the strong-billed Magpie and the Kingfisher (Halcyon), even rarer. Within two years this paradise of birds has become a wilderness and the quietness of death reigns where all was melody.

On Hawaii, centuries after the Polynesian rat came ashore, the Norway rat made it to land from Western ships. The maraudings of the Norway rat are not mentioned much, and it may have simply piggybacked onto the damage done by the smaller Polynesian rat, elbowing it aside but causing little broader ecological stir.

That was not the case in the late 1800s, when some believe the second European rat—the same black rat implicated in the extinction of the Laysan rail decades later on Midway—reached Hawaii. From 1892 to 1930, an estimated 58 percent of the remaining Hawaiian forest bird species were drastically reduced in population or went extinct. The decline was so mysterious that one observer in 1912 called it "one of the wonder tales of ornithology."

A wonder of horrors, no doubt.

One researcher, I. A. E. Atkinson, began to speculate about whether rats might be the cause of that striking decline. The black rat, also called the roof rat or ship rat, had been assumed to have arrived at about the same time as the larger Norway rat, also called the brown rat. But evidence of a huge population explosion among black rats in the late 1800s, coupled with a population crash of forest birds, made Atkinson think maybe that timeline wasn't accurate.

Atkinson began to dig into the background of the two rat species and found that a rat is not just a rat. Black rats differ from Norway rats in important ways. Norway rats are better swimmers, making it more likely that they would have gotten ashore from ships anchored off the Hawaiian coast. Black rats are better climbers, however, making them a bigger threat to the native birdlife.

The key to the puzzle, Atkinson believed, was timing. The black rat was not present on the U.S. Pacific coast until the 1850s, and the Norway rat was the most common species aboard ships. Then there was an inexplicable shift in the kind of rat—from the Norway rat to the black rat—found aboard European vessels.

The final piece of the puzzle bringing the poor-swimming black rat ashore was the construction of wharves in Hawaii at which ships could tie up, making it easy for the black rats to scramble ashore and establish populations on the main Hawaiian Islands. On Maui, the seminal event may have been the construction of a breakwater at Kahului Harbor in 1908, which allowed ships to anchor close to the island's wharf. The rats just roared ashore, according to Atkinson's reconstruction of events.

Better climbers than Norway rats, the black rats found forests of trees filled with birds that didn't know what to do when faced with them. Observers at the time repeatedly noted the presence of large numbers of rats in trees, with one Honolulu rodent control effort snaring about a third of its rats in the trees. A great number of rats were found even at high altitudes.

Though the rats doubtless preyed directly on birds, mainly by raiding eggs and young in nests, they likely also competed for the birds' food supply. Rats eat insects, fruits, and snails, dietary staples of many native birds. One writer wondered whether the disappearance of the 'o'u on Oahu was due to rats gobbling up the fruits of its favored ieie vine:

> Why the Ou should have become extinct on Oahu and remain abundant in far more restricted forests on Molokai and Lanai is by no means clear, but with regard to the former island, it may be noted now that over extensive areas it is often difficult to find a single red Ieie fruit, which the foreign rats have more or less eaten and befouled, and they may thus have indirectly brought about the extinction of the Ou, even if in times of scarcity of the fruit they do not actually prey on the bird itself.

Nature has a way of evening things out, however. Though the rats' population may have exploded after their introduction, eventually limits on the food supply, disease, and other factors caused their numbers to level off or decline. Even if this occurred sometime in the early 1900s, the damage to native bird populations from the combination of disease, habitat destruction, and the invasion of the black rats may have been so devastating that some never recovered.

Studies in the Hanawi Natural Area Reserve have shown that black rats, Polynesian rats, and mice all are abundant. In just six nights of trapping in 1985 and 1986, researchers caught nearly 300 black rats, 158 Polynesian rats, and 132 house mice.

The rats were plentiful enough to leave some researchers with unpleasant memories that the intervening years haven't faded. Marie Ecton, who logged long hours sitting quietly watching the po'ouli nest, said that one day at the spotting scope, a rat ran right up her leg.

In those studies researchers discovered feather fragments in the stomach of one rat, but they found that their diet consisted mainly of insect larvae, fruit, insects, and snails. Though there remains evidence that the black rat is a predator of birds, managers of the Hanawi Natural Area Reserve charged with staving off extinction of the po'ouli were also concerned that the rat was a competitor for food.

The two po'ouli specimens collected by researchers shortly after the bird was discovered were held in museums and used for reference. Researchers examined the stomach contents of these "type specimens," to see what the birds were eating.

The two stomachs contained bits and pieces—jaws, shells, and shell fragments—of 293 snails, many of them tiny. Though the examination also revealed a significant number of spiders, beetles, wasps, and even fruits from the olapa tree, snails made up 63 percent of the contents, and the researchers concluded that they had on their hands the only known honeycreeper whose diet consisted mainly of native Hawaiian snails.

Rats, unfortunately, also like to eat snails. Concerns about their efficiency at this task goes back some time, as Baldwin detailed on Oahu in 1887:

> The agencies now threatening the wholesale destruction of these little gems of the forest are the rats and mice, which have become very abundant in mountain forests, particularly where there are no cattle. Their ravages are not confined to the shells whose habitats are on the

ground, but extend to those found on trees. It is not uncommon to find around the charnel cells of these noxious little animals hundreds of empty mutilated shells.

A more recent example of the rat's effect on native snails was documented in 1993, when researchers reported that a population of native snails crashed by 80 percent when rats and carnivorous snails invaded. "We suspect that only rapid rat-control efforts prevented the total extirpation of snails at this site," they wrote.

Having retreated to Hanawi, the po'ouli had to compete with rats for food. But that wasn't the only tribulation the bird faced as it made its last stand.

As dramatic as Hawaii's bird diversity once was, it was nothing compared with the islands' profusion of snails. With a vast array of colors, patterns, sizes, and lifestyles, Hawaiian snails once numbered at an estimated 770 different species, more than 99 percent of which were found nowhere else on earth.

Like the islands' native birds, however, the snails have not fared well. Experts estimate that between 60 and 90 percent of Hawaiian land snail species are now extinct. And in freshwater streams and ponds, there are now more introduced snail species than there are natives.

Introduced snails have made their way to Hawaii in a variety of ways. Many have been accidentally shipped in potted plants, agricultural products, and cargo. Others have been brought in intentionally for aquariums, for gardens, and as biological controls. The track record of these introduced species is mixed, with some never gaining a foothold and others appearing to blend in well with native species. But still others have been an unmitigated disaster.

One example of such an environmental disaster starts innocently enough. In 1936, a woman living on Oahu was traveling home from Taiwan. Looking to add some extra pizzazz to her garden, the woman tucked two giant African snails into her luggage and headed back to Hawaii. The snails, though doubtless not happy about their accommodations, survived the trip. Another group of the same snails arrived a few months later from Japan, ordered by a man who wanted to raise and sell them.

At least some from these two original colonies escaped and multiplied, becoming established in enormous numbers. As the wave of giant African snails spread across the islands, state agricultural officials scurried to find ways to eliminate the pest. And what better to kill a snail than another snail? Through the 1950s and 1960s, the state intentionally introduced fifteen new species of carnivorous snails in the hope that they would eliminate the pest.

Luckily, not all of the carnivorous snails became established. But three carnivorous species did gain a foothold, including the rosy wolf snail, *Euglandina rosea*. It is hard to overstate the devastation that this snail has wrought on Hawaii and on every other island where it has been introduced. One snail expert called it a "major scourge of the terrestrial [snail] fauna."

Euglandina rosea is the Terminator of introduced snail species. Native to Florida and the U.S. Southeast, the rosy wolf snail is well named. Its shell is reddish, and like the animal for which it is named, it is a voracious predator. It tracks its prey by following their slime trails, but moving two to three times as fast. Though it eats small snails whole, it grabs larger snails and, when they retreat into their shells, sticks its elongated upper body into the shell openings, tearing them apart with its sandpaperlike tongue, called a radula, and eating them in pieces.

Hawaiian snail researcher Michael Hadfield has watched more than once as populations of native snails he was studying were invaded by rosy wolf snails. In one case, he had been following a colony of two hundred native Hawaiian snails in the Waianae Mountains of Oahu for five years, observing the snails' individual growth and the dynamics of the population as a whole. Then, on returning to the site in August 1979, researchers found only empty shells. Not a single snail from the native *Achatinella mustelina* species was left. Amid the *Achatinella* shells were also shells from the rosy wolf snail. Hadfield wrote in 1980:

> It was the appearance of the introduced predatory snail *Euglandina rosea* that most clearly coincided with the disappearance of all snails from the study site and the ridge above and below it. Specimens of *E. rosea* were first seen on these slopes, below the study area at elevations of about 1000 feet, in December 1974. By 1977, the predatory snails were found near the study site. In August 1979 a reconnaissance of the area showed dead shells of *E. rosea* to be abundant, and living achatinellids, as well as members of all other snail taxa previously seen in the area, were absent. . . . It must be concluded that predation by *E. rosea* was the "final" cause of extinction of the population of *A. mustelina* on the Kanehoa trail.

Ironically, the giant African snail turned out to be impervious to the control efforts by carnivorous snails but appears to be declining on its own.

Knowing that native Hawaiian snails make up a large part of the po'ouli's diet, and with the rosy wolf snail's depredations in mind, the Maui Forest Bird Recovery Project mounted its own study of snail populations in Hanawi. Over four years, from 1996 to 1999, researchers counted snails.

Though they didn't find any rosy wolf snails, allowing them a brief sigh of relief, they did find another introduced carnivorous snail, the garlic snail, *Oxychilus alliarius*. A quick check of its background provided them with little comfort. Though it lacked the fearsome reputation of the rosy wolf snail, the garlic snail, for those interested in saving the po'ouli, was little better.

The garlic snail is thought to have been introduced accidentally in 1937 from Europe. But by the time it was first reported, in 1945 in East Maui, it had been there a while and was widely dispersed. The destruction that garlic snails were wreaking on native snail populations became apparent in 1984, when Mike Severns detailed the results of surveys on which he embarked to find native Hawaiian land snails on Maui.

Severns was repeatedly puzzled and disappointed by the absence of native Hawaiian land snails on his travels. Finally, on the Maui coast below the Kipahulu Valley, he encountered six species of introduced snails, one of which was the rosy wolf snail. This, he figured, explained the absence of native snails.

But as he traveled from the coast upland through the valley, the rosy wolf snail became scarcer and scarcer, as did four of the other five species. When he reached the top of his study area, he found only one of the six introduced species—the garlic snail—but these he found in abundance. As Severns described it:

Endemic snails remained in the upper forest in reasonable numbers, but only in the trees, not on the ground. Meanwhile, *O. alliarius* was impressing me both with its peculiar garlic odor, evident as I walked through the forest, and by the numbers of dead shells on the ground. I did not find one living ground-dwelling endemic snail in the forest of the valley. Indeed, I found only one living ground snail in the entire upper study area, *O. alliarius.*

His account encompassed more than one survey and more than one area on Maui. "I could scoop them up by the hundreds from the leaf litter," he reported from Mount Helu. "In more than 150 hikes on the island of Maui, I have never been disappointed. It is everywhere."

Though researchers surveying Hanawi found garlic snails and observed them preying on native snail species, they also found that the numbers of the larger snails that the po'ouli feeds on, called Succineidae, were actually on the increase.

The evidence presents a mixed picture of the impact of introduced snails on the po'ouli's native prey. At the time of the survey, in all likelihood the entire po'ouli population had fallen to just three individuals. Without po'oulis to eat them, it may not be surprising that some snail populations were increasing.

That lack of clarity, however, would vanish when biologists turned their attention to yet another invader of the Hanawai Natural Area Reserve: feral pigs.

Joining the rats and snails in invading the po'ouli's last redoubt were nature's bulldozers: wild descendants of domestic Polynesian and European pigs moved into the Hanawi Reserve in the 1970s and tore up the po'ouli's habitat.

To understand the impact that wild pigs had on the po'ouli, it's necessary to understand just how the po'ouli used the forest to meet its needs.

The po'ouli was a specialist of the lower layer of the rainforest. It foraged for insects and snails on the ground and in lower portions of trees, prying up bark and lifting patches of moss and lichens looking for its food. A 1990 report on the po'ouli's behavior said that it used the understory and the subcanopy extensively and that the bird was observed on at least three occasions foraging in the ground layer. Researchers said they may have missed the bird foraging there more, however, because the thick underbrush may have concealed it from view.

Pigs helped solve that particular problem.

When the po'ouli was discovered in the early 1970s, there appeared to be enough of a population to make a stand in the section of rainforest they called home. Researchers observing the po'ouli through the 1970s and early 1980s noticed not just the precipitous drop in bird numbers, but something else as well: more pigs, a lot more. They reported a 473 percent increase in the level of pig activity at the very time the po'ouli's numbers were declining. And according to conservationists familiar with the story of destruction on the Hawaiian Islands, the pig played as important of a role as the other pest invaders.

The problem with pigs is how they live. Everyone knows pigs are messy, but outside the family farm, they're not just messy, they're destructive. They dig up the forest floor in search of earthworms and the tasty underground parts of plants. Also, with no sweat glands, pigs have to wallow in mud or water to stay cool. And in the tropics, they need to stay cool quite a bit.

This digging and wallowing destroys and clears out the forest's lower layer, the very layer on which the po'ouli depended, and trample the ground and compact it. This activity not only opens up the forest, but also increases runoff and enhances erosion. Perhaps more importantly, it destroys the ground layer where some insects spend their daylight hours hiding before moving to the trees at night to forage.

Pigs first arrived on Hawaii more than fifteen hundred years ago, brought here by the humans who crossed the ocean to make the islands their home. But these first Polynesian pigs are not thought to have had much of an impact on native forests. They were probably husbanded carefully by the first Hawaiians, who kept a sharp eye on them and tended them close to home.

The feral descendants of the European domestic pigs seem to have caused all the problems. Unlike Hawaiians, Westerners allowed their pigs to run free, at least initially, hoping the pig would establish itself and provide a food source for future travelers. Cook released the first batch of pigs on Niihau Island the same year he discovered the Hawaiian Islands.

Left to their own devices, the European pigs reverted to their wild ancestry and today look more like the European wild pig than they do domestic swine. They have long snouts, erect ears, and foul tempers. Boars can top two hundred pounds, and males and females alike do quite nicely on the islands.

Averaging five young in two litters per year, the pigs have no natural predators, and there has been little besides human hunting to stop them from spreading across the islands, digging and wallowing as they go. The pig activity not only damages the forest floor, but also spreads the seeds of the alien plants that have become common in the Hawaiian lowlands. Pigs feed on the introduced plants, move into less disturbed areas, and deposit seeds in their feces.

In recent years, scientists and natural resource managers have realized the ecological damage that pigs are causing and have taken steps to control them in several places, including the po'ouli's home range of Hanawi.

Research has shown that ecosystems can recover from the damage once pigs are removed, but slowly. One study in Hawaii Volcanoes National Park showed that the microarthropod community, responsible for decomposing and recycling nutrients in the soil, was devastated by pig activity. When the pigs were eliminated, it took seven years for the population to rebound.

But with po'ouli numbers in free fall in Hanawi, the birds did not have years to wait for their habitat to recover from pig damage.

9

THE HAWAIIAN FOREST
BIRD SURVEY

NEARLY THE ENTIRE 259-PAGE VOLUME OF WINSTON BANKO'S "History of Endemic Hawaiian Birds," part of a series of avian history reports put together between 1979 and 1990, is taken up by individual accounts of thirteen Hawaiian bird species, starting with the lesser amakihi and ending with the po'ouli. Almost every account has several pages of descriptive information, references, notes, and appendixes.

The po'ouli account, however, is not only last in the volume, but also the least. It totals a mere two paragraphs, followed by a half-page listing of five references. Banko summed up the knowledge of the po'ouli's status and distribution—where it was found and how it was doing—accumulated over the previous eleven years in a few spare lines:

> The Po'o Uli has the most recent and shortest history of any Hawaiian bird. Casey and Jacobi (1974) de-

scribed and gave this new genus and species its Latin and Hawaiian names from two specimens collected at 6500 feet elevation on the northeastern flank of Haleakala, Maui, on 15 and 17 of September 1973. The HOLOTYPE was deposited in the B. P. Bishop Museum and the PARATYPE in the American Museum of Natural History (Casey & Jacobi 1974).

Marshall (1975) stated that only 12 individuals were identified during the 1973 Hana Rain Forest Project and that this species was found only in a 60 ha (150-acre) tract between 5300 and 6800 feet elevation in the Ko'olau Forest Reserve. Shallenberger (1974) reported that "a 15-20 second observation," presumably of a single individual, was obtained (ca. 0.5 mile northeast of Pu'u'alaea) during a 6 to 13 April 1974 field trip. Conant (1979 reports, pers. comm.) documented two sightings (1 at 6400 and 1 at 6600 ft elev.) 0.5 mile northeast of Pu'u'alaea near the head of Hanawi stream on 21 and 22 June 1976. Little else of the status and distribution of this species seems to have been reported.

Banko had missed a sighting—by Sheila Conant in 1975—but was otherwise right. Little of the bird's distribution or its status in the forests of Haleakala had been reported, even though it was immediately recognized as endangered. The po'ouli was listed under the Endangered Species Act a bit more than two years after it was first seen by human eyes.

Biologists working with the po'ouli in the late 1990s and early 2000s regretted the early delay in gathering knowledge. Struggling to restore a population from just a handful of birds, they said the po'ouli's best hope would have been to take the steps they did—banding, studying their habits, rehabilitating habitat, and even captive breeding—earlier in the po'ouli's history, when the population was thought to be two hundred instead of three.

If that had happened, then hikers on Haleakala's wet northeastern slopes might still hope to hear a quiet *chik* call and see a dim flutter of brown and black zoom past and alight on a nearby moss-covered ohia tree to begin its search for insects and snails.

Biologists who worked with Hawaiian forest birds in the 1970s and 1980s agreed that hands-on management then would have been best. But at the time, it was a far-off dream. So little was known about the po'ouli and other native birds with which it shared the forests that even if they had the go-ahead, the money, and the expertise, they wouldn't have known which bird to start with. Cameron Kepler, a U.S. Fish and Wildlife Service (FWS) biologist on Maui from 1977 through 1987, says:

> Nobody really knew how many birds were up there, their distribution, what their habitat requirements were. Sure, you could say the po'ouli was rare, but was it rarer than the Maui parrotbill? Should we work on the crested honeycreeper, or the nukupu'u? Maybe Bishop's 'o'o is still up there. We simply didn't have the comparative information to say that the po'ouli needed more work than the Kauai 'o'o.

The po'ouli's problem—perhaps its fatal one—was that it was not the only mystery bird, and certainly not the only one in trouble, in Hawaii's tangled forests.

In the months after the bird's discovery, there was a flush of excitement about the world's first new bird in more than a decade. Life for Tonnie Casey and Jim Jacobi got more hectic.

Not only were they doing their own academic work and toiling on the written description of the po'ouli, but they also were repeatedly returning to the rainforest, shepherding scientists, photographers, and others who wanted to see one for themselves.

In January 1974, six months after the bird's discovery, Casey commented that she and Jacobi had been pressed into service because they were the only ones who could recognize the po'ouli's call. But Casey didn't seem to mind playing tour guide. She remarked that she had been trying for months to convince several of the people on the trip to come and visit the forest.

Members of the Hana Rainforest Project worked in the area through December 1973. In November, Casey's advisor, Andrew Berger, went in with David Woodside, the state biologist who collected the museum specimens. Jacobi led a trip in February 1974, seeing a pair of po'oulis. Casey led trips in April and August, which proved to be particularly fruitful.

"This last trip was very successful," Casey wrote Dean Amadon on September 3, 1974. "One day Walter, Dave Woodside, Andrew . . . and I saw 7 individuals—and one was a fledgling still being fed! That sure was an exciting day! Unfortunately, we didn't get off the transect to see what the birds' range might be."

Despite the success of the August trip, most visitors to Hanawi were frustrated by the terrain, weather, and tangled forests. Berger described his November trip with Woodside as something of an endurance test: "15 miles, beginning at 10,000 feet, down to about 7000, over a ridge at some 8300, and then down to the tent basecamp at 7100 feet on the northeast slope of the crater. Temperatures between 45° and 50° F, and some 10 inches of rain over the two-day period. We did not see the new species, but weather conditions were terrible, as they will be most of the time from now til June or July."

Robert Shallenberger, who accompanied Casey on the April 1974 trip, said the visit was almost entirely socked in by rain, which let up for just a few hours during the week they were there. Shallenberger recalls that it rained so hard they were tentbound for several days, "going out only to pee and to re-dig the trench that kept water from flowing through" the tent. "It's one of the few places I have camped where there's a premium for places on a slope."

Despite the steady march up Haleakala's furrowed sides in those early months, little research was done. The focus was on seeing a po'ouli and getting a photograph, film footage, or recording of its call. "We were following up on Tonnie's work," Shallenberger says. "She was showing us where she saw the bird." The trips "were not well-planned, with no specific research agenda."

That's not to say that no scientific work was going on at the time. Outside the forests, the two collected specimens were examined, recorded, and safely stored at the Bernice P. Bishop Museum in Honolulu and the American Museum of Natural History in New York. Casey and Jacobi toiled away through that first winter on their description of the new species, to be published by the Bishop Museum's *Occasional Papers* series later that year.

The paper gave the scientific world its first description of the po'ouli. It listed the bird's scientific name, *Melamprosops phaeosoma;* gave thoughts about its conservation; and described its behavior:

> *Melamprosops* appears to feed exclusively on insects . . . moving methodically over branches and trunks of trees, picking and prying at the cracks and crevices in the bark. On one occasion, a bird was seen hammering at a

branch with its bill, apparently in search of food, reminiscent of the manner in which the 'akiapola'au (*Hemignathus wilsoni*) often feeds.

The only vocalization thus far heard from *Melamprosops* is a single distinct call note: "chik," uttered sharply and harshly. It is very similar to the notes given by the Maui creeper (*Loxops maculata newtoni*), and *Pseudonestor*. However, it is distinct enough to be distinguished from those two birds.

The article recommended that the po'ouli be listed under the U.S. Endangered Species Act, that the bird's habitat be preserved, and that research into its status and distribution be given a high priority.

The federal government took Casey and Jacobi's listing recommendation almost immediately. On April 21, 1975, twenty months after the bird's discovery, the government published a notice proposing that the po'ouli be listed as an endangered species. Five months later, on September 25, 1975, with the state of Hawaii in "general agreement," the federal government added the po'ouli to its growing list of endangered species.

In listing the bird as endangered, FWS Director Lynn A. Greenwalt found that though the bird's history was unknown, its decline was likely caused by habitat alteration, mosquito-borne disease, predation by rats, and possible competition with non-native birds.

The listing was supposed to trigger a cascade of activities leading to the species' recovery, including designation of critical habitat, drafting of a recovery plan, and actions to recover the species. It triggered very little, however, at least right away.

For the next several years, not much new was learned about the po'ouli. In 1978, Walter Bock at Columbia University and the American Museum of Natural History published a detailed description of the po'ouli's tongue, which he said indicated that the bird was indeed a new species of Hawaiian honeycreeper. State biologist Woodside said he went into the rainforest perhaps four times between the bird's discovery and his retirement in 1979. University of Hawaii students also periodically visited the forest, Woodside said. Though it was clear even then that the bird was in trouble, the state did little, leaving the problem to federal biologists.

The po'ouli, though not abundant, was sighted with some regularity. Casey's field notes for the period indicated that she saw the bird repeatedly during the first years. Woodside also had some unreported sightings of his own. On one trip with a friend from Cornell University, they saw eight or nine po'oulis over five days. His friend had wanted Woodside to collect some specimens, but he went home disappointed. Woodside hadn't taken his gun.

On another trip, Woodside and Casey began to look in other parts of the forest for po'oulis, east and west of the main transect where the birds had been discovered. They didn't find any, but for the first time, they began to notice damage to the forest from feral pigs that were moving into the area, tearing up the understory as they did.

Casey was an exception in this period of low activity. Though often alone, she continued working in the forest. She had graduated from the University of Hawaii in the spring of 1974 and begun studies for a master's degree at Colorado State University. Every summer through 1979, Casey was camped in a tent on Haleakala's damp shoulder.

"I worked on the insectivorous foraging guild: the parrotbill, po'ouli, and creeper. I got quite a lot of data on the po'ouli," she says.

Though Casey was occasionally joined by visitors—her mother made one trip up and an ornithologist boyfriend another—for the most part, she kept a lonely vigil. John Kjargaard, the Hana Rainforest Project's organizer, had begun working at nearby Haleakala National Park and arranged for her to check in regularly by radio, just in case.

"I spent a lot of time by myself," Casey recalls. "There was this guy on the coast. I don't remember his name, but I remember his number, number 75. I'd call him each night and say I'm fine. He'd call John: 'She's fine.'"

Casey's field notes from the time are rife with po'ouli sightings. They record numerous sightings each year from 1973 to 1976. Her notes get thinner after that, with only single sightings in 1978 and 1979. There were several more in 1982, by which time the bird's decline was becoming apparent to those who worked in the forest.

During those years, Casey tracked details of the bird's diet, observing it eating berries, grubs, caterpillars, spiders, and two kinds of snails. She sighted a couple of juvenile birds and several pairs. She recorded hearing several calls from the birds, including the *chik* call noticed by other researchers, as well as a whistling *whee-it,* a husky *chip,* and a rapid *chi-chi-chi.*

On one trip in June 1975, Casey drew a po'ouli to her by mimicking the bird's call. She watched it for about five minutes and was rewarded with what may have been the first sighting of a po'ouli eating a snail. Casey wrote in that day's field notes:

It came forward . . . not searching for insects but coming towards me. It was alone. The weather was foggy and misty off and on. The bird hopped towards me, chipping every time I chipped and eventually was within about 10 feet. I had not yet used my binoculars. After it got a good look at me, it continued to look for food. At

one time I saw it pluck a round, shiny object. I thought
it looked like a dark colored snail.

Years later, Stephen Mountainspring, who worked as a
federal biologist on Maui through much of the 1980s, praised
Casey's work, urging her to preserve the unpublished data
because it was "pretty unique stuff."

By the late 1970s, three federal biologists were working on
the Hawaiian Islands. John Sincock had been studying the birds
of Kauai for many years. J. Michael Scott was a more recent
arrival. Cameron Kepler was the newest of the three, posted to
Maui in 1977. By that time, the wheels were already in motion
to pierce the veil of ignorance that shrouded Hawaii's mountainous forest bird habitat.

The lack of knowledge about Hawaii's native birds presented a tremendous problem for those at the FWS charged
with their conservation. They had to make decisions that could
affect a species' future but were flying blind. Though they knew
many Hawaiian birds were in trouble, they simply didn't know
how much trouble they were in.

The answer was the Hawaiian Forest Bird Survey. Scott's
brainchild, the effort would be a massive survey of the state's
forest bird habitat, unprecedented in scope and ambitious in its
aims. Running from 1976 to 1983, it sought to exhaustively
catalog the distribution, population size, and density of Hawaiian
forest birds. The effort covered all native forests above one thousand feet in elevation on Hawaii, Maui, Molokai, and Lanai,
as well as the known distribution areas for endangered birds
on Kauai. About a third of the territory covered by the survey
had never been explored by ornithologists.

The survey was larger than any ever conducted and involved thirty-four observers hiking down preestablished routes
from the tops of the islands' volcanoes until the forest gave out

at a settlement, agricultural area, or in some cases, the sea. Scott, Mountainspring, Kepler, and Fred Ramsey wrote in their introduction to the survey's results, published in 1986:

> Despite earlier studies, in 1976 we knew little about the current status of most native Hawaiian forest birds, because vast areas of the islands were still ornithologically unexplored. As recently as 1973, a new genus of honeycreeper was discovered on the island of Maui and even by 1980, the nests, eggs, and young had been described for only 11 of 37 nonextinct passerine birds. In 1976, recovery plan drafts for Hawaiian forest birds were largely statements of the need for information on the basic biology of endangered forest birds.

The survey's authors said the lack of information was due to the difficulty of working on the windward slopes of Hawaii's volcanoes, in conditions similar to those found on Haleakala by members of the Hana Rainforest Project.

According to Kepler, the survey took over biology in Hawaii, with Scott recruiting so many of the islands' biologists that his team was dubbed "Scott's Army."

Plastic flagging tape marked the survey's transects, with stations established by a metal tag fastened to a nearby tree. Working in pairs, the observers got up before dawn and hiked downhill, stopping at sampling stations usually spaced about 147 yards apart. Working from 5:15 until 9:15 A.M., they would hike to a station, drop their packs, and watch and listen for eight minutes, recording every bird they saw or heard, and estimating the distance to the bird. Then they'd move down the mountain to another sampling station, stop, and do it again.

To provide consistency, they conducted the survey only for the first hours of the morning, when the birds were most active.

By 9:15 A.M., they made camp for the day, spending the rest of their time collecting supplemental information.

Carrying all their gear in backpacks, a single transect took five to twelve days to complete. When they were done, they went back up the mountain, moved over a couple kilometers, and did it again.

"Just doing the walking was a chore," recalls Kepler, who covered dozens of transects. "We'd go in at the top with a backpack with full gear and we'd come out X days later, depending on how long it took. We'd get up before dawn, eat breakfast in the dark, and start hiking to reach the next station."

Botanists came later, stopping at the same stations and recording plants and forest structure. Bird surveys were done from May to August. The botanists had a bit longer to complete their work, but "nobody wants to do an excessive amount of work in those forests in the winter, because they're really really wet and surprisingly cold," says Kepler.

When it was done, the Hawaiian Forest Bird Survey had sampled 9,940 different stations, recording 240,000 individual birds of fifty-seven species. More importantly, it had created for the first time a map of the populations and ranges of the largest concentration of endangered bird species in the United States.

"It's like there was a cloud, a fog, a mist bank over a whole mountainside of data, and the Forest Bird Survey provided some shafts of sunlight into that, so you can start inferring what the terrain is like, and then as the fog lifts with more knowledge, you get to see more clearly what's there," Mountainspring says.

The Hawaiian Forest Bird Survey energized the conservation community in the state, providing just the sort of information needed to prioritize conservation planning and demanded by administrators in making funding decisions. "By the time this was done, we knew all the habitat correlates of the birds— where they were, where they weren't," Kepler says. "You could overlay maps of protected land and determine which areas were protected, which areas weren't protected."

Work on Maui was conducted in 1980. Observers clambering around Haleakala's rainforests encountered only three po'ouli, despite observations at fifty-three stations over thirteen square kilometers where researchers believed the birds lived.

"We got to Maui and found the po'ouli, but not many of them," Kepler says. "There was a pretty specific area that the bird was found in. We looked all over the main forest on Maui and had an area of about two square miles where we knew the bird was."

The survey provided the first public population estimate for the po'ouli: 141. Because of the low number of sightings, however, the figure carried a large margin of error: plus or minus 280 birds. Despite that margin of error, the estimate provided an important number that could be compared with earlier unpublished data and subsequent figures.

Together, the estimates painted an alarming picture: the po'ouli population had fallen by between 80 and 99 percent from 1975 and 1981. Densities for the bird had fallen from seventy-five per square kilometer to just four. In the meantime, pig activity skyrocketed 475 percent. Over time, Mountainspring says, "this little, shy bird gets less and less widespread and more rare. By the time we get there, it's pretty much a flickering ember."

After the survey was completed, Kepler and Mountainspring began spending a lot of time in the po'ouli's home range. They trained field workers, and with teams and alone, each logged many nights in the forest.

But the po'ouli didn't cooperate in the effort to gather information on its habits and life history, needed in order to do more intensive management. It proved such an elusive study subject that Mountainspring decided to focus instead on the Maui parrotbill. "You'd be in there a whole week and only see it once," he says of the po'ouli.

Through the mid-1980s, Kepler and Mountainspring became more and more worried by what they saw in the forests of Hanawi. Po'ouli numbers were declining, and increasing numbers of pigs were wiping out the forest understory. And the pigs' wallowing wasn't just clearing out the vegetation that the po'ouli relied on for the snails and insects it ate. It was also causing extensive erosion of the sloped forest floor, endangering the forest itself.

To measure the erosion, the pair pushed long gutter spikes into the ground, marking the soil level on the nails. When they returned a year later, some spots had an extra inch of the nail showing. "In areas there really was massive soil loss," Mountainspring says. "The erosion was so horrific there."

It quickly was becoming apparent that to save the po'ouli, they'd have to save its forest home. Feral pigs were ripping out the understory, rooting for food, and creating open wallows where ferns and shrubs had been. The forest was becoming more park-like and a more barren home for the po'ouli.

By 1984, state and federal biologists had completed the second draft of a recovery plan for the po'ouli. The first had been completed in 1976, and though it called for sweeping action to save the po'ouli, at the time there was little knowledge and less money to implement it.

"They called for heroic efforts to get a handle on the disease problem and possible predator control relative to rats, cats, and mongooses. All of the recovery plans called for a backup captive propagation effort, but it was pie in the sky at the time. We thought it would be nice to do, but we had no idea it would be possible," Woodside says of the early plan.

By 1984, however, things were changing. Because of the Forest Bird Survey and the continued work in Hanawi, it had become apparent that po'ouli numbers were in a steep decline. And though other problems certainly were plaguing the bird, biologists felt that the pigs needed immediate attention. Hanawi was under assault, and without the forest, there would be no po'ouli.

The recovery plan for the po'ouli, called the Maui-Molokai Forest Birds Recovery Plan, also covered the Maui parrotbill, nukupu'u, Maui akepa, crested honeycreeper, Hawaiian (Molokai) thrush, and Molokai creeper. The plan said that the birds' home was under such stress that recovery for all the species depended on preserving the forest. "It is clear that the stresses now encountered by these species are entrenched within their habitats, and without major commitments of time and money more species will certainly be lost."

The plan talked about slowing the spread of alien plants, establishing a second population of the birds, and captive breeding. It mentioned learning more about the birds' biology and addressing other threats, such as eliminating standing water that could be breeding spots for disease-carrying mosquitoes.

But the report's action plan makes plain what its drafters saw as the biggest problem facing the forest and what they thought the main solution should be: fences were needed to keep feral pigs and goats—and in some areas, cattle and axis deer—out of the forest habitat, and then managers could kill those that remained inside.

For Kalapawili Ridge and the Koolau Gap, it recommended stock-proof fences from the west wall of the gap to the north Kipahulu Valley sidewall; above the north wall of Haleakala's crater and the north wall of Kipahulu Valley; and from Hanakauhi north. Once the fences were up, the plan recommended eradicating enclosed goats and pigs in five years.

The plan was similar for other areas.

For the Waikamoi forest, extend one fence and construct another, then eliminate cattle, goats, and pigs.

For the Koolau Forest Reserve and the Hana Forest Reserve, including all known po'ouli habitat, eradicate goats and get rid of pigs on the north side of the fence constructed for the Kalapawili Ridge and Koolau Gap.

For Kipahulu Valley and Haleakala National Park, build a fence, kill the goats, and get rid of the pigs. For the Manawainui Planeze, build two fences, eradicate the goats, and control the pigs.

It was unclear whether the steep, gullied mountainside that the po'ouli called home could be saved, or even if fences could be strung over such rugged terrain in such inhospitable weather. But the po'ouli was declining, and finally government officials charged with its care had decided to act.

10

PRELUDE TO A FENCE

IN 1968, DON REESER ARRIVED AT HAWAII VOLCANOES National Park on the island of Hawaii to start his first full-time job with the National Park Service. He also walked into the middle of a war between native and alien species, being fought in part by park staff and local hunters.

Reeser, with a degree in wildlife management and the experience of a temporary job at Glacier National Park under his belt, quickly chose sides. He joined the fight against feral goats and pigs waged by Park Service personnel. Unlike those who came before, however, he would eventually win the battle by wielding an unlikely and unassuming weapon: a fence.

Non-native plants and animals have long been a problem on the islands. These hardy invaders brought by humans have been toughened by nature's battle for survival on the continents. They often overran native species that for millennia had not had to face competitors, predators, or disease.

At Hawaii Volcanoes, there were numerous invaders, but just one was considered public enemy number one: the goat.

Introduced by the first Europeans to visit Hawaii in 1778, the goat overran the islands. Tough, prolific, able to subsist on a wide range of vegetation, and with no natural predators, its numbers boomed. Within seventy-two years, there were so many goats in Hawaii that a hide export business shipped more than twenty-six thousand goat skins to the U.S. mainland in its first year alone. Despite the thousands killed for skins, there were plenty left behind, eating, eating, eating . . . and making little goats.

As Reeser and a coauthor wrote in a 1972 report on goats at Hawaii Volcanoes National Park:

> In less than 200 years, goats chewed their way from the seashore to the tops of island peaks and back down again, by which time they numbered in the tens of thousands, had eaten some species into extinction, and threatened the existence of many more. Moreover, the resultant forest destruction has been one of the major causes for the declines in populations of native, endemic, nectar-feeding birds of the remarkable and unique family, Drepanididae [Hawaiian honeycreepers], and perhaps birds of other families as well.

At Hawaii Volcanoes, goat control was a long ingrained tradition. Personnel realized almost as soon as the park was created in 1916 that it could have goats or native vegetation, but not both. Mainly through hunting and roundups, more than seventy thousand goats were removed from the park since its creation. Despite the vast numbers removed, however, an aerial survey in 1970 estimated that fourteen thousand goats remained, eating, breeding, and eating some more.

Reeser wrote in 1992 that because goats reproduce quickly, the goat "control" programs were anything but. Though park personnel could claim so many thousands of goats removed annually, all they were doing was skimming off surplus population. "Drives and hunts were only effective in keeping the goat population young and healthy and vigorously reproducing."

When Reeser arrived at Hawaii Volcanoes, large sections of the park were kept close-cropped. Though goats ate all vegetation to the ground, they preferred native Hawaiian plants, the very ones the park rangers were trying to preserve.

The attraction to native plants was understandable. Because of the long millennia with no mammalian herbivores, the plants lacked the defenses, such as thorns, tough bark, and bitter-tasting chemicals, that allowed continental cousins to survive browsing and grazing. Island biologists called native plants "ice cream plants," so defenseless and tasty that the goats, cows, and sheep always went for them first. "If one popped up, it got eaten by a goat right away," Reeser said.

Worse, the goats didn't limit themselves to native grasses and shrubs. They went after the trees, too. They ate saplings as soon as they sprouted, chewed the bark off older trees, and had the potential to destroy forests.

By the time Reeser came to Hawaii Volcanoes, rangers worried that it was too late. As the goats cleared out native plants, alien species adapted to their constant chomping moved in. The park was becoming not just a grazed pastureland, but one consisting of foreign, exotic plants.

The staff was concerned that the park had passed a tipping point and already changed permanently—that introduced grasses, now established, would outcompete native grasses. As in some horror movie where the villain becomes the victim's only hope, the goats, they feared, may be the only thing holding the alien weeds in check and keeping the situation from getting worse.

To answer that question, park personnel built a series of fenced-in areas. Called exclosures, because they were designed to keep livestock out rather than in, the areas allayed fears that an environmental tipping point had been passed and provided dramatic evidence of the robustness of native vegetation. They showed both that it was not too late for Hawaiian plants and that a fencing program was a viable solution.

The most famous exclosure was built in 1969 at Kukalau-ula, where the goat population was heaviest. When the fence went up, the landscape inside and out resembled a closely mowed lawn.

Two years later, things were starkly different. A photo taken at the time shows a few goats grazing on a sunny landscape. All around the exclosure, the ground looks largely barren. In the black and white image, the grass outside the fence is cropped so short that it is difficult to see what the goats are eating other than dirt. But in the middle of the photograph, where the exclosure's fences run off into the distance, inside grow grass and other plants, low but several inches tall, apparently healthy and a marked contrast to the nearly bare ground outside.

Meanwhile, inside Kukalauula's wire walls, a botanical resurrection had occurred.

When the fences went up, there were no native plants at all in the grazed stubble they enclosed. In two years, though, native plants had become reestablished, pushing invading grasses out of roughly half the fenced-in area and proving that the goat was not needed to keep foreign grasses in check.

Among the native plants was one never seen before. A native legume—a type of bean—left botanists scratching their heads, wondering where it came from and how they'd missed it. They named it *Canavalia kauensis*. It is thought to have been an "ice cream plant," eaten as soon as it sprouted. Its seeds, scientists believed, had lain dormant in soil too dry for it to grow. Once the goat browsing ended and grasses appeared, the soil became shaded and retained the moisture the plant needed.

The exclosure at Kukalauula and others showed that Hawaiian plants could recover if given a break from the goats. Reeser's predecessor at the park, Dave Morris, had developed a plan to do just that. It involved a strategy that had been used before unsuccessfully, but with a twist.

The park's boundary had been fenced in the 1930s, but the park was so large (333,000 acres)—and the boundary fence was so porous—that efforts to hunt out the park's goats failed. By the 1970s, the boundary fence was a mess. Long sections were falling down, posts rotted and wire rusted.

Morris understood that even if the boundary fence were intact, it would be impossible to hunt down every single goat: the area was too large. Some would always escape and reestablish their numbers. So his plan called for enclosing smaller areas within the park, small enough that hunters could be assured that they had eliminated every single animal. When Morris left in 1970, he left his plans behind with Reeser, who took over as the park's wildlife ranger.

In the early 1970s, relations between the park and the local hunting community soured. Sport hunting was not allowed in the park, but local hunters knew that goats were being hunted, and they wanted in. The hunting community lobbied heavily for a policy change. Finally National Park Service Director George Hartzog heard them and ordered the creation of a new goat control program that included citizen participation.

Park staff hated the idea. They couldn't see how outside hunters would be more lethal than their own past efforts. And if they weren't, they'd take just enough goats to keep the herd healthy. Instead of fulfilling its mission to preserve a unique native ecosystem for the enjoyment of every American, the national park would become a goat game farm.

"You were either going to have a national park or something else, a public hunting area or something. But if you were going to have a national park, you had to get rid of the animals and do some restoration. It was obvious to me," Reeser says.

The park staff reluctantly went to work, writing rules and regulations for a citizen hunting program that they didn't believe in. Then, in an effort to get a positive outcome, they dusted off Dave Morris's fencing plan, added a few more fences here and there, and released it at the same time.

When the two programs were announced, it was apparent to the hunters that the ultimate goal was to rid the park of goats, the last thing they wanted. So they switched gears and began criticizing the plan that they had lobbied for so fiercely.

With the hunters in an uproar, Hartzog returned. He assured the community that the Park Service didn't intend to eradicate goats from the park. That calmed the hunters, but it raised the ire of the national environmental community.

Through the summer of 1971, conservation organizations barraged the National Park Service with letters about the goat control policy. Amid all the turmoil, the Hawaii Volcanoes' park superintendent left, and in August 1971, Bryan Harry took over.

Harry's arrival signaled a sea of change at the park. He quickly grasped what was going on, understood the environmental damage being done by the goats, and bought into a program to eradicate them.

Harry pressed for funding for the fencing program, threatening to go ahead anyway if additional funds weren't approved. With the help of the Youth Conservation Corps, a three thousand-acre exclosure was finished a year later, in July 1972.

When they set about clearing it of animals, they found the task more difficult than they had imagined. At first citizen hunters came in to shoot the goats. But as the goats got scarcer, interest waned. "Nobody wants to hike too far for an animal and then have to carry a goat back out," Reeser wrote in 1992.

But park personnel understood that it was critical to clear them out completely. "That was a chore, to get the last one," Reeser said. "We always thought we had them, but boom, we'd see a few more."

That was the beginning of the end for the goats. Money came in to put up fences, and the staff set to work. Personnel went out for a week at a time, putting up fences all day long. They had drives, rounded up goats, and then sent in the hunters to finish off the remaining ones. Sometimes they used helicopters to get the last few.

"I tried to instill the idea that it really wasn't important how many goats or animals you took out, it was how many were left," Reeser said. "For some of [the hunters], it wasn't very satisfying, but taking out the last three or four was more valuable than taking out 100 [earlier]."

With goats running wild all over the islands, others were looking for a solution to the same problem. Just across the channel, on Maui's highest point, the staff at Haleakala National Park was watching closely.

11

A FENCE
IN THE FOREST

IN 1976, JUST UPHILL FROM MAUI'S COOL, MOIST FORESTS
where the po'ouli lived, Ron Nagata led the first fencing trip at
Haleakala National Park.

The fencing at Haleakala would set the stage for fencing in
the po'ouli's home on state land downhill of Haleakala National
Park in the years to come. Haleakala's lower fence would one
day also protect the upper reaches of po'ouli habitat. A volunteer
with the Sierra Club, Nagata led a team of five people who, in
two weeks' time, laid the first mile and a half of fence at
Haleakala designed to keep out cows and goats.

Like Hawaii Volcanoes where Reeser was waging war on
goats, Haleakala was under assault from introduced grazers that
were eating the park's vegetation to the ground and altering its
plant community's natural composition.

In 1978, Nagata quit his volunteer work to take on a paying job as a Haleakala backcountry ranger. In 1980, he became the park's first permanent resource manager, in charge of overseeing its natural resources and protecting them when necessary.

In addition to fencing out goats and cows, the park began to target feral pigs. The pigs, whose rooting was also beginning to destroy the po'ouli's forests downhill of the park, favored wetter areas than the goats and required fences with several inches buried below the ground to be effective.

Haleakala's fencing, Nagata says today, is not a job to be finished, but an ongoing project. The fence he worked on as a volunteer so many years ago was of simple barbed wire. Park personnel have since upgraded that to a power fence, then upgraded it again to hog wire to keep both pigs and goats out. Now they're upgrading parts of it again to keep out a new threat—axis deer, which were introduced as targets for hunters and which can leap shorter fences.

Even as Haleakala National Park was putting up its fences, changes were becoming apparent in the wet rainforest downhill where the po'ouli lived. Says Fish and Wildlife Service (FWS) biologist Cameron Kepler:

> It seemed to us that the po'ouli was on the way out. What really hit us was not only how restricted the po'ouli was, it was the correlation with the vegetation. It wasn't too hard to connect the dots: the pigs were changing the forest floor that was important for the po'ouli. The whole thing looked like if you don't control the pigs, you're going to lose that bird.

Kepler had led the team that wrote the Maui–Molokai Forest Birds Recovery Plan, and by mid-1984, he set out to implement its recommendations: fence in the po'ouli's forest and eliminate the pigs.

In June, he sent a memo to Allan Marmelstein, the service's Pacific Islands administrator based in Honolulu. Titled "High Priority Management Needs on Maui (Forest Birds)," it laid out the problem and the solution. It proposed an 197-acre fenced unit to begin management and recovery of the po'ouli and other forest birds. Kepler pointed out that they'd have to work with the state, since the forest was on state-owned land. He estimated the project would cost $50,000 per mile for three to four miles of fence.

Other memos followed, to both state and federal officials, emphasizing the direness of the situation and the need for immediate action to save the po'ouli from extinction. The forest's po'ouli population had fallen 90 percent from 1975 to 1980, Kepler wrote, and another 90 percent by 1981. Pig damage in the forest had increased dramatically since 1980, and po'ouli were gone from parts of the forest where they had lived five years earlier.

Marmelstein joined the fight and began to seek funding. He warned in April 1985 that pigs were out of control in Hanawi, with potentially dire consequences: "There are currently no efforts (including sport hunting) to control the pig population due to the remoteness of this area. The understory of the forest has been obliterated in many places, bare ground is resulting in some areas. . . . The current situation suggests the Po'ouli may be on the verge of extinction." Kepler warned a few months later, in July 1985, that "this species will likely become extinct if steps are not undertaken now to eliminate pigs from Poo-uli habitat."

It took more than a year, but the U.S. government approved $200,000 in funding: $20,000 for three miles of pig-proof fence, $150,000 to put the fence up, and $30,000 to remove the pigs.

In September 1985, the service concluded an interagency agreement with the National Park Service (NPS), which agreed to put its fence-building expertise at the disposal of the FWS.

By October 1985, Marmelstein, Kepler, and Ernest Kosaka, who had become the FWS point person on the project, had stepped up their efforts to get the state onboard.

Marmelstein made his case in an October 4 letter to Susumu Ono, chairman of the state Board of Land and Natural Resources, citing the drop in po'ouli numbers, the birds' limited geographic range, and the dramatic increase in pig damage. Marmelstein pointed out that fences were part of the Maui-Molokai Forest Birds Recovery Plan, and that the federal government had already allocated money for the project: "The allocation of limited, unencumbered funds to this office from the fiscal year 1985 appropriations provides us with an opportunity to implement recovery actions which may prevent extinction of the Po'ouli." But because the proposed project was on state land, they couldn't continue without the state's blessing. "We believe that this fencing project is urgently needed, and that you will agree with this assessment," he wrote.

State officials, however, were unsure that fencing was a good idea and showed little urgency. Over the next three months, the state tried to ensure that the proper paperwork was filed and that it wouldn't get stuck with the project's bill. Their correspondences showed little concern that a remaining tract of intact native forest be preserved to secure the future of an imperiled native bird.

When asked about the situation years later, Marmelstein said that the state wasn't necessarily hostile to the idea, but that it didn't agree that the fence should be first among its priorities. Others, meanwhile, indicated that funding was always a concern for the agency, and that they were further hamstrung by the lack of a management plan for the land.

In his 1985 letter to Ono, Marmelstein asked for advice about which permits would be needed for the project to go ahead. Although state officials insisted that the proper permits be obtained, they weren't sure which those were, according to records of telephone conversations and meetings over the next three months.

It seemed certain that a special use permit was needed from the Natural Area Reserves System Commission (NARSC), since the po'ouli's home forest was in the process of being named a Hawaii natural area reserve, an important, positive step on the state's part. But there was uncertainty whether a Conservation District Use Application was also necessary, and, if so, whether the state or the FWS should file it. There was also talk that county special management area requirements would have to be complied with, and, in January 1986, the state told the FWS that an Environmental Impact Statement would have to be filed.

Throughout this process, there were signs that the state had little enthusiasm for the fencing effort. On October 31, 1985, a state official refused to meet with Marmelstein, saying "there was nothing to discuss." On November 7, Ono wrote to Marmelstein that they hadn't decided whether the project was a good idea: "As with the overall judgment of the proposed fencing project at this time, we can properly deal with this only as you develop your project plans and there is more information made available to us."

The NARSC refused to act on the special use permit at its November meeting. NARSC Executive Secretary Robert Lee wrote on November 8:

> Although the purpose of the project appears to be in line with the management objectives of the Natural Area Reserves System, the permit request contains little or no detail on method and procedure, the potential

adverse impact on the native ecosystem, and the management of the installed project. Considering the scope and character of the project, these should be elaborated upon. We perceive our staff review and recommendation for a subsequent NARS Commission evaluation to be largely a matter of weighing the benefit of the project against detrimental effects that likely will occur to achieve that benefit.

Lee attached to the letter a copy of the management policy for the NARSC, which includes among its objectives several that clearly supported removing pigs from Hanawi: "preventing further biological degradation," "restrict invasion and occurrence of established exotic biota," "reduce or eliminate established exotic biota," and "eliminate . . . exotic biota before they become established."

By early January, three months after Marmelstein's letter to Ono asking about permits, the state still wasn't sure which ones were needed, according to records of a phone conversation between NARSC Executive Secretary Lee and Kosaka of the FWS. Lee also revealed another state concern to Kosaka: that it not get stuck with the bill to manage and maintain the fence once it is built.

While the state was dithering over permits and dragging its feet on the paperwork, it was also adamant that its turf be protected. Lee chastised Cameron Kepler for not waiting for the state to issue a special use permit for his research in Hanawi, warning Kosaka during one of their January conversations that Kepler's permitless work was "technically illegal," and that the state could confiscate equipment used in it, including helicopters that touched down in the reserve. But bigger problems were on the horizon that would eventually kill the project for more than three years.

In mid-November, thirteen people from the NPS, FWS, and the Bishop Museum in Honolulu, along with a representative of a private fencing company, traveled to Hanawi to conduct research and begin figuring out where the fence should go.

They spotted three po'ouli while on the trip, which was encouraging, but as they attempted to traverse the steep slopes, twisted trees, and treacherous gullies, they began to realize that putting up this fence was going to be tougher than they had thought—and more expensive. According to a memo from the trip: "The places where the fence might be built are as inaccessible areas as imaginable. Getting people and material to these sites will be difficult. Putting the fence up on these densely vegetated, sometimes narrow ridges, will also be difficult."

To avoid the risk of a washout, instead of just crossing the area's many streams where the fence encountered them, it would have to run up and down their banks to reach natural obstacles such as deep pools and waterfalls. That would lengthen the fence's course and its cost. "A longer fence will mean higher material and labor costs," the memo said. "All material and people will have to be flown in by helicopter. We knew this already; nonetheless it will be expensive. . . . Techniques like rolling out the fence material for ease of construction, done in open areas, simply can't be done in this forest."

University of Hawaii botany professor Cliff Smith, who headed a university–NPS collaboration through which project funds were funneled, puts it more succinctly:

> The fencing in these areas was not easy in the first place. The logistics are horrendous. We'd done a lot of difficult areas before, but Hanawi was a totally different ballpark. Here we were, working in an upper elevation rainforest with deep ravines, trying to work out where we could fence and where we couldn't. . . . We spent an

incredible amount of time on the ground assessing fencelines and things like that. It was nightmarish.

By mid-December, it was becoming apparent that they might not have enough money. The state had no money for the effort, something Marmelstein had been aware of the previous April as he sought federal funds. And it was beginning to look like the $200,000 in federal money would not be enough.

In December, Kepler began to express concern about funds for the project, and by the end of January 1986, his fears became a reality. During a meeting on the twenty-ninth, the planners decided that the initial estimate of $50,000 per mile, derived from the fence construction at Haleakala, was too low. Much too low.

They doubled that estimate to $100,000 per mile for the most difficult parts of the forest, and all the zigzagging increased the fence length too. Their new estimate: 4.6 miles of fence, which would cost between $230,000 and $320,000.

They were busted.

They'd spent roughly $32,000 of their initial $200,000 budget already. Fifty rolls of hog wire were sitting in storage at Haleakala National Park. They had invested eighteen months in the effort and aligned federal agencies behind it. Pigs were still tearing up Hanawi, and they were ready to go. Given enough time, the state even might have figured out what permits were needed.

But without enough money to finish the task, they couldn't even start. They had a bid from an outside contractor for $185,000 for the fencing, but after reexamining what it entailed, they doubted it could be done for that.

"Quite frankly, we underestimated the enormity of the job," Smith says. "I think that the original estimate had been grossly off, that's what the problem was. Then when people began to realize how much was involved, it became very apparent that a totally inadequate amount of money was going into the project, and we backed off."

The fencing project slipped into low gear and then into neutral. No more money was forthcoming from Washington, D.C., and the state didn't have any for it in the first place.

In April 1986, the project's special use permit application was withdrawn and changed to allow continued study. In September, Haleakala National Park superintendent Hugo Huntsinger issued a plea that the project not be lost. Kepler was leaving, and Huntsinger feared that momentum for the fence would leave with him. Huntsinger wrote:

> I believe that this project will have a very positive impact upon critical habitat adjacent to the park, and thus is beneficial to our own efforts to save threatened native habitat and associated endemic species which are listed as endangered. We have already expended a considerable amount of time and funds for planning and supplies in support of this USFWS project and I would hate for it to be lost at the last minute.

The project wasn't lost, ultimately, but time was. Three years would pass until it was resurrected. During those three years, pigs continued to run free through Hanawi, and the po'ouli lost more and more habitat. Though three birds were seen during the November 1985 trip to explore fence feasibility and the nest was spotted in 1986, no po'ouli were seen at all in 1987 and, though some were spotted in 1988, none were seen in 1989.

October 1989 saw renewed interest in the fencing plan. In his final months in the area office, Marmelstein had arranged an additional $50,000 for the project. The state, in the intervening years, had completed a management plan for Hanawi, an important step in a process that would make the area the state's premier forest bird sanctuary.

Michael Buck, who would become administrator of the state's Division of Forestry and Wildlife in the 1990s, worked as the NARSC coordinator from 1987 to 1989. Spurred by a large grant and interest from The Nature Conservancy, Buck spent a year visiting the reserves and drafting management plans, which would allow active management of what he says until then had been essentially "paper parks."

With the management plans in place and the money ready to be used, the state was finally prepared to move ahead. Further, since the project was aligned with management objectives, no permits would be needed.

Not only was the fencing project back, the urgency was as well: "Although this is not the best time of year to begin work in Hanawi because of the weather, it was generally felt that work should start as soon as possible," wrote John Engbring in a November 1989 memo to Kosaka.

The state appeared to have allayed its concerns that it would get stuck with a bill for the project, accepting overall supervisory responsibility.

"A consensus was quickly reached that the Maui Office of State Forestry and Wildlife was the appropriate agency to supervise the work," Lloyd Loope, a Haleakala National Park research biologist, wrote after one meeting.

The paper trail shows smooth sailing from there, with regular extensions of the interagency agreement that provided the project's administrative structure, requests for required progress reports, and the additional release of funds to allow the work to advance.

In the intervening years, the project had grown. Instead of the single, 350-acre enclosure described in the 1986 Environmental Assessment, the project envisioned four separate adjoining enclosures of about two thousand acres, with more than ten miles of fence. It would wind up taking ten years to build and cost $1 million.

Now that the administrative battle over the fence had been won, the fight with Hanawi's treacherous terrain, twisted trees, and unrelenting rain could begin. Much of this work was overseen by Bill Evanson.

During the summer of 1990, Evanson was working not for the state, but for Haleakala National Park. He walked the park's fence that season, inspecting as he went. Evanson, in his second year as a seasonal park ranger, had left a better-paying job as a paralegal on Oahu to work on this Maui mountaintop. He had exchanged his office job for days outdoors, toiling in Haleakala's thin, crisp air, where panoramic views of Maui, the Pacific, and nearby islands could be had for the effort of raising one's eyes.

"I left my job as a paralegal on Friday and started as a ranger on Monday," Evanson says. "I did a complete 180-degree turn. I took a big pay cut, but I'm a lot happier."

In his two years at Haleakala, Evanson had done various jobs in addition to fence inspection. He had gained renown for eliminating a potentially disastrous introduction of rabbits, likely from a kindhearted pet owner unaware of the destruction their unchecked breeding can cause. By the time Evanson had set to work, an estimated one hundred rabbits were scattered over 197 acres.

As Evanson neared the fence that day in 1990, he could hear the state fence crew at work downhill in the Hanawi Natural Area Reserve. He looked into the misty forest for a time, and then heard a helicopter approaching. Evanson knew the pilot and waved. The pilot picked him up and gave him a tour of the Hanawi fence project from the air.

"The area was always talked about as being the home of the po'ouli and of many rare and endangered forest birds," Evanson says. "It was always kind of like a no-man's land . . . the deepest, darkest reaches of the forest on Maui. It's situated in the wettest, cloudiest portion of the island, and so it had this mystique to it. I thought, 'Cool, awesome place, cool new project, great, important thing to be doing.'"

Down below, the fence crew was led by Randy Salomon. Salomon was a paniolo, Hawaiian cowboy, who had spent years rounding up cattle, putting up fences, and working with helicopters in difficult, remote terrain. He had taken the job at the urging of his son Derrick, who was working on the crew.

Derrick says that the job was the hardest he's ever had, making his stints in the military and sailing across the Pacific seem easy by comparison. Despite the difficulty, however, he felt that it was an honor to help with such an important task. He was struck by the forest's harsh beauty, with its dry streambeds that a moment later could be a head-high raging torrent and its fifty-foot-wide gullies that look almost crossable until one realizes they're 150 feet deep. During his years in the forest, he saw many native birds, including the po'ouli.

Randy was less taken by the forest—and less surprised at what he found there. A longtime hunter, he had spent time in other native forests and knew he was in for a strenuous, wet job. Still, he kept at it, year after year. He enjoyed the challenge and the sense of accomplishment from a job so tough that few would do it.

By the time Evanson took his tour, the Salomons had already sited the fence, helicoptering over the proposed fence line and then walking and flagging it. For the portions they'd finished, they cleared the forest with chain saws and dug a trench to bury the fence bottom. They pounded in the posts and rolled out the fence.

After working all day, they slept in an eight-by-ten-foot metal shed that could be picked up by helicopter. When they finished a section, the helicopter would pick up the shed and move it to a new site, leaving the old camp to be reclaimed by the forest.

The helicopter airlifted supplies and materials as well, including three-hundred-pound fence rolls. The crew carried their tools back and forth to the work site, though, including a forty-pound manual post pounder—a large weight that slid up and down on a piece of pipe—and a seventy-five-pound gas-powered rock drill for rocky sites along the route.

A year after Bill Evanson's helicopter tour of the fencing operation, he heard about an opening with the state that would put him in Hanawi as the project's supervisor. He jumped at it.

One of Evanson's first tasks was to go into Hanawi and see how the work was going. Before he left, however, his supervisor called him in to deliver a cryptic warning about Randy: "Don't piss him off; he's doing a very good job."

The helicopter flew Evanson into the grasslands above the reserve. He walked downhill, following the fence to its lower line, where it turned to cut across the slope.

Evanson immediately saw the fence's impact. A swath of brush and trees was cleared from the fenceline. With the po'ouli so scarce, Evanson became concerned that the very act of fencing might harm the bird: "Fencing is a high-impact activity. Obviously, you're going to have to cut trees. But when you're in endangered forest bird habitat, you have to wonder."

He threw his gear into the fence crew's cabin and followed the sounds of the rock drill, eventually coming upon Randy, Derrick, and a third worker.

Evanson watched them work for a few minutes and then went over to talk to Randy Salomon about how the bottom of the fence was being installed. Randy listened for a bit and then lit into Evanson, telling him to let them do their work and to get off the job site.

Evanson left, understanding his supervisor's warning. Derrick later said that Evanson and his father mixed like oil and water. They avoided each other after that, with Evanson leaving Randy in peace to put up the fence.

Whatever their personal disagreements, Evanson and others gained an appreciation for Randy Salomon's work ethic. He was a notoriously hard driver, pushing his crews to get the fence up. They worked through the rain and were always wet. They'd had a friend weld metal cleats to the bottoms of their boots to give them traction in the mud and just kept moving.

Even Derrick had trouble keeping up sometimes. His father was such a fast hiker, it seemed all he ever saw of him was his back.

"My father is not someone who messes around. If it's pouring rain, we're working," Derrick says. "We were up there to work, so work we did. We thought it was an important job."

Randy had a morning exercise routine that dropped jaws, doing one thousand push-ups while he waited for the coffee to boil. He says that the jungle was a tough place to work, and he felt the exercise got him ready for whatever it would throw at him that day.

According to Evanson, state work crews just couldn't keep up and didn't like Randy's prickly demeanor, so eventually they stopped trying to send state crews up when the Salomons were working. "We had regular DOFAW [Division of Forestry and

Wildlife] employees who tried to go up there and supplement them, but they could not work with him. The guy would wake up, eat no breakfast. He'd drink a pot of coffee, and he and his son would do a thousand pushups every morning, in sets of a hundred. They intimidated the hell out of our guys, who were mostly fat and cigarette smokers."

But the fence went up, and fast. In the first year, 1990–91, 2.5 miles of fence were constructed, almost twice the 1.3 initially projected. In the second year, 2.2 miles were put up, almost a mile more than the 1.4 miles expected.

The original fencing plan called for four individual adjoining units to be built. This allowed pig removal to begin when the first unit was done, rather than waiting for the whole project to be finished.

When the first unit was completed in 1991, Evanson immediately set out to clear it of pigs. Though hunting with dogs had been the preferred method in the 1970s, research since then had confirmed that snaring coupled with hunting—sometimes from a helicopter in open areas—was most effective.

Evanson admits that snaring could be gruesome, but says that a properly set snare would dispatch a pig within minutes. "When I first saw one, I thought, 'Oh god, this is ugly. There's got to be a better way.' I subsequently came to realize that in remote areas, snares work twenty-four hours a day, seven days a week. They don't complain about the weather, don't need overtime, and don't want to eat pizza. There is no better way. Snaring is one of the oldest hunting methods known to man."

After studying pig movement within Hanawi, Evanson cut and flagged trails needed to set the snares. As it had the scientific expeditions, the weather plagued the fence crews and the pig removal effort. Evanson says they had to cancel about 70 percent of their scheduled helicopter flights because of wind, rain, and clouds.

"It was a humbling experience to be in the area when the weather came in," he says. "It would rain all day, every day. You'd eat your lunch in five minutes. Your sandwich was a sponge while you were eating it under your raincoat, trying not to get it wet."

The first unit had about twenty pigs in it, and by 1993, it had been pig-free for more than a year. Evanson eventually developed a two-year rule of thumb: it would take about two years to remove all the pigs from a newly enclosed unit, and another two years for the vegetation to recover. But once it recovered, the difference was spectacular, causing several observers to comment about the regrowth of the forests' ground cover, which was particularly dramatic when viewed in comparison with damaged forest outside the fence.

"There were ferns coming up everywhere," says federal biologist Thane Pratt. "It was just astonishing. You could stand at the fenceline and see, Okay here's *inside* the fence, and here's *outside* the fence. It was so different in just a couple of years, it's just amazing."

Though the vegetation was recovering, in the early years of the fencing, po'ouli sightings were scarce. Evanson and others became concerned that all the noise might be having an adverse impact on the bird.

"We flew lots of helicopters at low-level elevation," Evanson says. "I'm talking on the treetops for an extended period of time, hauling men and material. The helicopter is an extremely noisy and objectionable thing. I can't imagine how it could not have affected the bird."

Those concerns, coupled with Evanson's confidence that he could successfully eliminate pigs from a larger area, led to a decision to eliminate one of the interior fences. That would create a single larger unit where original plans had called for two smaller ones. Cliff Smith, who oversaw the administrative collaboration that provided the project's funding, echoed Evanson's concerns in a 1993 memo to the FWS:

> Our belief is that fence construction (i.e. habitat disturbance) in endangered forest bird habitat such as Hanawi should be kept to an absolute minimum. Research has not yet been able to determine the limiting factors for these rare species of forest birds, but experience tells us to err on the side of prudence. Who knows what effect our fence building has had on the Poʻouli, but the 1992 Maui Forest Bird Survey detected none of these birds. In retrospect, putting a fence down through the heart of Poʻouli habitat might not have been the best idea, but the state of what we know about managing ecosystems is fluid and ever changing.

While Evanson was wrestling with pigs and fence crews, Smith was wrestling with pigs and animal rights. Animal welfare laws passed in the 1980s regulated the use of laboratory animals and required the university to set up a review board for animal research. According to Smith, there was a lot of confusion over how to execute the laws, and the pig removal project happened to be before the board as it worked through that confusion. The result was an enormous amount of angst over the best way to remove the pigs. Smith says:

> Towards the latter part of it, we did have to deal with how you kill animals like that in these sorts of situations. We had to consider shooting, poison, and all sorts of different techniques, and it wasn't enough to tell the committee it was our opinion—we had to have evidence. Most were pretty skeptical of the whole idea of hunting being an acceptable method of animal control.

Smith says that snaring was selected almost by default; hunters just wouldn't do it. "Getting people to go hunt in these areas consistently in a regular pattern—you can go in there, and its just torrential rain for days on end—it was just impossible to get people to do it. Snaring was our ultimate answer, because everything else was just horrendously difficult."

And as with Hawaii Volcanoes' goats, unless they got all the animals, they were just wasting their time.

12

BACK FROM THE DEAD

BY THE EARLY 1990S, FEARS WERE STIRRING THAT THE HAWAIIAN Islands had lost another bird.

Poʻouli had been sighted in the 1980s, but the emotional high of finding the nest in 1986, with its treasure trove of biological information and hopeful assurance that the birds were still breeding, faded as the years passed.

No poʻouli were spotted in 1987, but in 1988, five were observed between the east Hanawi and west Kuhiwa gulches. The joy at seeing the birds was tempered by the extensive pig damage that was also found. The sighting report noted that "the Kuhiwa Plateau was devastated by pigs, and most of the activity was fresh. All that remained of the understory was a few uprooted ferns and some scattered ʻakala. Erosion had exposed the underground roots of many ohia."

Andrew Engilis Jr., who reported the sighting, said they found no poʻouli at all in the location where they were originally discovered. Rather than rejoicing at the sighting, he described the alarming "apparent collapse of the range of Po'ouli."

After that, the birds disappeared. There were no sightings in 1989 or 1990, though at long last, fencing operations began in Hanawi. The fencing was the first hands-on action to protect the forest and its unique avian inhabitants. It came seventeen years after the po'ouli was discovered, fifteen years after it was listed as endangered, and six years after Cameron Kepler warned that the bird would go extinct if something weren't done immediately.

In 1991 no birds were seen, though the first of the three fenced units was completed and pig removal began, another hopeful step in the recovery effort. That same year, positive changes were afoot in the Honolulu office of the Fish and Wildlife Service. Robert Smith, the Service's assistant regional director in Portland, Oregon, had taken the extraordinary step of asking to be demoted and sent to Honolulu.

Smith had spent years working on recovery of the spotted owl and other mainland species, but over the course of several visits to Hawaii had come to understand that "a true extinction crisis" was underway there.

Smith came to Hawaii with the ear of those above him in the FWS bureaucracy and the energy born of his conviction that Hawaiian extinctions could be stopped.

His arrival in Hawaii also roughly coincided with the government's loss in a lawsuit that required the listing of two hundred Hawaiian plant species under the Endangered Species Act. Together, those factors brought significant new resources to conservation programs.

The Honolulu office, which oversaw conservation in Hawaii and on far-flung islands such as American Samoa, Guam, and Palau, had been managing with as few as seven staff before Smith's arrival. By the time Smith hired Karen Rosa as a recovery biologist in May 1991, the office was already up to eleven and had begun an era of growth that would bring it to fifty-two by 2007.

Smith's tenure would also see the construction of a new avian captive breeding facility, renovation of Hawaii's existing one, and the hiring of The Peregrine Fund to run them. It would also see the creation of several programs to recover native birds, including key programs for the po'ouli.

Despite those developments, however, by 1992, people were getting worried about the po'ouli. The Maui Forest Bird Survey—a major effort that went right through the middle of po'ouli territory—came up empty.

Ronald L. Walker, the state's wildlife program manager, put those worries into words in May 1992, when he testified at a U.S. Senate hearing on the administration of the Endangered Species Act in Hawaii:

> As recently as three weeks ago in concert with . . . the Fish and Wildlife Service and private landowners, we have done a major survey of forest birds on the island of Maui, and went right through the middle of the habitat of the po'ouli which is a very rare bird on Maui and saw zero, none. That would indicate at least by that one survey that it is either extinct or in very little numbers.

But that same year, there was a glimmer of hope that at least a few survived.

Rebecca Cann, part of a scientific team working in Hanawi, was hiking down a marked but uncleared transect. After three hours of bushwacking, she'd had enough. She told the other team members to push on ahead and pick her up on the way back.

Cann found a level spot on the steep hillside and sat quietly, watching the forest around her. During her two-hour wait, a strange bird appeared that she didn't recognize. She watched as it picked its way along the tree trunks, realizing later that it was a poʻouli.

When other members of her party returned, she told them what she'd seen. Together, they waited for a while, but the bird didn't reappear.

Cann's sighting did little to soothe anxiety about the bird. Its long absence and the Maui Forest Bird Survey's failure to find any had rattled people beyond the point where they could be assuaged by a single unconfirmed sighting.

It was during the poʻouli's continued absence that state officials overseeing the fencing began to wonder whether the short-term impact of their work had been too severe, even for the long-term benefit to the forest.

But the poʻouli hadn't succumbed just yet. In September 1993, Betsy Gagné (formerly Harrison) and Tonnie Casey, two of the original Hana Rainforest Project members, teamed up with federal biologist Thane Pratt to scout Hanawi prior to a new study of the forest's endangered birds.

The project, a collaboration among state, federal, and private conservation organizations, aimed to gather biological information such as life history and breeding habits in preparation for a more intensive hands-on recovery program. The project would focus on the Maui parrotbill and crested honeycreeper, endangered birds that still had large enough populations that they could be studied.

Birds with vanishingly small populations, like the poʻouli, would be added only should the opportunity present itself. According to Pratt, by this point they had begun to lose hope that the poʻouli still existed. "We went up for a few days to scout around the Frisbee Meadow area and the former nest site a couple of ridges to the east. We felt that the poʻouli was very close to extinction. It had disappeared from its historic haunts."

But Casey, Gagné, and Pratt succeeded where others had failed. Searching the forests near the nest site, the team saw two po'ouli—or one bird twice. Either way, the confirmed sighting generated a buzz of excitement.

"Betsy Gagné, Tonnie Casey and Thane Pratt saw po'ouli!" Karen Rosa of the FWS wrote in a telephone conversation record on September 13, 1993. "They checked one of the old sites and saw them. . . . We'll get more info from them later."

The sighting not only created a surge of excitement among state and federal biologists, but also prompted a sigh of relief from those working on the essential but potentially disruptive Hanawi fence.

"Unsuccessful efforts to locate the Po'ouli during the 1992 Maui Forest Bird Survey and later by the Forest Bird Research Project had raised questions about our preservation efforts, particularly how fencing may have affected the Po'ouli. Confirming the Po'ouli still exists has not only boosted our morale, but the morale of people all over the islands who work to preserve native species," Bill Evanson wrote in a fencing status report.

The sighting turned out to be the last, however, near the place where the po'ouli was first discovered. The research project focused on the parrotbill and crested honeycreeper got under way shortly, and though the project's researchers logged many hours in the forest, they found no po'ouli in the area where, twenty years earlier, a college student had seen three sitting on a single branch.

It would be bad enough if it were just the po'ouli clinging to existence. But unfortunately for Hawaii, the po'ouli had plenty of company.

By the early 1990s, more than a dozen bird species hadn't been seen in years—some not for decades. Their names read like a ghostly echo of long-ago Hawaii. Polynesian words once spoken by everyday people pointing out a creature in a nearby tree or bush had become entombed in books, scholarly articles, and lists of the lost or nearly so: 'alala, puaiohi, 'o'u, 'o'o'a'a, kama'o. The missing birds also included other denizens of Hanawi like the po'ouli, whose rarity not only engendered mystery, but also sparked debate about their continued existence: the Maui nukupu'u and the Maui 'akepa.

Some of the lost birds singlehandedly illustrated the stunning diversity of Hawaiian birdlife, such as the greater 'akialoa, which sported an enormous curved bill that reached as long as half its body length.

In 1993, two researchers, Michelle Reynolds and Tom Snetsinger, embarked on a project to determine whether these birds still existed. They realized that though the broad-based bird surveys provided critical information, they were inadequate for truly rare species.

Rare birds were unlikely to be encountered under the rigid conditions that gave the Hawaiian Forest Bird Survey and its successors their statistical power. Researchers walking preset transects and conducting counts for predetermined periods created a snapshot of the forest in time. But rare birds needed a more focused effort or they would be missed, or seen so infrequently that the sightings were meaningless in determining an overall population.

Reynolds and Snetsinger designed a survey that would target these rare species, called the Rare Bird Search. By focusing their search effort, they would determine whether the birds had been missed by earlier efforts or were no longer there to be found.

"There had not been a concerted effort that was intense enough and specific enough to give a little more confidence whether [a] bird was around or not," Reynolds says, adding that with the broader surveys, "if a species is very rare, the chance of hearing a vocalization during that eight-minute count is pretty slim."

The greater 'akialoa and other birds targeted by the Rare Bird Search had been missing for years. The 'akialoa's last confirmed sighting was in 1965 on Kauai. Today considered extinct, it may well have been long gone even by the time of the Rare Bird Search. But they wouldn't know without looking. Reynolds says:

> The last surveys that were done had not picked up most of these rare species. Even back in the eighties, when these species were picked up, they were picked up in very low numbers, and the po'ouli in particular had not been detected during the last survey they had done on Maui. It was a very expansive survey and it covered much of the bird's range, and none were detected.

Reynolds and Snetsinger prepared exhaustively. They studied scientific literature on their targets, listened to birdsong recordings, and visited museums to view specimens that existed only in collections. They studied the songs of other Hawaiian species so they would know if they heard something different in the forest. They examined all former sightings so they would know the birds' historic ranges and be able to identify likely habitat that remained unexplored.

According to Reynolds, this was the first survey where 100 percent of the effort was focused on searching specifically for these particular birds. "We tried to pick out areas where these birds were most likely to be found, either historically or because of habitat quality."

From August 1994 until April 1996, teams searched Hawaii for the ghosts of its forests. Reynolds' effort was focused on two places where the most endangered species existed: the northeast slope of Maui's Haleakala volcano and Kauai's Alakai Swamp. Rare Bird Search teams also visited Hawaii, Molokai, and Oahu.

Altogether, teams mounted twenty-three expeditions, logging 1,685 hours in the field. They found seven of the thirteen birds. The other six they concluded were extinct: kama'o, 'o'o'a'a, Bishop's 'o'o, 'o'u on Kauai, greater 'akialoa, and kakawahie, a bird from Molokai.

The po'ouli was among the birds they did find, and in numbers high enough to spark a desperate effort to pull it back from the brink of extinction.

Tom Snetsinger had worked in Hawaii for several years before the Rare Bird Search began. Though he had visited many of the state's forests, he had never set foot among the tangled trees of windward Maui. "My experience there kind of took my breath away," he says. "It felt like the Hawaii of old. In the areas where pigs were removed and fenced, you'd find [plants like] lobelioids, cyaneas. It seemed much more intact than any other place I'd been up until that."

The two researchers established something of a routine for getting into, working in, and leaving the remote forests. Flying in by helicopter, they hiked from the landing site to a remote camp. They conducted day hikes from there, traveling as far as possible while leaving enough time to get back by dark. When they had covered all the territory they could from that camp, they loaded up their backpacks and headed even farther out. They traveled as lightly as possible, sleeping in hammocks strung between trees, with a tarp above to keep the rain off. And this being Hanawi, rain it did.

The two conducted nine expeditions on Maui. They searched extensively through the po'ouli's known home range, between the upper forks of the Hanawi stream where the bird had been discovered and where Gagné, Casey, and Pratt had the two sightings in 1993. They found nothing, however.

On August 22, 1994, the two set out for the Kuhiwa unit. The largest of the three units to be fenced, Kuhiwa remained little explored. At the time, fencing was still two years from completion and pigs had free access.

It rained steadily for their first week, bringing work to a halt. Though they could—and often did—hike in the rain, looking for birds was pointless. The mist would roll in and binoculars fog up, making them useless. Not only couldn't they see, they couldn't hear the birds either, since the rain's steady drumbeat on heads, hats, and hoods obscured birdcalls, often the first hint that a bird was near. Not that the birds would call in the rain anyway. Like humans, birds hunkered down in the rain, waiting for it to let up.

After several days without a break, Reynolds began to consider leaving. She knew that other researchers working in the area had a helicopter pickup planned in a day or two, and as she and Snetsinger were a full day's hike out, they would have to make a decision soon.

But on August 30, the downpour gave way to a drizzle, light enough that they could survey the nearby forest. After days of inactivity, the two loaded up and finally got moving.

A little after 9 A.M., they were heading down an old Hawaiian Forest Bird Survey transect. They reached a wide, steep-sided gully, one of many carved by the area's streams. Just below the spot where the stream plunged in a forty-five-foot waterfall, Reynolds heard a single *chip* call, like that of the Maui creeper, a common honeycreeper that calls the forest home.

Reynolds looked in the direction of the sound and saw not a creeper, but a po'ouli, sitting on an olapa branch about thirty feet away.

"I was so excited I shouted, 'Tom!' which was not a good thing, because it might have scared the bird." Reynolds says. "It was very, very exciting, after wandering around in the wet for so long, to actually see one."

Snetsinger came up just before the bird flew off, and then the two began to move downhill again. After about five minutes, they came upon not just one po'ouli, but a whole family: a male, female, and juvenile, begging with a high-pitched twitter and being fed by the parents. They were just fifteen feet away.

"It felt like it was the discovery of the millennium. It was completely symbolic of what we hoped would happen," Snetsinger says. "The rains had lifted. It wasn't quite a rainbow shining on a family group, but it sort of felt that way at the time."

The two just sat and watched the birds, forgetting about the recording equipment and cameras they'd lugged for days through the forest. Reynolds recalls:

It was a very magical moment. We were able to watch them for less than five minutes. The birds left and we said, "Oh, we forgot about the recording equipment in the back of our packs." We forgot about the cameras and all those things that one would use to document a sighting. But if you were to take off the pack and pull all that stuff out, you'd miss the observation. That's when we decided, "We don't have to catch that helicopter; we can stay in another ten days."

The two were disappointed, however, when they stayed for several more days but did not have another sighting.

"They're so secretive and cryptic and difficult to find," Reynolds says. Still, "I just thought it was amazing that we never saw them again after that initial sighting."

Follow-up trips through the area logged two more sightings and one po'ouli's call. All together, the Rare Bird Search found five or six individual po'ouli.

News of the po'ouli family spread fast. Within a week, state and federal officials were scrambling. Though some voiced concern that continued fencing in the Kuhiwa unit would disturb the birds, others said the fencing was so critical that it had to be expedited, though routed to avoid po'ouli populations.

There was also immediate talk of beginning a new project, focused on the po'ouli. Adding the po'ouli to the existing parrotbill and crested honeycreeper project was discussed but rejected, because the po'ouli site was several hours' walk away and the crew would have to spend too much time in transit.

"The birds were located in a very difficult spot, far from the camp at Frisbee Meadow," says Thane Pratt, then a biologist with the U.S. Geological Survey's Biological Resources Division. "Also, part of their territory included a deep chasm that was marginally accessible. I got to see the male, viewed across the gorge."

Pratt, who had set up the parrotbill and crested honeycreeper project, had a sense of urgency. They'd gotten another chance with the po'ouli but had to move quickly. Pratt remembers:

> There was a lot to do right away to set the project up: hire a crew for the po'ouli project, establish camps closer to the birds, comprehensive population surveys, and predator control. It was also hard to know what the bird needed. Plus, decisions had to be made among the agencies responsible about what to do with the remaining po'ouli.

Pratt had a feeling that the po'ouli's back was to the wall, hemmed in by Frisbee Meadow on one side and the Kipahulu

Valley on the other. Both were well known and neither held any po'ouli. This was in all likelihood the last population.

By September 16, just two weeks after the sighting by Reynolds and Snetsinger, word had gotten out. Requests from birders wanting to visit the site were coming in. Pratt didn't want people visiting the area and inadvertently harming the environment or the bird. He was concerned enough to write a memo asking that maps of the site distributed at a Hawaii Forest Bird Recovery Team meeting be treated as confidential:

> At our last meeting, I passed out an account of the Po'o-uli sighting. It is probably now buried deep in your stack of papers gathered during the meeting, and I'd request it stay there out of harm's way. Attached to the report is a map showing the location of the birds. Though we aren't expecting a stampede of birders, the first inquiry has come in. So, please regard the map as confidential information, and don't distribute it. The bird, and particularly its habitat, are sensitive to traffic by individuals unaware of the hazards their presence may cause.

Within a month, FWS officials were beating the bushes for personnel and funding for the new project, to conduct intensive data gathering and habitat management focused on Hanawi's rarest birds: the po'ouli, the nukupu'u, and the Maui 'akepa.

"Now that these extremely rare species are known to still exist, we have what may be the last opportunity to reverse the fate of these, and perhaps other, endangered Maui forest birds," said a flyer sent to The Nature Conservancy asking for its support. "A two-year project has been designed to save the po'ouli and nukupu'u (and possibly the equally rare Maui 'akepa) through a combination of research and population management."

The flyer described a project that would first exhaustively search the forests to determine how many po'ouli still existed and color-band them. This would allow researchers for the first time to track individual birds, determine their ranges, and learn about their life histories. They'd focus on breeding status, control cat and rat predation, and study the feasibility of captive propagation.

The following summer, the new project was up and running. It was called the Maui Critically Endangered Species Project, but memos and meeting minutes often referred to it as the Po'ouli Project. Pratt provided overall guidance and ran the administrative side of the project, which was authorized for two years and funded at $200,000 per year. Paul Baker, a British Ph.D. who'd been in Hawaii since 1993, headed the fieldwork.

Baker had his work cut out for him. Despite decades of study, the list of what wasn't known about the po'ouli in 1995 was lengthy. The population estimates from the early 1980s were obsolete. Just a few years earlier, some had thought it possible that the bird was extinct. Now that it was known that at least some existed, it was up to Baker to find out how many.

Details of the bird's basic biology were also vague. Little was known about breeding behavior, courtship, and parenting, illuminated only by the observation of a single pair nesting in 1986. Even such basic information as the sexes of the remaining birds—critical in assessing the species' future—and how long the average po'ouli lived was unknown.

It was time to get to work.

Hired in July, Baker put a field team together in a few months. The team members' first trip to Hanawi was on September 13, and they had established a field camp by October. From there they immediately set to work on one of the project's main goals: finding out how many were left and where they were.

Over the next nineteen months, Baker and his crew spent 729 person-days searching new areas, locating birds, and repeatedly revisiting areas where birds were found, covering 1,730 acres of tangled, dense, dripping forest. By the middle of 1996, the search crew had located six po'ouli, but search as they might, they came up with no others. In October, Baker reported that it appeared that six were all there were.

The crew then began to get to know the individual birds, with Baker denoting four distinct home ranges. With only six birds, recovery was definitely a long shot, but at least there appeared to be a mix of sexes, including two pairs.

Home Ranges 1 and 2 each had birds thought to be male and female. Home Range 3 held a lone male. Home Range 4 was the shakiest of them all: a lone bird detected by a single call.

The next year was a devastating one for the po'ouli. The bird in Home Range 4 was never heard from again, dropping the known population to five. Worse, in July, both pairs lost a partner: the male in Home Range 1 and the female in Home Range 2 both disappeared.

The remaining po'ouli population totaled three: a bird thought to be male in Home Range 3, a bird thought to be female in Home Range 1, and a bird thought to be male—that would ultimately become the last po'ouli—in Home Range 2.

Banding the po'ouli so they could be tracked with certainty was one of the project's goals. But the birds frustrated Baker and his crew, eluding capture time and time again. Finally, observing that the po'ouli often flocked with Maui parrotbills, Baker shifted strategy and began banding parrotbills. He figured if he could tell with which parrotbills the po'ouli were associating, he'd have a better chance of catching them. He also began using recordings of parrotbill calls in an effort to draw the po'ouli into the long, fine mist nets. Baker later wrote:

> On 15 January 1997, while on a ridge at 1700m eleva-
> tion in Unit 3 of the reserve, I heard a pair of Maui
> Parrotbill approaching me. I set up one 6m mist net and
> used playback of Maui Parrotbill calls and song to lure
> the birds into the net. The female Maui Parrotbill ap-
> proached the net with an adult male Poouli close behind.
> The Poouli disappeared in the foliage in a nearby ohia
> tree, but the Maui Parrotbill flew away. A minute later,
> the Poouli reappeared in the same tree and flew straight
> into the mist net. This was the first Poouli ever captured.

Baker was fully aware of the momentousness of the occasion. Not only was he the first person to hold a live poʻouli, but
he was likely holding one of the last of its kind. He was excited
and felt a sense of accomplishment at finally netting one of the
birds that had eluded capture for so long. "At last we were getting somewhere," Baker says. "The number of sightings was just
ridiculously low. My thought was to just get the bird processed
and get it back out there, while getting every last molecule of
detail we could from holding it."

They worked quickly, examining the bird close up, measuring
it, banding it, and extracting a few feathers for sexing. Baker later
published a detailed description. At the time, he was pretty sure
the bird was a male, as its behavior was aggressive toward the play-
back calls. But the sexing tests indicated that it was a female, and
for years biologists assumed that it indeed was a female until it was
captured for breeding, resexed, and found to actually be a male.

Recalling that first poʻouli years later, Baker says its bill was
broader than he expected, and it seemed capable of crushing
tougher things than snails. He was also struck by its similarity to
chickadees and house sparrows. He tells of a lasting image from
the encounter:

When I let the po'ouli go, he went and perched on a branch about six feet from me and just sat and looked at me. My colleague who was with me and had a camera in her hand had the power off and didn't get the picture. The bird just sat and looked at me like, "What are you?" I looked at it like, "I'd like to know more about you, too."

After a long moment, the bird hopped to a higher branch. The two humans finally gathered their wits about them and shot a few pictures, and then bird was gone. Now that a bird had been banded, researchers could know when they were seeing this individual in the forest. And they soon found that the bird stayed in its own home range.

By 1997, researchers had become fairly certain that just three po'ouli were left, living in three separate home ranges. Baker summed up the situation that would face conservation biologists for the next seven years: "Given a fairly sedentary nature and the long distances between home ranges, it is unlikely that the remaining Po'ouli in the Hanawi NAR may wander into each other's home ranges. . . . The remaining birds cannot find each other and attempt to breed." Sadly, he noted, "We presume the Po'ouli to be on the brink of extinction."

In 1996, Hanawi's Kuhiwa unit—where the sole known po'ouli population lived—was finally fenced in. But the last pig wasn't removed until the next year, when the population was down to just three birds.

Though pig damage had been associated with the po'ouli's decline, it wasn't the only factor thought to be at work. Figuring out what the other factors were and managing those threats also fell to the Po'ouli Project.

Knowing that po'ouli favored native snails as a food source, project field crews surveyed snail and insect populations. And understanding that introduced predators could devastate a bird that evolved in their absence, they worked to control rat, cat, and mongoose populations.

A 1985–86 study of rats in Hanawi found that the forest had one of the highest rat densities in the state. Those who worked in Hanawi had their own stories of rat abundance. Randy Salomon, who led fencing crews for years in the forest, says he was surprised at how many rats there were. In the morning after a rain, the smooth mud on the trail would be covered with tiny rat footprints all the way from the cabin to the fenceline. They were careful to bag their garbage each night, Salomon says, but it wasn't unusual to wake up to find rat droppings on the table in the cabin.

Though there was no direct evidence that rats were harming the po'ouli, there was also no reason to think these birds were exempt from the marauding of this common tree-climbing predator. So the project established a grid of poisoned bait that field crews hoped would reduce rat numbers dramatically. Just over a year after the project began, two grids of 120 stations each were centered on the home ranges where the pairs had been seen, in an effort to protect any breeding birds.

By early 1997, the project planned to take on two other known predators: cats and mongooses, with 40 cat traps and 125 mongoose traps.

Some people were demanding more. Tonnie Casey in particular was a vocal proponent of more intensive and widespread rat control. Casey was in touch with conservation officials in New Zealand, an island nation whose native birdlife, like Hawaii's, had been suffering from the scourge of introduced predators. In New Zealand, they didn't just put rat bait on the ground; they spread it aerially, covering far larger areas and in some cases showing dramatic results.

"One day I saw a po'ouli hopping through a pilo bush," Casey says, recalling a lesson learned years earlier. "The next day, I was sitting in the same place watching the same bush, and I saw a rat following the trail exactly where the po'ouli went." She thought it would be easy for a rat to track a bird like the po'ouli. "They're very slow moving. They don't fly well. Rats can track them right down."

Rats did their damage at night, eating eggs, nestlings, and even adult females, and the result could be a catastrophic loss of female birds. Thus Casey believed the danger from rats was not prioritized high enough. She cited one New Zealand study, where officials thought they had a population of nineteen kokako, blue wattled crows, but when they looked closer, they found that all were male. "All the females were gone; they'd all been predated. You think you have a population, but they're all males. It's really a scary thing."

Though state officials shared Casey's concerns about predators, by October 1996 they were starting to worry about the forest itself. The bait grids required cutting trails and making regular visits to resupply the stations. They were also concerned that crews might inadvertently carry in the seeds of invasive weeds stuck to backpacks or clothing. The intensive activity began to stir concerns that the effort, however necessary to save the po'ouli, was exacting too high a cost on the forest.

Bill Evanson, who oversaw the Hanawi fence construction as the state's Maui District Natural Area Reserves Systems specialist, and state wildlife biologist Fern Duvall met with Po'ouli Project leader Baker. The two told him he needed to shift attention away from rodent control and back to learning more about po'ouli biology. Rodent control should be centered only around possible po'ouli nesting sites, they said.

"The rat control work was a controversial part of the po'ouli program," Evanson says, adding that some people were willing to do anything to save the bird, regardless of the cost. But while trying to save the po'ouli, they had to be careful not to kill the forest. In response, Baker scaled back traffic on the trails by having crews check stations monthly instead of weekly.

Sensing the growing discord, Robert Smith, head of the FWS Pacific Island Ecoregion, tried to get everyone back on the same page. He requested a meeting with Hawaii Division of Forestry and Wildlife administrator Michael Buck and officials from New Zealand, who had also been in touch with Casey. Smith wrote Buck on October 21, 1996:

> Some individuals are concerned about possible damages to the forest as a result of increased human impacts associated with predator control. Others are worried that predator control efforts may be doing little in terms of actual protection of the endangered forest birds but costing a lot in terms of field crew time. And, still others believe we should do everything possible to continue and expand predator control activities in the Natural Area Reserve.

The conflict continued, however.

In early 1997, Earl Campbell came on the scene. Campbell had worked at the U.S. Department of Agriculture field station on rat control in agriculture, which was very similar to rat control in conservation areas. He immediately joined the Toxicant Working Group, which was meeting on predator control issues in Hanawi.

Campbell shared the goals of others on the working group, and there was broad agreement that something had to be done to control predators, particularly rats, in the po'ouli's forest home. Though most believed that aerial broadcast would be a useful tool, Campbell thought that expectations concerning it were unrealistic.

One problem was that the New Zealand sites where there had been dramatic successes were offshore islands. The islands' limited area allowed high-dose aerial dumps without either the associated public outcry or the poisons affecting other land uses that would occur in a setting such as Hawaii's main islands, where many communities, concerns, and interests had to be considered. On Maui, upland forests serve as watersheds, which nearby communities didn't want to see tainted. Further, the poison being considered, diphacinone, had not been licensed for aerial broadcast in the United States. That fact alone meant that exhaustive, expensive, and extensively documented studies had to be conducted before the federal government would allow its dispersal.

"People really had grossly unrealistic expectations on what people could do with rodenticide in the United States," Campbell says. "I don't think people understood what it would take to get this data."

Campbell's greatest concern, particularly with forest birds such as the po'ouli, was a rodent irruption, or population spike. Rather than being stable over time, rodent populations fluctuate depending on conditions. Irruptions could be caused by high food abundance, low mortality, or unusual fertility. Numbers would eventually fall back to more sustainable levels, but the rats could do a lot of damage before that happened.

In one Waikamoi Forest experiment, infrared cameras were aimed at rat bait to record what animals were eating it. This occurred during an irruption with so many rats that they chewed the wires and damaged the cameras. Yet Campbell was astonished to find Maui parrotbills successfully nesting in Waikamoi that season.

Casey was convinced, however, that the rats had to be controlled and that aerial broadcast was the way to do it. She and Campbell tangled more than once at the meetings. Casey says:

> We never got anywhere. We'd sit around a big table. In the law, you can do an emergency drop, so let's do an emergency [rodenticide] drop and then worry about what the people in Hana think. It was one fiasco after another. Nobody wanted to do it. Nobody wanted to risk it. I don't know what they wanted. They wanted to see the bird go extinct, I guess.

Campbell, for his part, says that though Casey was a great advocate for the po'ouli and her heart was in the right place, her studies did little to advance the cause. He was critical of their design and the data they generated, saying they were inadequate to justify the permits for which they all were working.

"I clearly frustrated Tonnie. She'd just blow up and yell at me . . . and then we'd move on," Campbell says. "Some people couldn't handle it."

It wasn't just Casey and Campbell who clashed during this period. With just six birds left, and then three, the stakes for po'ouli recovery were getting higher. With every day that passed, the last po'ouli were getting older.

13

FUNERALS
AND FRUSTRATION

BY THE MIDDLE OF 1997, THE POʻOULI PROJECT HAD RUN ITS course. The original project had been intended for just two years, and now planners put together a permanent follow-up: a collaboration of state, federal, and private entities—with the state in the lead role this time—that would spearhead forest bird recovery in Hanawi. Though poʻouli recovery was a major goal, the project would also try to aid Maui parrotbills, crested honeycreepers, and other rare birds. The new effort was called the Maui Forest Bird Recovery Project, with the name emphasizing a shift from study and habitat management to recovery of the birds.

The project was headquartered in a former warden's home high above the Maui town of Makawao, on a fantastically winding road that twists its way up Haleakala's northern slope. The former prison, several hundred yards downhill, houses one of the state's two captive-breeding facilities, run at the time by The Peregrine Fund.

Officials hired Mark Collins to spearhead the project. He would be the first of three coordinators between its hopeful creation and the death of the last known po'ouli in 2004.

The project got a rough start, however. The two years of Collins's tenure were difficult ones for po'ouli recovery. Though important milestones were achieved in the field, most critical being the capture, banding, and sexing of the two other known birds, the way ahead became muddied. The result was years-long delay in hands-on management, whose outcome might have been different if undertaken with younger birds.

Collins was a wildlife biologist who had prior experience with Hawaiian and endangered birds. He worked on a rat control project in Hakalau National Wildlife Refuge on the Big Island and, years earlier, in the late 1970s, had toiled on the massive Hawaiian Forest Bird Survey. He'd also worked with the endangered Bali myna, releasing captive-bred birds to bolster a wild population that was estimated at just fifteen in 1990.

It's unclear whether Collins himself was the source of the difficulties or whether he was merely a lightning rod for the tension among recovery team members. It is clear, however, that some view his tenure unfavorably.

Collins describes a rough ride almost from the start, with morale-sapping delays, personnel problems, and disagreements over the proper path. Ultimately, he says, he was squeezed out of the post.

Just weeks after being hired, Collins attended an annual conservation conference in Honolulu. He says he was pulled aside by Michael Buck, administrator of the Hawaii Division of Forestry and Wildlife. Buck ran the division that had operational oversight over the project. Buck was, in effect, Collins's boss's boss.

"What are we going to do about the po'ouli?" Buck asked him, according to Collins's account of the conversation.

Collins says he began recounting the story of New Zealand's black robin, drawing lessons from an effort that recovered the robin from a single breeding pair. Then he stopped.

"It turns out he wasn't really listening to me," Collins says. "That wasn't what he was referring to. He was thinking in the context of some kind of ceremony involving the Hawaiian people about the passing of the po'ouli. Here I am a couple of weeks into this, and they're talking funeral."

Collins also ran into trouble with recovery team members, representatives from state, federal, and private agencies who met regularly to discuss the status and direction of the Maui Forest Bird Recovery Project's work.

According to Earl Campbell, the USDA representative who worked on rodent control issues, the meetings accomplished little during this time. "We were getting lost trying to sort out important issues, but we weren't getting to the big issues. People were feeling overwhelmed."

And Buck questioned whether scarce conservation resources should be used on the po'ouli at all.

Collins's ideas to recover the po'ouli proved a hard sell. One was centered around capturing and moving one bird into another's range in hopes that they would form a pair. He wanted to use supplemental feeding stations to keep the po'ouli near each other until a bond was formed. But some scoffed at the idea as little more than putting up bird feeders.

While some said Collins's leadership during the period was lacking, Casey and Campbell among them, others defended Collins, saying that some of the animosity may have come because Collins was pushing to implement recovery actions and started doing things on his own.

Collins today defends his ideas as well as his actions. The supplemental feeding proposal, he says, was extensively researched.

The technique has been used in a variety of settings, including such high-profile recovery efforts as that of the California condor.

Sharon Reilly, who oversaw day-to-day operations of the Maui Forest Bird Recovery Project as wildlife biologist for the state Division of Forestry and Wildlife, felt enormous frustration that decision makers were hemming and hawing. She believed the road ahead was clear. Though the po'ouli was critically endangered, similar efforts were going on around the world. To her mind, there were clear steps that had been proven in the field. The birds had to be banded, which was accomplished by Paul Baker and then by Collins's crew, and then bled to get a blood sample. The blood would allow a host of tests, including more reliable sexing, and is routinely done in the field.

These steps should have been done as a matter of course, she says. Instead, because of the birds' rarity, every step was reexamined and reconsidered. Reilly says:

> What was going on with the po'ouli was nothing new. People had been working in Hawaii with birds for years. People had been working with these small passerines all over the world for years: banding them, bleeding them, translocating them. But it was as if people were blinded by the fact that these were now critically endangered species and held back from making a decision.

Outside the meeting rooms, work did progress in the forests. The field crew eventually netted the two po'ouli that had eluded Paul Baker, banding them and taking feather samples.

By January 1998, it had been two years since two po'ouli had been seen together. With the banding and ongoing monitoring of po'ouli home ranges, it was apparent that the remaining birds would not stray into one another's territory. Searches for additional po'ouli populations had come up empty. The hope that there were unknown birds left in the existing home ranges was fading, because every time a field team member saw a po'ouli, it had a band on its leg.

If the remaining birds were going to meet and breed, it looked as if it would take a human hand to make it happen. Though that seemed obvious to some, there was still considerable disagreement over the right course. Others felt that given the nature of Hanawi's forest, one could never be sure there weren't unseen birds out there somewhere. Interfering with the known birds might disrupt unknown interactions and relationships, which would be disastrous in such a small population. Still others believed that scarce resources shouldn't be used in an intensive hands-on effort and instead should be diverted to making the forest healthier, which would benefit the po'ouli as well as other birds, insects, snails, and plants.

By February of that same year, the DNA results on the feathers taken from the two birds captured so far—including the first one caught in 1997 by Paul Baker and thought by him to be a male—came back. Both birds in Home Ranges 1 and 2 were female, according to laboratory results.

This added another level of tension to recovery efforts. They had to step up work to capture the Home Range 3 bird. If testing came back that that bird too was a female, then recovery efforts would appear to be in vain. That the Home Range 2 results were in error only became apparent years later, after the bird was caught for breeding in 2004.

Within two months, not only had the Home Range 3 bird been caught, but its feathers had been tested. The state crowed its relief in a press release on April 30: "It's a boy!" With no sign of another po'ouli population, and just three birds known to exist, the release labeled the po'ouli the "world's rarest bird."

"For the Po'ouli there may only be three birds, but as long as there are birds of two sexes, there is always hope," Reilly said in the release. "To save this species, we will need to intervene."

Even this happy moment was clouded with tension. Because the sexing technology had been developed recently, the recovery team sent the feathers to other labs to confirm the results.

Confirmation was not forthcoming. The new results conflicted with the initial findings. Worse was the fact that none of the results—even the new conflicting ones—were rock solid. One testing company official said later that it was difficult to be sure without known male and female samples against which to compare the results.

In effect, po'ouli recovery officials thought they knew the birds' sexes, but they couldn't be absolutely sure.

"That was frustrating," Collins says. "It led to the desire to do more tests. It didn't help our cause that the results got muddied."

In April, Division of Forestry and Wildlife administrator Michael Buck convened a panel of experts for a po'ouli recovery planning session. Though Buck's letter said the meeting's goal was to build "mutual understanding of the available options . . . for Po'ouli recovery," he later described the meeting as something of a counseling session for those who had cared for a dying friend: the po'ouli.

Buck says that because he had lived through the death of both his wife and father, he recognized what was going on with those involved in the recovery effort and what was behind the disagreements. "I had a whole different perspective on grieving and on how to manage this issue. What we were really doing was managing an extinction. I knew that going in, and what I was seeing all around me were the kinds of things people do when they're grieving: blaming someone, fear, all those kinds of things. I had kind of a unique perspective on this."

To Buck's mind, the po'ouli was as good as gone, and his goal was to ensure that those on the recovery team would be able to continue to work together on other projects. If the federal government wanted to dump a lot of money on the po'ouli and it wound up helping other forest birds, so much the better. The state was managing ten other species as endangered as the po'ouli and didn't have the money to focus on the po'ouli on its own.

Twenty-nine people from a variety of government and conservation agencies attended. According to the minutes of the meeting, Buck stood up first and acknowledged both the extraordinary nature of the po'ouli's recovery situation and the weighty responsibility on those in the room. He called it a defining moment in Hawaiian biodiversity. More personally, he then said he believed that everyone was scared by the situation, and he reminded them that there was no right answer.

"I was trying to talk to people about how you have an extinction in a culturally appropriate way," Buck said later. "No one wanted to have that dialogue, especially no one at the federal agencies. It's unheard of."

Other attendees at the meeting expressed their opinions on the proper path for po'ouli recovery, with several following Buck's lead and setting aside their official positions to speak from the heart. Robert Smith, who headed the Fish and Wildlife Service's (FWS) Pacific Islands Ecoregion, apologized on behalf of the government. Because of its uniqueness, he said, the po'ouli should have received a higher priority in government efforts.

Despite Smith's acknowledgment, the lesson that delay would only further the po'ouli's decline appeared not to have been learned—or at least not heeded. Though these birds of unknown lifespan were already several years old, four more years of planning and paperwork still lay ahead before a single po'ouli was translocated, and six more years passed before one would be captured for breeding.

In hindsight, the causes for the delay are apparent. A reading of the minutes indicates that the handful of people in the room, who were the most influential over the po'ouli's recovery, were split over what path to take. And with the stakes as high as they were, people would not be budged easily.

Many of the comments voiced support for captive breeding, understandable given both the growing track record of success in Hawaii and the fact that some sort of manipulation appeared necessary to bring together territorial birds living in separate home ranges. Not everyone agreed that this was the path to follow, however. Some pointed out that earlier captive-breeding efforts with species of extreme rarity had at least one breeding pair to start with. That was not the case here. The remaining po'ouli were independent adults. Managers would have to not only successfully bring the birds in and keep them alive— no small trick on its own—but also play matchmaker to a bird whose breeding habits were virtually unknown.

Alan Lieberman, who headed up The Peregrine Fund's offices on Hawaii, said at the meeting that the famed conservation organization would be willing to embark on a breeding program with wild-caught eggs, removed from a nest in the forest, incubated, and raised to adulthood in captivity. This presented enormous difficulties, however. Over the thirty years that the bird had been known to humans, only two po'ouli nests had ever been seen—built by the same pair that rainy spring in 1986. Since the three known birds weren't breeding, that meant field crews would have to not only find other po'ouli, but nesting ones.

By the meeting's end that day, no consensus was reached on the issue of hands-on management. Those in attendance did agree that more effective predator control, including aerial broadcast of rodenticide, was needed, and that if a nest was found, eggs should be collected for captive propagation. They also agreed to look again for more birds, west of the current population site.

Instead of bringing people together, the meeting had high-lighted divisions over hands-on management that would color the next recovery phase: writing an environmental assessment that would set the stage for action.

Mark Collins didn't like it when he was asked to get the process moving by drafting six alternative strategies to recover the po'ouli. The alternatives would be the foundation for an environmental assessment, which would have to go through draft and final phases and was designed to elicit public and expert comment at hearings and in written testimony. It would take some time.

"With a critically endangered species, you don't have time to go through the writeup of an environmental assessment and take it to the public and go through the process," Collins says. "There was no real desire to save this bird. They'd rather have the funeral."

Collins drafted six alternatives outlining options with increasingly intrusive management. They were variations on four ideas: leave the birds alone but step up protection of the forest; catch them and hold them in a forest aviary; catch one bird and move it to the home range of another and let it go; or catch all three birds and bring them into captivity.

After he'd drafted the alternatives, Collins got an angry phone call from Cyndi Kuehler, a key aviculturist working for The Peregrine Fund. Kuehler was upset that he'd included captive breeding as an option—which would effectively involve The Peregrine Fund in the project—without consulting the organization.

"She just rips me a new one, saying how dare you include us in bringing the bird in," Collins says. "She was *really* upset."

Collins says he hadn't mentioned The Peregrine Fund by name in the document, but felt that in listing possible options, he had to include captive breeding.

What irked Kuehler was that Collins's alternatives were written up in the form of a management plan that favored captive breeding, according to Alan Lieberman. In the absence of an environmental assessment or recovery plan, he says, the management plan would guide po'ouli recovery actions. Lieberman says it was "a serious oversight" to draft it without consulting them.

Either way, Collins says that The Peregrine Fund signed up to breed endangered birds in situations like this when it agreed to manage the Hawaii captive-breeding facilities. Collins also felt, however, that The Peregrine Fund shouldn't be forced to take on such an important job if it didn't want to. There were other aviculturists who might be interested in the challenge.

Collins wasn't the only one chafing at the delay. Sharon Reilly, his supervisor at the state Division of Forestry and Wildlife, wanted to get ready to implement a recovery plan as soon as it was selected. She suggested moving ahead on parallel tracks—drafting an implementation plan, testing field aviary design, and doing test translocations, for example—so that when the environmental assessment process was done, they'd be ready to go. But she was told to wait, that there was no sense trying something that may not happen.

"There were things we could have been doing in the interim," Reilly says. "Things were being put on a single rail versus two rails and moving forward simultaneously."

By September 1998, the draft of the environmental assessment was ready. It laid out the problem, history, and setting and discussed proposed actions. The six alternatives were aired at three public meetings and received fifty-four letters of comment. Much of the discussion centered around three ideas: continue habitat management with no active manipulation of the birds; capture all three and bring them into a breeding facility; or move one po'ouli into the range of another in hopes they meet and breed.

Perhaps because of their clarity, the responses tended toward either leaving the birds alone or capturing them and trying to get them to breed. Most of those who supported leaving the birds alone emphasized that poisoning and trapping predators and continuing other management of the forest had to be stepped up. The status quo wasn't working. Several of those who supported stepped up habitat management also supported translocating a bird into the home range of another.

There was considerable support for captive breeding, but among the dissenters was one powerful voice. The Peregrine Fund had an immense reputation for its success in a number of breeding programs, not least those of the peregrine falcon and California condor. It also had success in breeding Hawaiian forest birds in captivity, perhaps lending additional support to the idea that the organization could do it again. But in an exhaustive, forty-six-page comment on the proposed alternatives, The Peregrine Fund said no.

Written by Kuehler, the response said the organization would raise po'ouli from eggs collected from the field, but under no circumstances would it handle adult po'ouli brought in from the wild. Though there had been captive-breeding successes before—even of birds of very low numbers—they weren't birds like this. Not all birds are the same, Kuehler wrote, and small insect eaters like the po'ouli presented a riddle that bird-keepers, breeders, and scientists hadn't yet been able to solve. In more than one hundred years of birdkeeping, there had never been a successful breeding population of insectivorous passerines. Further, the death of one or several birds captured for breeding programs is not unusual. An effort to breed a bird as little known as the poʻouli, without even a single breeding pair, was bound to fail. The Peregrine Fund would have no part of it.

Despite the detailed scientific argument, some say the reason behind The Peregrine Fund's position was actually much simpler: fear of failure. Among them was Smith, who headed the FWS Honolulu office. He said the state and The Peregrine Fund were of like mind on the issue. "The Peregrine Fund . . . did not want to tackle the task for fear of failure, or perhaps more kindly and accurately for concern that they could not succeed. In my view, the state shared this view, as well as the notion that poʻouli habitat may already be unsuitable due to changes both known and unknown."

Lieberman responded to such charges at a public hearing on the environmental assessment, denying that the risks involved with captive breeding poʻoulis had scared The Peregrine Fund, saying that instead of their having "cold feet," their refusal was due to "a cool head" prevailing.

With The Peregrine Fund unwilling to take on captive propagation, state and federal officials explored other options, inquiring whether the Honolulu Zoo would be able to accept the birds for captive breeding, but the zoo said it didn't have appropriate facilities.

The result of all this consultation was presented in the final Environmental Assessment for Proposed Management Actions to save the Poʻouli in April 1999. The preferred action was a hybrid plan of increased habitat management coupled with a translocation attempt that represented the best hope of getting the birds to meet and match in their forest home.

As the environmental assessment had gone from draft to final version, the field crew, which had been universally lauded as trained, energetic, and ready to go, had begun to come apart at the seams. According to Reilly, the repeated delays and make-work to keep the team busy sapped morale. "You had an amazing group of people just busting butt, working in some of the harshest field conditions on the planet, doing whatever they can do, not really given a voice yet also not allowed to do what they were hired to do." Additionally, the crew also disagreed with Collins over the direction of recovery, feeling that the birds should be left alone.

Not helping morale were allegations of sexual harassment against one male member of the crew, Collins said.

A female crew member approached Collins one day and asked whether she should warn new female volunteers about a crew member who had made romantic overtures toward her. When she rejected those advances, she told Collins, the male crew member treated her badly.

Collins said he followed the personnel manual and reported the incident to the Research Corporation of the University of Hawaii, which was part of the complex administrative network that supported the project.

The report sparked an investigation that involved interviews with team members and past interns but led to no disciplinary action. After that, Collins was stuck trying to figure out how to schedule his fractured four-person crew for ten-day stints in the forest alone with each other. He eventually scheduled the accuser and accused together, and on the morning they were to leave, the male crew member refused to go.

Collins says he threatened the guy, saying that the helicopter was on the way, and if he didn't go, he could be fired. The crew member refused but, after hiring a lawyer, retained his job.

By this point, Collins says, the list of people he had fallen out of favor with was growing. He felt he was in bad favor with the Research Corporation of the University of Hawaii. He didn't see eye-to-eye on recovery goals with Division of

Forestry and Wildlife administrator Michael Buck. And he'd had a falling out with The Peregrine Fund—though Lieberman said their disagreements were professional, not personal.

"I was basically squeezed out. They didn't feel like I was the right guy. They felt like I was a loose cannon," Collins says. "I was getting somewhat isolated."

In 1999, Collins left for a job with the West Maui Mountains Watershed Partnership, and the Maui Forest Bird Recovery Project had no coordinator for several months. Reilly stepped in temporarily, moving from the state Division of Forestry and Wildlife to the project's headquarters in Olinda. It was spring 1999, Reilly says, recalling that the jacaranda trees were in bloom. But a few months later, she left as well, and Buck asked Randall Kennedy, the Natural Area Reserves System program manager, to take over. At that point, Kennedy says, the project was in low gear, with just one technician aboard.

It took several months, but in 2000, they finally hired Jim Groombridge to take Collins's place. Groombridge, who had received a doctorate in zoology from Queen Mary College at the University of London, had worked on a well-respected bird recovery program on the Indian Ocean island of Mauritius.

Though the environmental assessment had recommended translocation as the favored recovery strategy, Kennedy said they needed to go through another round of review, focused on implementation this time. With Groombridge's participation, reviewers made two important decisions. First, they decided to move ahead with the translocation. Second, they determined that they would not let the po'ouli go extinct without trying everything possible to save it. They would keep captive breeding open as an option should the translocation fail. "It was an action plan to keep the po'ouli from going extinct," Kennedy says.

Now that they finally had a green light on translocation, those involved in trying to save the po'ouli had much to do. With each passing year, the last po'oulis were getting older, and biologists still didn't know how long the birds lived.

Before the translocation could take place, field crews needed to ensure that the very actions they were planning to save the po'ouli didn't kill it. They had to test procedures on a surrogate species to make certain that they were safe and effective. They selected the nonendangered Maui creeper, a small, yellowish green forest bird that shared Hanawi with the po'ouli.

Things were finally moving ahead, not only in the field, but in the meeting room as well. Groombridge's experience on Mauritius—which was facing some of the same issues as Hawaii—his confidence, and his easygoing manner quickly won people over.

The trial translocation with the Maui creeper took all of 2001. Headed by Groombridge, the Maui Forest Bird Recovery Project ran three mist-netting expeditions, in December 2000, March 2001, and January 2002, capturing and transporting eighteen Maui creepers. With the variable weather not allowing them to rely on helicopter transport, the team members decided to hand-carry the birds in plastic holding cages, traversing two routes, one half a mile long and the other one and a half miles long, using two transport methods.

Though Baker and other field workers had captured and banded all three po'oulis, the translocation would be the most hands-on treatment the birds had yet received. They would be netted, checked, put into a box, carried over rough terrain, and observed before being released. With three birds left, the researchers couldn't afford an accident. And after years of planning, they desperately wanted to avoid failure. So they designed two different transport methods that aimed to minimize discomfort and stress, trying out both on creepers.

They divided each plastic transfer box in two. One side held two small perches, and on the other was suspended a nylon sock into which a soft bag holding the bird would be placed. The bag, a tried and tested method of keeping a bird immobile while transporting it, would sit suspended, safe from hitting the box's walls.

The hike typically took one or two hours. On arrival at the release site, the crew reexamined the creepers, drew blood, and then let them go. Researchers examined the blood to determine stress levels, which led them to favor the more open perch arrangement for transporting the po'oulis.

But the field crews noticed another trend that was a cause for concern: the released creepers overwhelmingly returned home.

Eleven of the eighteen creepers were observed back in their home ranges within five days of their release. Nevertheless, researchers planned to push ahead with the po'ouli anyway. Creepers and po'ouli were different birds and might not respond the same way to translocation. And the researchers hoped that once the male and female po'oulis saw each other, their bonding would overcome any desire to return home.

By the time the creeper translocation experiment was completed, the researchers were ready. They had traversed the routes laid out for moving the po'ouli over and over. Eighteen birds had been netted, bled, put into transport boxes, and carried on foot through the rugged forest. None had died.

They decided to make their first attempt at po'ouli translocation in the 2002 breeding season, between March and May. They secured permits and made preparations.

The plan was designed to maximize the chances that the two birds would meet. Researchers would capture the male first, tag him with a radio-tracking device, and release him back into his home range. This would allow the field teams to monitor his location and release the female—also radio tagged—near him.

Support teams and equipment were set up. The researchers had a small holding cage fitted with a video camera. They had an avian intensive care unit that could control internal temperature and oxygen levels, and a supply of snails. They had a veterinarian on site during each capture trip, one of whom remarked that he was impressed at how remarkably well equipped the field veterinary facilities were. They had anesthesia and surgical tools, antimicrobial drugs, and diagnostic equipment. If the bird got badly injured, they could provide emergency care in the forest for three days. That was necessary insurance in case the weather kept away a helicopter to take the bird to a veterinary hospital. If the worst happened and the bird died, they would salvage what they could and harvest tissue for preservation at the San Diego Zoo's center for Conservation and Research in Endangered Species.

Long years of contentious planning and meticulous preparation were done. It was finally time for action.

Nobody had told this to the male po'ouli, however. He may have held the future of his species in his loins, but he had other plans. Researchers chased him through the forest from New Year's Day to Valentine's Day 2002. They logged twenty-one days and spent 157 hours trying to mist-net him. They spotted him repeatedly, eighteen times during those weeks, but just couldn't catch him.

Ultimately, Groombridge gave up and shifted the crew's attention to the female, catching her on April 4, well into the nesting season, after another eight days of effort.

"We got better at seeing it," Groombridge says of the male. "We got very close to capturing it, but in the end, time was of the essence. We got very lucky with the weather. We decided to shift focus to the female and try to bring her down, which was what we achieved."

David Phalen, a veterinarian from the University of Texas A&M, flew into Hanawi for the capture attempt. He described it this way:

> The next day began the same way. By noon it was beginning to dawn on me that these researchers had done this same thing day in and day out for 10 weeks, often in much colder and wetter weather. Surely with the failure to capture the po'ouli, their spirits must have been flagging. Two hours later, everything changed. All the radios began barking at the same time; the female had been caught, and it was being carried by land to our camp.
>
> We hurried back to camp and got our all the supplies. The translocation team made the trip 45 minutes faster than any of the previous dry runs. Steam rose from their bodies as they came into camp. The po'ouli was taken from the transport box and carefully examined. It seemed somewhat indignant but otherwise fine.

The bird was held in the field aviary for two hours, to make sure she weathered the trip well. Her calm demeanor and the fact that she began eating right away—not just snails, but also the waxworms that would be part of a captive diet—had broader ramifications, as it helped convince researchers that po'ouli would adjust well to permanent captivity.

The failure to capture the male meant that researchers weren't sure exactly where he was. So they made their best guess and released the female in the spot where he had been last seen.

She roosted there overnight, and early the next morning, the team fanned out to track her. Hopes were high that she'd stay in the male's home range.

But by 9 A.M., spirits sank. Successive locations with the radio tracker showed that she had begun the long journey home, alone. By evening, she was back in her home range, and observations over the next nine days showed that life had returned to normal for her. She was spotted twenty-one times, and on nine of those, she was with her familiar chums, the Maui parrotbills with which she had a long history of associating.

The translocation had failed. But though no breeding pair was established, the field crews learned some beneficial lessons—about both themselves and the bird. According to Groombridge, "We actually did some hands-on management of the species, and the team proved to itself it could work with something that was extremely rare and do something that is relatively technical. We used a radio transmitter, kept the bird in the field, tracked the bird, all in a very difficult environment."

On June 25, 2002, members of the Po'ouli Working Group met on Maui to discuss what would happen next. They chewed over alternatives from the environmental assessment, including another translocation attempt. Ultimately that—and every other alternative except captive breeding—was rejected.

In the interim, The Peregrine Fund had turned over management of the captive breeding facilities to the Zoological Society of San Diego, with which The Peregrine Fund had a long, close relationship. And the same personnel was in place, as Alan Lieberman and Cyndi Kuehler had stayed on. With some reluctance, the San Diego Zoo agreed to take part in the captive-breeding operation.

In January 2003, a permit was issued by the FWS, and the Maui Forest Bird Recovery Project was again ready to go.

14

BREEDING IN CAGES

SKELETONS DOTTED THE PRAIRIE, THE GHASTLY REMAINS OF A buffalo hunt four years earlier. The travelers stood, looking, and understanding in a way they hadn't before where all the buffalo had gone.

Bodies lay thick along the trail leading through the buffalo range. None were living; only bones remained, bleaching in the sun. Skeletal limbs rested where they fell, necks outstretched as if for one last breath. The skinners who had set to work after this eastern Montana hunt had left the great beasts' heads untouched. The dried skin still bore its shaggy fur, reminding the travelers that the creatures once roamed the prairie, and causing them to mourn their loss and the great slaughter as if it were yesterday.

The year was 1886. William T. Hornaday, the U.S. National Museum's chief taxidermist, was in Montana searching for the buffalo, or North American bison, which had once thundered across the prairie by the millions. Hornaday was among those

189

concerned about the buffalo's disappearance. Despite its once vast numbers, it appeared to be on the road to extinction.

Ironically, Hornaday was looking to kill a few more, albeit for what he believed was a good cause. He wanted to create new museum exhibits that would mobilize the public on the buffalo's behalf.

Hornaday's expedition found just a few buffalo that year, including a lone calf they named Sandy and brought back to Washington, D.C. Sandy eventually died and became part of the stuffed exhibit. The party also found two bulls, one of which they managed to kill.

By the end of the year, the months of fruitless searching made such an impression on Hornaday that when he finally came across a group of fifteen buffalo, he left them alone, gathering specimens instead from the plentiful skeletons. Hornaday's concern led to one of the earliest efforts to breed an animal—the buffalo—for conservation purposes. That endeavor in turn led to the founding of the U.S. National Zoo.

Captive breeding as a conservation tool has come a long way since then. Unfortunately, so has extinction. The World Conservation Union estimated in 2004 that the rate of known extinctions over the last one hundred years was between fifty and five hundred times higher than it would have been without humanity's interference. If possible extinctions are included, the unnatural extinction rate rises to between one hundred and one thousand times higher.

Extinction can be a natural process. As individuals have life cycles and are born, grow old, and die, so do species. Little is natural, however, about today's extinctions.

Around us today, the "lasts" march into oblivion, joining a parade that has been filing slowly into history for centuries. The last Steller's sea cow, a gentle giant of the sea, is thought to have died in 1768, just thirty years after it was discovered—and tasted—by humans. The last great auk, the world's original penguin and native to the North Atlantic, was seen in 1852. The last passenger pigeon, whose flocks once darkened the skies, died in 1914. The last Tasmanian tiger, with a kangaroolike pouch, died in 1936.

On Hawaii, extinction is a part of the modern reality. Plants and snails and insects have all joined the archipelago's birds in their fight for life. The very diversity that makes the islands special gives them more to lose.

Almost 800 species have gone extinct worldwide in the last five hundred years, according to the World Conservation Union. The last two decades alone have seen twenty-seven documented extinctions in the wild with many more species likely or presumed extinct.

Extinction has touched all kinds of creatures: wallabies and wolves, mussels and moths, wrens and rats. Browsing the World Conservation Union's Red List shows that many of the 784 extinct species were so unfamiliar to people that they had no common names. Known only by their scientific names, they were gone before we really knew them.

Past extinctions are just the warm-up, however. More are on the way, possibly a lot more. Some scientists say we're on a path to match the great extinctions of the past, such as the one that ended the dinosaurs' reign. By the middle of this century, according to one estimate, as many as 30 percent of all species may be extinct.

Sixty-five species sit with one foot in the grave. Already extinct in the wild, they are hanging on in zoos, research facilities, and other captive settings. The World Conservation Union knows of more than sixteen thousand species that are threatened with extinction. But it also knows that number is far too low, since it is based on assessments of just 3 percent of the world's 1.3 million known species. These assessments just trace the outline of the global extinction picture, and the emerging image is alarming.

Twelve percent of bird species are threatened, as are almost one in four mammals. Conifers are among the few plants that have been completely assessed, and one in four of these are threatened.

Problems are especially acute for amphibians, which are dying all around the world, sometimes with astonishing speed. The Costa Rican golden toad bred normally in the Monteverde Cloud Forest in 1987. In 1988, only two females and eight males were found. In 1989, just one male. The toad hasn't been seen since. As many as 122 amphibians have disappeared since 1980, with 9 extinct and another 113 not seen in years. A 2004 World Conservation Union assessment showed that 43 percent of the world's amphibians were declining, and a third were threatened with extinction. Because of amphibians' permeable skin, scientists believe they serve as the proverbial canary in a coal mine for environmental change. If that's the case, the canary's telling us we may be in trouble.

Given the complexity of the web of life that sustains us, we can't be sure how all these extinctions will affect humanity. Nature is unlikely to respond meekly, predictably, or in ways that humans won't notice as three in ten plants, animals, fungi, and insects go extinct.

The effect of large-scale decline was illustrated in the link scientists established between the collapse of the North Carolina scallop fishery and shark overfishing in the North Atlantic. Though voracious, sharks are slow to both breed and recover from overfishing. A collapse in shark numbers in recent decades has led to an increase in populations of skates, small sharks, and rays. Rays eat clams and scallops, and scientists believe their overabundance hammered the North Carolina scallop fishery and led to harvest declines in Virginia and Maryland.

As with sharks, declining numbers are not just seen in rare species. The pathway to extinction isn't always the po'ouli's, with an obscure species in a remote location declining and eventually disappearing. Sometimes the road starts with abundant numbers and widespread populations that are progressively thinned until they disappear from different locations, one by one. The beginnings of such a broad range reduction may have been picked up in 2007, when the Audubon Society warned that twenty common U.S. birds lost more than half their populations over the last four decades, including common terns, eastern meadowlarks, rufous hummingbirds, and evening grosbeaks.

The reasons for species decline are numerous. The Audubon Society cites habitat loss, changes in agricultural practices, pesticides, invasive species, and global warming in the troubles of backyard birds. More broadly, experts add overharvesting and pollution to the list.

There are many approaches to fighting species decline. Overharvesting can be fought with tougher laws and vigorous enforcement. Polluters can be fined and forced to clean up their mess. Introduced species can be eradicated, as goats and rats have been from some islands. As removing alien insects and weeds once they've become established can be difficult, if not impossible, the fight focuses on preventing their introduction, snuffing out early infestations, and limiting their spread once established. Habitat loss can be counteracted by protecting existing conservation lands and bringing more land into reserves and parks. Fighting environment change, particularly global warming, depends on mobilizing world governments to reduce its causes.

Unfortunately, many of these problems don't appear in isolation. Each declining species faces a unique mix of factors.

Solutions, therefore, need to be individualized and are far easier said than done. Captive breeding is an important tool and an element in many recovery efforts, though its use remains controversial.

A modern success story is the Arabian oryx, an antelope once found across the Arabian peninsula. By the 1960s, it was confined to the Rub al Khali desert on the border of Oman and South Yemen. A striking animal with a white coat and long, straight horns, the last wild oryx was shot in Oman in 1972. Luckily, a breeding program at the Phoenix Zoo, begun in 1963, had brought together wild-caught and zoo-bred animals to form a captive population.

The species bred well in captivity, and, in 1982, a small herd was released in the Jiddat al Harassis desert, followed by other releases in 1984, 1988, and 1989. Today there are fifteen hundred oryx living in the wild and in zoos around the world, most of which are descendants from the Phoenix Zoo's original herd. The oryx is the first case of a species extinct in the wild being successfully reintroduced through captive breeding.

The oryx isn't the only animal whose conservation success is due at least in part to captive breeding. At about the time the last wild oryx was being killed, biologists on the Indian Ocean island of Mauritius were nervously eyeing a small native falcon. The Mauritius kestrel, which fed on tree-dwelling geckos, had been in decline since settlers began cutting down the island's forests. The use of pesticides such as DDT made things worse. By 1974, the Mauritius kestrel was possibly the world's rarest bird, with just six known individuals.

Starting in 1973, biologists used a variety of techniques to increase the kestrel population, including captive breeding. They tricked the wild birds into producing two clutches of eggs annually by removing the first and incubating it artificially. The adult birds, thinking their eggs were lost, laid more and raised the second brood themselves. The artificially hatched chicks were fostered in wild birds' nests or raised in captivity to be released later or held as breeding stock.

The captive-breeding program was slow to get off the ground. Luckily, pesticide bans began to help the remaining wild birds, and the wild population slowly crept up to about thirty in the 1980s.

When captive breeding got on track, it accelerated the wild birds' recovery. Thirteen captive pairs produced 139 young through 1993. The released kestrels helped boost the wild population to more than 200, including roughly 60 breeding pairs. The program was successful enough to put itself out of business. It was discontinued after the 1993–94 breeding season because the kestrel population was judged to be restored.

In the United States, captive programs are under way for nearly 500 species, according to a 2004 Fish and Wildlife Service tally. While that number includes long-term storage of plant seeds as insurance against future population declines, 143 animals—everything from mammals to bugs—are also being bred in captivity. Some owe their continued wild existence to captive propagation, including the black-footed ferret, California condor, Mexican gray wolf, and red wolf.

In 2006, scientists reported an important success in Hawaii's reintroduction program for the puaiohi, a small Kauai thrush. From 1999 to 2001, conservation officials reintroduced thirty-four captive-bred puaiohi into Kauai's Alakai Swamp. Ten females and two males bred with wild and released birds. Though predators destroyed 38 percent of nests, breeding behavior and success were similar to that of wild puaiohi. It marked the first recorded wild breeding of captive-bred endangered Hawaiian passerines.

Captive breeding remains controversial for several reasons, however. Though most recognize it as a potentially valuable tool, some also raise concerns. Among criticisms are captive programs' disproportionate share of scarce conservation dollars, their use as a substitute for politically difficult field-based measures, and more broadly, the effects of captivity on subject animals.

Scientists and conservation workers look at the mounting numbers of species in trouble and can't help but wonder how bad it could get. In 1986, a small group of researchers tried to answer that question, examining how many animals could be maintained in captivity should their wild homes be wiped out. They examined the possibility of creating what they termed the Millennium Ark and said that, barring a catastrophe for the human race, wildlife can expect a "demographic winter" from peaking human populations to last between five hundred and one thousand years. After that, wilderness areas would again begin to increase.

The researchers said that two thousand species of large land animals may have to be captive-bred in order to survive. That total doesn't include the many species of plants, insects, and other types of creatures whose existence would also be threatened.

They put faith in technology to help them through the demographic desert. They predicted that within two hundred years, cryogenic technology would be sophisticated enough to allow some species to be preserved frozen rather than in zoos. If correct, that means we only have to figure out how to house the animals for two centuries to avoid losing them. Either way, the need is far beyond the capacity of zoos for even the initial two hundred years.

So how many creatures could zoos hold? A 1996 estimate falls far short of two thousand. Andrew Balmford, today a professor of conservation science at the University of Cambridge, and colleagues estimated that no more than five hundred species could be helped through captive breeding. To increase capacity, Balmford recommended ending zoos' love affair with large, expensive animals, even though they draw in visitors. Instead, he wrote, zoos should focus on species that breed well in captivity and can be readily reintroduced to the wild to free up space for the next patient.

But some say the answer can't lie with zoos. With the World Conservation Union's estimate of sixteen thousand species in trouble—and counting—even an optimist has to admit the number is beyond the capacity of humans to keep in captivity. Carsten Rahbeck in a 1993 examination of captive breeding as a biodiversity conservation tool wrote:

> It is hard to imagine specific programmes for each of the immense number of species that are in danger of extinction within the next decades. . . . The sad fact is that the number of species in need of conservation action is so immense that it is hopeless to make specific actions for them all. The main goal must be to save as much as possible of the biodiversity of the Earth.

Many believe that since they can't be saved in cages, species must be saved where they are now: in the field. An advantage of conserving declining species in the field is that the per-animal cost of conservation can be far less than in a lab or a zoo.

A 1990 analysis of an elephant and rhino conservation program in Zambia's Luangwa Valley showed that the programs were ineffective because they were starved of funding, receiving less than 10 percent of what was needed to combat poaching. But compared with the cost of maintaining elephants in the London Zoo, keeping them alive in the Zambian bush would have been fifty times cheaper and had the additional benefit of conserving several hundred impalas and thousands of trees, birds, insects, and other creatures.

The successful field-based recovery program of another "world's rarest bird" is often cited in reference to the po'ouli. The Chatham Island black robin, native to a small group of islands off the coast of New Zealand, recovered from just a handful of birds in 1980 to 250 by the late 1990s.

The birds initially declined when their native forests were cut, and then introduced rats and cats moved in to finish them off. They nearly succeeded. In 1976, the remaining seven birds were relocated to Mangere Island, where 120,000 trees had been planted to restore the island's forests. By 1980, the population hit its lowest point. With just five black robins left, one of which was a female, the species teetered precariously on the edge of extinction.

The black robin had an important advantage over the po'ouli, however. Among its five remaining individuals was a breeding pair, the female called Old Blue, and the male Old Yellow.

A program to save the black robin protected nests from predators, provided supplemental feeding, and fostered young robins in the nests of a related bird. As in the case of the Mauritius kestrel, recovery workers doubled the black robin's natural production by removing the first clutch of eggs laid by Old Blue and putting them in the nest of another bird—in this case the Chatham Island tit—to be raised. Old Blue would then lay and raise a second clutch, increasing the population faster than possible if left to her own devices.

By 1989, the black robin population had grown steadily, reaching one hundred birds. As in the case of the kestrel, the conservation program was judged a success and discontinued.

In the po'ouli's case, some argued that money should not be spent on captive breeding. Repairing the birds' endangered habitat, they said, had to have top priority, because habitat problems led to the po'ouli's decline in the first place. If not fixed, other birds would soon follow. Even if the po'ouli didn't recover, the habitat would be healthier for the forests' remaining denizens.

Nearly two decades earlier, Bronx Zoo general director William G. Conway argued that such an extreme habitat-centered focus could provide conservation victories, but they'd be hollow if they came at the cost of charismatic, keystone species:

> Even where nature reserves protect landscapes which still appear natural to the casual eye, the original configurations of large vertebrates are unlikely to survive, except where the refuges are very extensive. Such depleted reserves would certainly remain invaluable, but the preservation of a segment of grizzly bear habitat without grizzly bears, condor country without condors, or the Mountains of the Moon without Mountain gorillas seems like saving the husk without the kernel.

Critics also argue that captive-breeding programs are sometimes preferred not because they're the best strategy, but because they're politically expedient and let decision makers more easily balance competing uses of wilderness.

Alan Rabinowitz believes that was the case with the Sumatran rhino in Borneo. Rabinowitz, who wrote about the rhino's recovery program in 1995, said that poaching for its horn and habitat loss were well-known factors behind the animal's decline. Recovery goals, starting in 1979, emphasized protecting rhino habitat and the animals from poaching, as well as data collection and research.

In 1984, conservation officials decided to begin a captive-breeding program using what they termed "doomed" animals—those whose lives were in immediate danger from forest clearing.

The captive program diverted attention and resources, Rabinowitz said, but accomplished little.

By 1993, rhino conservation had consumed $2.5 million, with most going to captive-breeding programs with a dismal record of success. Virtually none of the money had been spent to improve the protection and management of wild rhinos, Rabinowitz found. Antipoaching laws had been passed but were rarely used to deter or prosecute those involved. Even habitat management took a backseat to economic concerns, with protection granted only where it would not interfere with logging or agriculture.

"Emphasis in time, money, and effort has been placed on the capture and breeding of rhinos, despite the fact that such activities alone, even if successful, would not solve the problem nor remove the causal factors of rhino decline in the wild," Rabinowitz wrote, adding that the presence of a captive-breeding program makes the failure of field-based conservation seem less serious.

The Sumatran rhino program isn't the only captive-breeding endeavor with less than stellar results. A 1994 study found that just 16 of 145 programs had successfully reintroduced captive-bred animals. An examination of captive breeding's track record two years later said it should be a last-resort strategy and always done with the goal of helping or reestablishing wild populations.

Noel Snyder et al., authors of the 1996 study, described several problems with captive-breeding efforts, among them similar concerns to those that plagued the Sumatran rhino:

Captive breeding can divert attention from the problems causing a species' decline and become a technological fix that merely prolongs rather than rectifies problems. Longterm solutions are often politically more difficult than captive breeding solutions, so it is tempting for managers to deemphasize efforts for wild populations once captive populations are in place. . . . Captive breeding can become an end in itself and may undermine rather than enhance habitat preservation by reducing the urgency with which this goal is pursued. The existence of a captive population can give a false impression that a species is safe, so that destruction of habitat and wild populations can proceed.

One study of Endangered Species Act implementation said the fact that recovery plans frequently included translocation and captive breeding was an indication that interventions were beginning too late, requiring drastic action, and adding to cost while reducing the chances for success.

The po'ouli's case, however, argues against the use of captive breeding as a last resort. When asked what lessons could be learned from the po'ouli, several commented that hands-on recovery programs, including captive breeding, should be begun when a population is still relatively numerous.

Establishing a captive flock of Maui parrotbills, for example, would create a second population should disaster befall wild birds concentrated in East Maui. Further, beginning captive propagation when there are still several hundred birds left would give aviculturists a margin of error as they learn how to keep the bird healthy and induce it to breed.

But some of captive breeding's problems are not just due to resources. Captivity changes creatures, making subjects less able to survive when released. The problem can be particularly acute when there is no wild population left from which the captive-bred population can learn upon being released.

201

One 2002 study noted that changes "deleterious in the wild" have been seen in insects, turkeys, rats, and fish. It sought to illuminate what happens in captivity by breeding fruit flies under benign conditions for fifty generations and then examining how well they competed for mates with wild flies. They did far worse.

The study had some good news, showing that the damage to wild fitness is reversible. Even that was tempered, however, by the fact that it took twelve generations for the flies to regain something close to wild fitness. Twelve generations may not be a long time for a fruit fly, whose lifespan is measured in weeks, but for larger, longer-lived animals, the need to stave off extinction for many generations under wild conditions may be impractical or impossible.

A study of captive-bred endangered mice shows that captivity's changes don't affect every individual, but instead reflect the increased survival of less fit individuals.

The study, published in 2003, examined the predator response of mice from the beaches of Alabama and Florida. It compared the responses of wild mice with those that had been captive for two, fourteen, and thirty-five generations.

While the wild-caught mice immediately bolted for cover when researchers waved an owl-shaped figure over a holding tank, some of the captive mice did and some didn't. That illustrates captivity's relaxed selection pressure, researchers said. Mice that don't bolt to the nearest hole at the first sign of a predator survive just as well as those that do. After a few captive generations, both types of mice are in the population.

Nature's goal—or at least that of the great gray owl whose outline was used in the work—is just the opposite of humans harboring captive populations. There is a constant cull in the wild of those too weak, too slow, or too unwise to head for cover.

The implication, the authors said, is that when a species is reintroduced to the wild, more animals will be needed than anticipated to reach a target population. Nature's first order of business on taking command of a captive-bred population will be to do a remedial cull.

Such a remedial cull has been a heartbreaking feature of some Hawaiian captive-breeding programs.

The recovery program for the Hawaiian crow, or 'alala, stalled in the 1990s when captive-bred individuals failed to breed or even survive very long in the wild. Of twenty-seven crows released between 1993 and 1999, twenty-one disappeared as a result of disease, predation, and possibly poor nutrition. Officials finally recaptured the six survivors in 1999. The last two wild crows disappeared in 2002. In 2007, there were almost fifty in captivity.

The captive-breeding program of the Hawaiian goose, or nene, provides lessons on the importance of coupling captive breeding with protection of appropriate habitat. The program began decades ago, in 1949. The breeding has been extraordinarily successful, with 2,150 captive-bred birds released into the wild as of 1997. The program has had less success, however, in raising birds able to survive after release. It has kept the nene a part of wild Hawaii—no mean feat, considering that in 1949, the population was down to 13 captive and fewer than 30 wild birds. But the wild population has only recently become self-sustaining, and only on Kauai.

The difficulty in this case may not be changes in the captive-bred geese, but long-term alterations to its habitat. With most lowland areas converted to agriculture and other human uses, some believe the geese have had such a difficult time reestablishing themselves because—like the po'ouli—they're being released in marginal habitat that was once a small part of their range. The geese are restricted to areas high on the islands' volcanoes that may not provide adequate food. As of 1997, there were an estimated 885 nene in the wild.

Several of the broader issues surrounding captive breeding and its drawbacks were echoed during the debate over whether to bring the po'ouli into captivity. The reality, however, was that by the late 1990s, those interested in po'ouli recovery had no good choices left. Even on exactly the right road, success would be a long shot. And there was nobody to tell them which road that was.

15

SAVING THE LEGACY

IN 1878, THE PIGEON HUNTERS WERE AT WORK IN PETOSKEY, Michigan.

The area's forests held one of the last major nesting sites of the passenger pigeon, which, like the North American bison, once had immense populations on this continent. Before the pigeon's destruction, the birds moved in massive flocks across the eastern forests. Flying up to sixty miles per hour, they descended to feast where the trees were fruiting most abundantly, ate their fill, and moved on to a new bounty in another part of the forest.

Clearing the forests for agriculture likely played an initial role in the birds' decline, but the final blow occurred over three decades starting in the mid-1800s at the hands of hunters providing meat to city markets. Researchers believe it may not have been the actual slaughter that did the most damage. The unceasing harassment at virtually every nesting site, however, led to fewer and fewer young to replenish the adults killed by hunters and natural causes.

In 1878, the Michigan hunters were merciless when they descended on Petoskey, as they had been other years at other sites. Using nets and guns and long poles to get even the young from their nests, they killed fifty thousand passenger pigeons per day in a five-month hunt. Later, when surviving adults had fled to a second nesting site and tried to breed, hunters tracked them down too, killing them before they could raise their young.

The ferocity and single-mindedness of the assault is almost as unimaginable as the extinction of a creature once so numerous that it is thought to have made up between 25 and 40 percent of the continent's birdlife, an estimated 3 billion to 5 billion individual birds.

One can't help but wonder what might have happened had the hunt been stopped that year. Though one of the last major colonies, the flock held millions of birds, a population with which most conservation biologists would be happy to begin a recovery program. With northeastern farms abandoned and forests regrowing, it might still be possible to stand in one's yard and marvel as flocks darken the skies on their way to warmer climes.

The Michigan legislature took a crack at it, making it illegal to net pigeons within two miles of a nesting area. But the law had little effect, and the killing went on. An effort was made again in 1898, when the state legislature considered a bill to close the season on passenger pigeons for ten years.

But it was far too little too late. From the once enormous bounty, the last passenger pigeon was seen in the wild two years later. And the last of the species, dubbed Martha, died in the Cincinnati Zoological Garden in 1914, bringing to a close an extraordinary chapter in the history of earth's wildlife.

Much has been learned about conserving species since 1878. Legislative efforts today have teeth that give them power, which also makes them the focus of much debate and controversy.

Congress outlawed hunting the bald eagle in 1940 and in 1966 passed the precursor to today's Endangered Species Act, the Endangered Species Preservation Act. In 1967, then U.S. Secretary of the Interior Stewart L. Udall designated seventy-eight species of mammals, birds, reptiles, and fishes as threatened with extinction. In 1969, the act was expanded and renamed the Endangered Species Conservation Act. In 1972, Congress passed the Marine Mammal Protection Act, which outlawed killing whales, seals, dolphins, and the like. And in 1973, it passed the Endangered Species Act, declaring that endangered species had ecological, aesthetic, educational, historical, recreational, and scientific value.

President Richard Nixon signed the Endangered Species Act into law with words that many would agree with today: "Nothing is more priceless and more worthy of preservation than the rich array of animal life with which our country has been blessed. It is a many-faceted treasure, of value to scholars, scientists, and nature lovers alike, and it forms a vital part of the heritage we all share as Americans."

Since that time, the landmark act has been praised as the strongest and most meaningful species conservation law in U.S. history. A 2006 estimate said that 227 species would have gone extinct without its protections, and by 2007, 14 endangered U.S. species had recovered enough to be taken off the list, including the American alligator, the peregrine falcon, and the bald eagle.

But with this being the case, why are so many who are working to conserve species driven to despair? One longtime biologist working in the Hawaiian Islands said in 2003 that conserving species was an ongoing challenge, that it was *always* too little too late, and that species like the poʻouli all too often slipped over the edge.

One problem with relying on numbers to determine the act's success is that extinction, oddly enough, is in the eye of the beholder. According to the Fish and Wildlife Service (FWS), just 9 listed species have gone extinct since the Endangered Species Act passed. That tally, however, doesn't include either listed species that haven't been seen for years and are likely extinct or extinct species that were never listed under the act's provisions. As of September 30, 2000, another 26 species were listed but presumed extinct, and a 2004 report by the Center for Biological Diversity said that 85 species that were not listed by the government at the time also went extinct, including the Ochlockonee Moccasin shell, a freshwater mussel from Georgia, and the Guam broadbill. The center's tally of species extinct or missing for a decade or more since the Endangered Species Act passed was 108, far higher than the FWS's 9.

To many people, extinction is a black or white issue—the last of a species is either alive or dead. But for those dealing with the practical realities of rare species conservation, particularly in places like Hanawi, certainty is hard to come by. It's possible, though not always easy, to prove that something is there. It's much more difficult to prove that something isn't, particularly when it was rare to begin with, and "there" is so inaccessible that just a handful of people visit each year.

That's part of the reason the government's 2006 Revised Recovery Plan for Hawaiian Forest Birds covers 10 species that have not been seen in more than a decade and may already be extinct. Included in that group is the poʻouli, which the plan refers to as "critically endangered," though the authors acknowledge that the bird may now be extinct.

Despite criticisms of those who oppose the act or who would improve it, its protections can be important. The Center for Biological Diversity said the failure to include needy species under the Endangered Species Act's protections was a "spectacular" and sometimes "purposeful" failure. "These species were not listed and thus were not protected by the ESA's prohibition on take and extinction. . . . Indeed, it was legal to drive them extinct."

That was illustrated by the case of the Valdina Farms salamander, which the FWS began reviewing for listing in 1977. After ten years of inaction on the listing, a local water district channeled floodwater into the only cave in which it lived, driving it to extinction.

The Center for Biological Diversity's extinct species list, which includes 49 from Hawaii, highlights the danger of delayed listing, one of the main controversies over the Endangered Species Act. Of the extinct species on the center's list, 67 never made it onto the government's endangered and threatened species list at all, and 18 were listed only after they became extinct.

A look at the species listed by the government as threatened or endangered shows what seems to be a skyrocketing number in trouble. From Udall's original 78 species in 1967, the list stands at 1,352 as of this writing. The rising number of species listed doesn't reflect the increasing danger to America's wildlife, however, but the ongoing battle over how quickly to list species as endangered or threatened. Far more species were in trouble even at the time of the act's passage than have been put on the list. In 1975, two years after the Endangered Species Act became law, the director of the FWS estimated that 7,000 species would need to be listed. A more recent estimate put the number at 9,206.

The government foot-dragging over species listing is a consequence of the act's strength. It can compel certain actions on behalf of endangered species and block others, which can anger powerful constituencies.

In the 1970s, the FWS was on the road to listing thousands of species when a lawsuit caused the nation's political leaders to have second thoughts. In 1978, the U.S. Supreme Court ruled in favor of a three-inch fish called the snail darter over the Tennessee Valley Authority and its nearly completed Tellico Dam on the Little Tennessee River. The $120 million dam was intended to create a thirty-mile reservoir for recreation, flood control, and power, but the court halted construction, saying that the dam endangered the fish. It also said that in passing the Endangered Species Act, "Congress has spoken in the plainest of language, making it abundantly clear that the balance has been struck in favor of affording endangered species the highest of priorities."

Eleven other major federal projects, including the space shuttle, were imperiled by the decision. It shook the halls of power and sent legislators scrambling to make their language a bit less plain and afford endangered species a priority somewhere below "highest."

It took a couple years, but Congress eventually exempted the Tellico Dam from the Endangered Species Act and amended the act in ways that slammed the brakes on listings in the late 1970s and early 1980s, causing almost 2,000 proposed listings to be withdrawn. The amendments made the listing process more complex and put a two-year time limit on a listing's completion. The lawmakers also began the process of transforming the act from a fairly simple yet rigid law into one that is more permissive and flexible. It has also become more complex, to the point where the act and its associated rules and regulations often may seem beyond comprehension.

Since the Tellico Dam case, listing decisions have become politically charged. Different administrations have had varied listing efforts. Republican president Ronald Reagan, for example, kept listings to a bare minimum, suspending the issuance of federal rules in 1981, including species listings, and ordering economic impact analyses to be conducted before any proposed listing. Listing increased dramatically in the early 1990s, with an average of seventy-three species per year from 1991 to 1995, though several lawsuits spurred the pace of listing.

Though some consider the slow pace of listings the greatest problem, the listing process is not the only part of the act that has drawn criticism. Even among those who support the law and its aims, there is an almost palpable sense of frustration that more hasn't been accomplished. Scientists and policy makers have searched for reasons why legislation so strong that it's become a political lightning rod has had so few successes.

Much attention has been focused on the quality of recovery plans, the blueprints to save species. Many findings have pointed out flaws in their design and implementation. In 1993, one startling report found that for a significant number of species, recovery goals for their populations were actually *below* their current population size and risked the species' extinction rather than ensuring their survival. The findings prompted the report's authors to comment that it appeared species were being "managed for extinction."

Studies of recovery plans have shown a slow improvement in their quality. In the 1990s, authors pointed out flaws such as a bias toward charismatic species like the bald eagle and grizzly bear and away from lesser known species that may be more imperiled. They also found shaky science underpinning planning, such as guesses of population sizes and little distinction being made between threatened and endangered species. More recent studies have shown that though recovery plans still have problems, they've improved over time.

Another issue that has gained attention has been political influence over the act's administration, though that seems clearly contrary to its design. Several authors—in addition to the U.S. Supreme Court in the Tellico Dam case—said that Congress had been particularly clear in its intent that science guide endangered species conservation programs. J. R. DeShazo and Jody Freeman wrote in a 2006 article on congressional politics and the Endangered Species Act:

> By mandating that scientific criteria determine listing and funding, and by clarifying this mandate over time, Congress has ruled out political considerations—such as the number of representatives on oversight committees with species in their districts, or party affiliation of those members, or whether those members sit on a House or Senate committee—as determinants of agency decision making. We believe that in its preference for scientifically grounded listing decisions, the ESA is unusually clear.

But as with road and bridge building projects, military base locations, and a host of other programs where lawmakers play politics, Congress just can't seem to help itself. Wrote DeShazo and Freeman:

> Our results are striking given the clear choices made in the statute that political considerations should not count. And yet they do: extinction may turn on the preferences of members of oversight committees, not

on the criteria established by law. Our study demon-
strates ... that members of Congress use their positions
on oversight and appropriations committees to prevent
the U.S. Fish and Wildlife Service from complying with
the specific provisions of the ESA. Listing and funding
decisions are influenced to a greater extent by a member's "institutional identities"—party affiliation, committee jurisdiction, and chamber—than by the act's
evidentiary requirements.

DeShazo and Freeman said the best-case scenario for an
endangered species was not necessarily to be tended by biologists with the best pedigree guided by a recovery plan based on
the best science:

The best-case scenario for your survival and recovery
would be that your geographic range falls within states
with exclusively Democratic representation; that your
elected members of Congress—especially your
senators—sit on committees with oversight and appropriations authority over the implementation of the
ESA; and that you are a mammal. . . . As it turns out,
who you are matters, but who you know—who represents you on committees—might matter more.

Spending decisions are more likely influenced if a con-
gressperson sits on the appropriations committee; listing decisions are influenced if he or she is on an oversight committee.
"As it turns out, the [Fish and Wildlife Service] is not acting on
its own when it deviates from statutory criteria. Rather, the
agency's listing and resource allocation decisions respond to

legislative principals whose preferences simply contradict what the enacting majority intended when it passed (or reauthorized) the law."

Other evidence of tampering with the Endangered Species Act's administration exists as well. A 2005 survey of hundreds of FWS biologists, ecologists, and botanists by the Union of Concerned Scientists found that almost half had been told at one time or another to "refrain from making jeopardy or other findings that are protective of species." Additionally, one in five had been "directed to inappropriately exclude or alter technical information from a USFWS [Fish and Wildlife Service] scientific document." The survey showed that in addition to scientific factors, economic considerations, the influence of political appointees, congressional interference, and the desires of local officeholders were also factors in the scientists' work.

An eight-year survey of five marine mammal recovery programs administered by the National Marine Fisheries Service provides another view of the considerations that go into endangered species protection decisions. The study, released in 2003, showed that decision makers in programs to recover the Florida manatee, northern right whale, Steller sea lion, California sea otter, and Hawaiian monk seal knew what decisions would get them into trouble and avoided conflicts with economic interests—even when the welfare of species was at stake. "The costs of making decisions that adversely affect various industries were often perceived as too great to risk. This is because the agencies rely on the support of elected officials, and that support is often tied to those officials' satisfaction with the agency's contributions to or lack of interference with local or regional economic gains." Thus conflict avoidance had become part of agency culture.

The study's author was sympathetic to the pressures facing agency heads, saying they are making complicated decisions with uncertain information, often with vocal advocates on several sides making their views known. All this is done under the threat of losing funds with the wrong decision. Still, he concluded, "leaders' decision-making in these circumstances rarely promoted species recovery goals."

The effect of all this political tinkering is that the FWS doesn't take its own scientific advice. In 1983, the service created a ranking system that uses a species' uniqueness, its potential to recover, and the degree of threat it's under to assign a rank for its recovery priority ranging from 1 to 18, with 1 being the highest.

A species under high threat, with high recovery potential, that is the only species in its genus would gain a priority rank of 1, for example. A rank of 18 would be reserved for a subspecies under low threat with low recovery potential. The po'ouli, with a high degree of uniqueness, high threat, but low recovery potential, was ranked 4 in the 2003–04 Recovery Report to Congress.

A 2002 study looking at whether species recovery dollars were directed by priority ranking showed that two of the system's three criteria—the degree of threat a species is under and its uniqueness, both high for the po'ouli—had little to do with actual funding allocation. Those with higher recovery potential, however, received more money. Funding also reflected special-interest priorities, with more money allocated to large, wide-ranging predators. The study also found that threatened and endangered species received similar amounts, despite the higher level of threat facing those that are endangered.

"Expenditures often fail to track priorities because of a combination of political, social and institutional barriers," the authors wrote. "Each barrier alone is important, but together they effectively limit the funds received by high-priority species that have low public appeal, that have little effect on the economy, and that reside on islands far from Washington D.C."

All this jockeying to influence endangered species spending does affect species recovery. A 2002 study showed that even if plans are based on sound science, they can be gutted by under-funding. This study examined the budgets for 243 species recovery programs from 1989 through 1995. It looked at how much money officials requested to implement their plans versus how much they got, then at how the species were doing.

The results showed that half of the listed species got 18 percent or less of their budget requests, and that a species' status was related to how much of its requested budget it received. Species whose populations were declining got just 15 percent of requested dollars, those with stable numbers received 27 percent, and those that were improving got 37 percent of requested funds.

The study's authors concluded that funding overall was less than 20 percent of what was needed. They pointed out that passing a law, even one like the Endangered Species Act, is no guarantee that money will be there to fulfill its mandate, and wrote, "Our current scenario is akin to starving hospitalized patients and then grilling the doctors about why more patients are not recovering."

In addition to political influence, lawsuits brought by conservation groups also affect endangered species spending. Lawsuits force the FWS to defend itself in court, and court decisions can force the agency to shift money from higher-ranked species to those on which the court orders additional funds be spent.

Researchers examined the influence of 109 lawsuits brought against the federal government from 1990 to 1999. They found that three times as many were brought on behalf of threatened species as endangered species, even though the latter, by definition, are in deeper trouble. Roughly half of the lawsuits involved just three groups: spotted owls, sea turtles, and grizzly bears. In 2003, the Department of the Interior declared the Endangered Species Act "broken" because of lawsuits' influence over how conservation programs were run.

One doesn't have to be a scientist to know that something is wrong with how this country finances endangered species programs. Any citizen can look at annual expenditure reports, broken down species by species, on the FWS website. Even a cursory glance shows that the numbers are badly skewed. Though 1,340 species were on the endangered and threatened species list in 2004, only a handful got the lion's share of funding. In fiscal 2004, the last year the FWS posted reports, just 20 species got half of the funding. Further, the 2004 report showed that 90 percent of the funding was spent on just 108 species, leaving more than 1,200 species to split the remaining 10 percent.

Some may reason that under this scenario, at least the most needy species are getting adequate funding, but judging by the number of threatened rather than endangered species in the top spots, need apparently doesn't play much of a role. The Endangered Species Act defines threatened species as those that could become endangered in the foreseeable future, and thus by definition, they are in less trouble than those that are already endangered.

Among the top ten entities—species, subspecies, and distinct populations—receiving funding, however, seven were threatened and only three endangered. Nine of the ten were western fish, including four runs of Chinook salmon, one run each of coho

217

and sockeye salmon, two runs of steelhead, and bull trout. The Steller sea lion, which preys on fish, was the lone nonfish.

Looking just at full species, only three of the top ten were listed solely as endangered; some others had both threatened and endangered populations. Chinook salmon got the most money, garnering $161.3 million, followed by steelhead, the Steller sea lion, coho salmon, bull trout, sockeye salmon, red-cockaded woodpecker, pallid sturgeon, chum salmon, and right whale. Of these, the woodpecker, sturgeon, and whale were the three listed as endangered.

The po'ouli that year, on an island far from Washington, D.C., and down to just three individuals, was ranked 389th, receiving $67,203 state and federal dollars.

Money for conservation programs seems to have always been an issue in Hawaii. The administration of Hawaii governor Linda Lingle acknowledged as much in announcing an increase in the amount she would request for the Department of Land and Natural Resources for 2007 to 2009. A press release issued by the department said the $103 million requested for its two-year operating budget was previously "inconceivable and unimagined" and "reversed the prior trend of annual cuts and lack of attention prior administrations gave to DLNR."

While the press release was undoubtedly as much a political document as a statement of historical fact, other sources not only agreed, but went a step further. One person involved with the po'ouli recovery program in the late 1990s decried the state's underfunding of the Department of Land and Natural Resources as "criminal neglect." Others working with the state at different points in the po'ouli's history cited budgetary factors as important reasons recovery work didn't move ahead. According to a key state wildlife program administrator, "There's no question that the administration and the legislature underfunded these sorts of things and always have."

David Woodside, the state wildlife biologist at the time of the po'ouli's discovery, said that early recovery plans involving fencing, captive breeding, pig removal, and predator control were viewed as "pie in the sky," partly because no one knew where the money to implement them would come from.

A decade later, when the FWS was pushing to build a fence in Hanawi to provide pig-free habitat for the po'ouli and other birds, the project collapsed because federal dollars appropriated for it were not adequate. Though the project was revived a few years later, the delay occurred at a time when the po'ouli's population was crashing. That delay may have been a critical one.

Scott Fretz, wildlife program manager for Hawaii's Division of Forestry and Wildlife, says that the fencing simply took too long, and that funding issues were among the things that delayed needed action until the 1990s, when there were just six po'oulis left and little could be done. "Appropriate action was not taken early enough, and we got into a situation where it was exceedingly difficult to recover the species."

U.S. Geological Survey biologist Thane Pratt, who headed the Hawaii Forest Bird Recovery team in the 1990s, says that more hands-on intervention earlier might have saved the po'ouli, even in the late 1980s. But funding was a problem, and the fence still had to be built. "By the time the Maui Forest Bird Recovery Project got going on the birds, there were less than six. It's really hard to do something with six birds, birds that are tough to find because they don't call and you can be in their home ranges and not see them."

It may be little comfort, as administrators scrounge for dollars, but Hawaii is not alone. A 1998 survey by the International Association of Fish and Wildlife Agencies on state spending on nongame wildlife programs said that though funding levels were increasing, they remained "mostly unpredictable and inadequate, making planning difficult and precluding formation of workable programs to restore declining species and to prevent nongame wildlife from becoming endangered." The association estimated that almost ten times the amount spent that year was needed to fully fund state nongame wildlife restoration programs.

A study published in 2006 indicated that states are playing a greater role in conservation of nongame species as time goes on and collectively are spending more on endangered species than the federal government. It also said, however, that the myriad programs in different states make it difficult to gauge their collective impact.

In Hawaii, anyway, the problem may be one of scale. Though it's the fourth-smallest state in the Union, Hawaii has more endangered or threatened species than any other, with 344. The next smallest state, Connecticut, has far fewer troubled species, with 21.

Pratt says that underfunding of Hawaiian bird programs is a recurring problem, and that even though most of the country's endangered songbirds are in Hawaii, most of the funding goes elsewhere. "It has to do with geopolitics. The electorate paying taxes is somewhere other than where the birds are."

The southwestern willow flycatcher garnered $11.9 million in 2004, the black-capped vireo $4.6 million, and the golden-cheeked warbler $4.5 million, all mainland species. The Hawaiian bird getting the most money was the palila, which was on the winning side of a lawsuit and got $3.09 million that year.

A 1992 U.S. Senate hearing examined whether Hawaii was being shortchanged when it came to federal endangered species recovery dollars. Witness after witness answered yes. Ronald L. Walker, the state's wildlife program manager in the Department of Land and Natural Resources at the time, put the problem succinctly: "Hawaii has two-tenths of 1 percent of the land area of the United States, but has experienced 75 percent of the nation's plant and animal extinctions. We have 40 percent of the country's endangered birds and 26 percent of its endangered plants."

Walker called the resources allocated to the FWS Hawaii office woefully inadequate. He said that one request for $132,000 in federal funds for ten endangered plants that year was granted just $1,200. The state sent the money back because it would cost more to do the associated paperwork.

Other witnesses at the hearing said that lawsuits were important factors in getting results for the palila, 'alala, and Hawaiian plants.

The funding complaints may have had an effect. A 2001 study of statewide spending on Hawaiian bird conservation from all sources through the 1990s found that $94.5 million was spent during the decade. The author said the amount rose dramatically from the 1980s because of lawsuits and conservation action under the Endangered Species Act.

Nevertheless, the study indicated that much more was needed for effective conservation programs. It specifically said that state conservation spending—roughly 1 percent of the state budget—should increase. State funding was inadequate enough that matching federal dollars were lost in some cases, and the Department of Land and Natural Resources budget was cut at a time when research on declining bird species was critical.

Though scarcity of money has been a recurring theme running through Hawaiian conservation and may have been an important factor in the early years of the po'ouli's recovery program, this doesn't appear to have been the case during its later years. Alan Lieberman of the San Diego Zoo, which handled the po'ouli's captive breeding, says he felt that their grant from the state was sufficient. Jim Groombridge, who ran the Maui Forest Bird Recovery Project during the translocation in 2002, says that the federal and state governments were funding the project quite well, and that the money was adequate to do what he needed.

With the difficulties of conservation in Hanawi, it seems that the bird had bigger problems than money. One observer says flatly, "The po'ouli didn't go extinct because of a lack of funding."

Despite all the criticism of the Endangered Species Act's implementation, few would think America's wildlife better off without it. The law undoubtedly has given the welfare of endangered species a "place at the decision-making table." Some say it's unfair to judge the law after just three decades, given the length of time that biological change can take. Thirty years is barely a generation for some long-lived species. The author of a paper looking at lessons learned since the act was passed said:

Most species do not reach the ESA's protected list until their populations are very small or dwindling rapidly. It takes time to turn around those declines. But even without that biological lag, it is simply unrealistic to expect rapid delisting. While the ESA has not fulfilled the rosy expectations that it would function as a con-servation "emergency room," providing intensive but relatively short term care until "recovered" species were ready to make it on their own, that failure is properly attributed to unrealistically optimistic expectations rather than to fundamental flaws in the act.

16

AFTER ELEVEN WEEKS

BETH BICKNESE'S SHOULDERS SLUMPED. SHE SIGHED A LONG, exhaled "Ohhh" as she read Alan Lieberman's e-mail. The captive po'ouli was dead.

It was the Saturday after Thanksgiving 2004. The San Diego Zoo vet had known the odds were stacked against the ailing bird half an ocean away at the Maui Bird Conservation Center. But when she woke up that morning undisturbed by a late-night phone call bearing bad news, she allowed herself a sliver of hope.

"I thought they'd call me if he died," Bicknese says. "I expected the call and didn't get it, so I thought maybe he made it through the night."

As she got up, her mind was whirring with medical possibilities, things she could suggest that Rich Switzer try to help the bird. Then she went to her computer and checked her e-mail. Bicknese recalls:

It's one of those things that was not a surprise, but I was still—deflated would be the best word. What a bummer, what a loss. I felt bad for the people working their hearts out, for the field biologists who spent hours and hours and hours to mist-net him. I ran what we'd done through my head. Was there anything we could have done differently? Then I thought, "They haven't seen those other two birds," and I realized I just probably touched the last po'ouli in the world.

When the po'ouli died, a whole new set of protocols kicked into action. Though they had hoped for the best, the scientists and administrators charged with po'ouli recovery understood that the captured bird would someday die and had made plans to extract as much information as possible from the body.

Oliver Ryder, head of the San Diego Zoo's Genetics Division, says the idea of collecting po'ouli genetic material came up in the years before the capture effort, as they discussed future possibilities. Though the focus was squarely on recovering the species, recovery officials also understood that if the bird died, having it in captivity would allow the preservation of its genetic material.

When Switzer woke up at the Maui Bird Conservation Center the morning after the bird's death, he got to work following the new protocols. He woke up Kirsty Swinnerton with a 6 A.M. phone call, asking for help harvesting the bird's tissue. Swinnerton went to the center, a bit nervous, given the high stakes. She asked Switzer if he shared her feelings.

After reflecting on the stress and exhaustion of caring for the ailing bird night and day for weeks on end, Switzer said, "I've been nervous for the last two months. Now nerves don't come into it. The bird's dead."

Together they harvested a variety of tissues to be sent to the San Diego Zoo and hustled the specimens to Kahului to make the noon Federal Express plane, the last of the day.

After spending months in the field trying to net the bird, Swinnerton was disappointed at its death, but she had known the end was coming. "I knew it was sick. I saw it a few days before. He was hopping around. This guy was wobbly and weak but still trying to function. I didn't think he was going to make it."

Lieberman's e-mail on the po'ouli's death didn't just go to Bicknese; it spread the bad news to others involved in the recovery effort as well.

"This is to inform you that the poouli has died," Lieberman wrote. "The critical tissues are being prepared for shipment to [the San Diego Zoo's center for Conservation and Research for Endangered Species] early this morning (Saturday). They will go out FedEx today. The body will be held for necropsy."

Paul Conry, administrator of the Hawaii Department of Land and Natural Resources, wrote to thank Lieberman and his staff, saying that despite the progress they'd made working with Hawaiian birds over the years, this miracle was not to be. "Sometimes it just doesn't work out the way we hope," he wrote.

While the tissue samples were on the way to the zoo's geneticists, the po'ouli's body was on its way to the zoo's veterinarians for a postmortem. Lieberman tracked the items, keeping the technicians aware of their progress and making sure the technicians were ready to begin immediately. Time was of the essence. Degradation could be delayed for only a short time. If tissues were going to be preserved, it would have to be done quickly.

The tissue samples arrived Sunday morning in excellent shape. The zoo's geneticists immediately set to work. Their task was to ensure the po'ouli immortality of a sort. They would separate the cells from this last bit of po'ouli tissue and encourage fibroblasts—common cells found in many body parts—to grow and divide until they had enough to freeze and preserve.

Frozen inside the nucleus of each cell would be the po'ouli's DNA. Those long, coiled molecules hold the blueprint of life, and as long as they exist, the story of the po'ouli, however bleak today, has not been completely told.

By shortly after noon on Sunday, November 28, the tissues were "being treated, prepared, separated, teased and coaxed into various broths and enzymes to make things happen," Lieberman wrote in an e-mail to the po'ouli group.

Zoo technicians separated the growing cells into two batches and let those batches grow. They divided them and grew them again, proliferating and dividing until they had an adequate supply of cells. To avoid changes in the cells induced by the culturing process, they worked rapidly, "walking a balance between growing lots of cells and minimizing the time growing them," says Ryder.

Before putting the cells into cold storage for good, the geneticists tested their viability. They froze several samples, waited a week, and then thawed them to see if they would still grow.

"It actually worked quite well," Ryder says. "It sometimes takes a month. Well within that time, we had frozen cultures and thawed them. We did that and they were fine. They grow great."

Ryder did an initial examination of the po'ouli's chromosomes, coiled blocks of DNA inside a dividing cell. An image of the chromosomes shows them splayed dark against a white background, looking like paint splatter, with the large major chromosomes standing out from the dotlike smaller ones.

"It was a poignant irony," Ryder reflects, "to be looking through the microscope to see the chromosomes of the po'ouli, to be the first person to look at them, and to know the bird is gone."

While Ryder's crew was teasing po'ouli cells apart and coaxing them to grow, veterinarian Bruce Rideout had a different challenge. By 10 A.M. Sunday, normally his day off, he was at the zoo with Lieberman to examine the po'ouli's body. The exam went pretty much as it would for any bird, but a bit more slowly and carefully. They made sure they complied with the protocols that accompanied such a valuable specimen.

The exam confirmed what had been suspected: this bird was very old. Rideout noticed lipofuscinosis, the remnants of cellular death that accumulate over time, evidence that it had had a long life. "That made it that much more a poignant exercise for me," Rideout says. "You realize what this bird had gone through and how long it had lived in a difficult environment in the face of a lot of threats."

Another major finding was that the bird appeared to have tolerated its malaria infection for some time. In other circumstances, this might have been cause for rejoicing, a sign that the po'ouli was finally developing natural resistance. According to Rideout, "We were surprised to find the bird had a malaria infection but appeared to be surviving with it just fine. There was no evidence of tissue damage or a lot of pigment accumulation in the liver that we often see with malaria."

It's hard to say how long the bird had the infection, but the disease appeared to be in an advanced stage. In its initial stages, the parasite replicates in the liver and other organs. The second stage occurs when the parasite gets into the bloodstream and circulates in red blood cells. Sensitive birds can die in either stage.

The po'ouli had malaria parasites in its red blood cells but no signs of damage in the organs. In his November 30 report, Rideout called the infection subclinical. "Although most native Hawaiian forest birds do not tolerate *Plasmodium* sp. infections well, this individual seems to have been surviving with a low-level parasitemia for some time. Surprisingly, there was no gross, cytologic, or histologic evidence that the infection was causing clinical problems."

The finding is a piece of the puzzle in the po'ouli's story, but Rideout and others cautioned against giving it too much weight. Though the bird's tolerance of malaria may indicate that the disease was not a big factor in the species' decline, it may instead be that the other po'ouli did die of malaria and this bird was a final, lone exception.

The examination also showed that a fungal infection called aspergillosis "significantly contributed to the bird's final decline." Rideout says that's not unusual in a bird in deteriorating condition. Aspergillosis is virtually everywhere in the environment and often takes hold as a bird's health is failing, blossoming as the immune system slows down.

"That's not an unusual finding in a bird that is declining from any cause," Rideout said. "It looked like the bird was very old. It began to decline in condition, and it acquired aspergillosis as a late secondary disease process.

"It could well have picked it up at the MBCC [Maui Bird Conservation Center], but that doesn't tell you anything about conditions at the MBCC, because it's completely ubiquitous, and this bird was exposed to a forest of aspergillosis and other related fungi throughout its life," Rideout said later. "In a wet environment like that, it's just everywhere."

Rideout reported that the body was in poor condition overall and that the immediate cause of death was due to multiple factors. He concluded that the bird's apparent advanced age was possibly a major factor in its demise.

In essence, the last po'ouli died from a cascade of causes leading to multiple organ failure. What the aging process started was exacerbated by the stress of the bird's capture and captivity. Once it began to fail and lose weight, aspergillosis went to work, hastening the end.

"Any one of them, by itself, would not have killed the bird," Rideout says. "But when you look at a geriatric bird that begins to lose weight, that's when it becomes vulnerable to secondary infections like aspergillosis, and these things start to converge on the bird and, all together, lead to spiraling decline and death. That's what happens to all of us."

Rideout believes that the bird probably had reached the end of its natural life, and if left in the wild, it would have died within a similar time frame, or more likely even earlier.

"My personal view is this would have been the end of the bird's life no matter what. In fact it probably would have died earlier if it had been in the wild," Rideout says, adding that at least in captivity the ill bird was kept warm and comfortable and had easy access to food and water.

Another finding was that the bird's testes were inactive, which Rideout attributed to the bird either being out of its breeding season or being too old to reproduce. Though it's possible all this effort was expended on a bird that was past the age of reproduction, Lieberman doesn't think so.

"Birds in the wild are alive and reproducing, reaching their end of their physical health and the end of their breeding life [at the same time]," Lieberman says. "With the po'ouli, since it was wild and still alive, it possibly could still have been reproductive. The fact it died so quickly of age-related factors, it was probably at the very end of its reproductive life."

While the veterinarians and genetic technicians were doing their work, recovery officials huddled with public relations staffers, preparing to notify the outside world. The endeavor to breed the po'ouli against almost impossible odds, begun with high hopes eleven weeks earlier, had come crashing to the ground.

On November 30, the release went out.

"We are always sad to lose an animal in our care. In this case, we may not have lost just a bird, but one of the last remaining vestiges of a species. It is difficult to realize that our last efforts to save this species rely on just two birds," Lieberman said in the prepared statement, which reflected the hopeful possibility that the poʻoulis in the forest were alive.

Gina Schultz, acting field supervisor for the Fish and Wildlife Service's (FWS) Pacific Islands office, focused on going forward:

> Our goal of saving the poʻouli is now very difficult and may not be achievable, but we must continue to try to save the species we have left. In addition to the poʻouli, we have 31 other endangered bird species in Hawaii that are threatened by loss of habitat, introduced predators, and diseases. Rather than giving up hope, we need to rededicate our efforts to save these unique birds that are such an important part of Hawaii's native forests.

Eric VanderWerf, the FWS's Hawaiian bird recovery coordinator, added a hopeful note concerning the two remaining poʻoulis: "Although we have not seen or heard them for many months, it may be that they have shifted their home ranges. All of the birds are old for forest birds, but birds have been resighted after long absences in the past, and we are not willing to give up all hope yet."

When the zoo staff was done with the poʻouli's body, the next priority was to preserve it as a museum specimen, making it available for future scholars. The zoo sent it to Helen James at the Smithsonian Institution, who prepared it and then returned it to Hawaii.

Today three poʻouli specimens are available in museum collections. One lies in a tall, gray cabinet in a room overlooking

Central Park in the collections of the American Museum of Natural History in New York. Its insides have been preserved in alcohol, in a jar in a crowded cabinet in the museum's basement.

Two more—the type specimen and the last po'ouli—are in the Bishop Museum's collection in Honolulu. The last bird was preserved with one wing outstretched, doubtless in order to show wing feathers otherwise obscured in the typical study skin. The effect, however, is of the bird forever pointing to the past or some unseen future.

In the field, the po'ouli's death brought work to a screeching halt. It triggered a reassessment of the captive-breeding program, stopping efforts to capture the next po'ouli.

But as the days and weeks went by without a sighting, whether they were or weren't trying to capture the next bird became academic. Crews began to focus on just finding it. They returned to the forest on November 30, but after several weeks of effort, they called it quits.

By this time, the Home Range 1 bird hadn't been seen since February 2004. The Home Range 3 bird hadn't been seen since December 2003.

The po'ouli recovery program had come to a standstill.

Rideout's finding that the dead po'ouli was geriatric sheds light on one possible cause for the disappearance of the two known wild birds. Swinnerton says:

> They were all old birds. They were banded as adults in 1997 and 1998. We don't know when they were born. The bird that died in captivity was a minimum of nine years old when it died. The other two were a minimum of eight years old when they disappeared. [For a small bird of this type] that's quite an age. There's an extremely good chance those birds were already ten, eleven, twelve years old.

While the po'ouli's body headed east for preparation and then back to Hawaii, its last living cells remained frozen at the San Diego Zoo. The cells are stored at minus 270°F, in containers bathed in liquid nitrogen vapor. They are held in large insulated tanks at the zoo's center for Conservation and Research for Endangered Species. A room containing nine such tanks, dubbed the Frozen Zoo, holds the po'ouli's genetic legacy, along with those of eight thousand other animals of six hundred different species and subspecies.

The oldest cells there were frozen forty-five to fifty years ago, according to the center's Genetics Division head, Oliver Ryder. The cells, he says, should remain viable for as long as ten thousand years, barring human error or a natural catastrophe.

With human and animal cloning in the science headlines today, it is perhaps natural to assume that the Frozen Zoo exists as kind of a high-tech Noah's Ark, conserving the DNA of extinct and endangered species so they can be resurrected through cloning in some better distant—or not-so distant—future. But when the po'ouli cells were added to the Frozen Zoo, they were the first of a potentially extinct species to join the collection. Though today the Frozen Zoo contains specimens of thirty-five to forty critically endangered species, some of which may well become extinct, "Bringing back extinct animals is not part of our mission," Ryder says.

Instead, the Frozen Zoo is a research collection whose aim is to bring knowledge gleaned from genetics to bear on preserving species in the wild. The collection exists not as a warehouse of the last remnants and last hopes of extinct species, but as a working library providing tools in the ongoing struggle to preserve those still living and help prevent extinction.

Po'ouli cells could be used to learn more about the bird in order to aid in the conservation of other Hawaiian species. Its

DNA, for example, could hold important information about malaria resistance.

As long as po'ouli cells exist, the question of cloning the bird and resurrecting it remain. Ryder acknowledges that he has fielded questions on the subject but says it's more complicated than it seems.

He bristles at the notion that having po'ouli cells somehow lessens the impact of its absence from the wild:

> There's so much we can learn about the po'ouli from its DNA, but ... there are all kinds of aspects of its biology we won't know. In no way do I want to come across as saying that having the DNA is a substitute for preventing extinction or for having a viable population. That's sort of a frustration of mine, when people say, "At least we have the cells." In some ways, I'm a celebrant of having the cells, but I'm also in the unique position to know how little that really means.

For now, at least, Ryder plans to commit his energies to preventing future extinctions, not reversing past ones. Still, he does feel a strong obligation to protect the Frozen Zoo's material for whatever uses technology may make possible in the future.

Part of the way they're doing that is by taking a lesson from computer technology and backing up their collection. Rather than keeping all the cells in one location, they grew enough to store them in two places. The main collection is at the Frozen Zoo, down the hall from Ryder's office. The other remains undisclosed.

Despite the presence of a backup, the staff is taking no chances with the main collection. The large freezers holding the specimens are thickly insulated and can keep their contents cold even if the power is cut off. The building has been built to strict earthquake codes and is stocked with food.

"Even in a hugely severe earthquake, we have a two-week window before we'd need outside assistance. Any of a half dozen people would hike in here. We'd live here and take care of the cells," Ryder says. "At the end of the day, I feel thoroughly convinced that the future will be glad we did this."

17

KNOWLEDGE AND
HOPE

THOUGH TODAY NO KNOWN PO'OULI REMAIN, THE SPECIES IS better understood than when the last one died. The captive-breeding effort provided an information bonanza. Conservation officials learned that the bird's demeanor in captivity is calm. They found that it would adapt to a diet different from what it ate in the forest and confirmed that their capture, transport, and holding techniques worked.

They also were reminded that the feather-based sexing techniques used in the 1990s were unreliable. Though Paul Baker's early observations had him convinced that the captive bird was a male, the sexing results came back female. That became the assumption until the bird was caught and blood tests showed it was male after all.

That discovery changed the characteristics of the final three-bird population. Instead of two females and a male, as previously thought, there likely were one female and two males. If known earlier, that difference wouldn't have made much of an impact on how recovery efforts were conducted. But the inaccurate test results brought up an uncomfortable third possibility, one that would fit the pattern of differential rat predation on nesting females.

"There is a very good chance we had all three males, which is why they were in discrete territories," Kirsty Swinnerton says. "That would explain why they never got together. The translocated bird was actually quite close to Home Range 2. I find it quite surprising they never actually met at some time in the nine years of their life."

Researchers also have learned more about what the po'ouli's natural range might have been, strengthening the fish-out-of-water view of rainforest po'ouli.

A 2006 study brought modern computer models to bear on the question of the po'ouli's diet. Researchers figured out how much energy it would take to live as a po'ouli in the cold, wet rainforest. They then compared that with the amount of energy a bird would get by eating snails all day.

The answer, it turns out, is not enough.

Though the birds could have scraped by at some times of the year, during the high-energy breeding season there's simply no way they could have eaten enough snails to survive. This is largely because snails require four times as much foraging effort to catch as insects. Researchers stopped the analysis when their models showed that the birds had to eat three times their body weight in snails each day to sustain themselves during breeding season.

The model ran an additional analysis, examining where the po'ouli would have to live if it truly was a snail specialist. It showed that home would have been in the more benign lowland areas of Maui—just the place where po'ouli fossil remains were found.

The finding that snails alone couldn't have sustained the po'ouli living in Hanawi confirms what has been suspected by some observing the birds' hunting behavior: that the po'ouli's dependence on snails may have been overstated.

The idea that the birds were snail specialists came from an analysis of po'ouli stomach contents, published in 1983. Paul Baldwin and Tonnie Casey examined the stomachs of the two birds shot for museum specimens, finding the remains of hundreds of snails. Though the stomachs also included insect parts and fruit, 63 percent of the contents were snail remains. That was taken as evidence that it was the lone snail specialist among its extraordinary family of birds, the Hawaiian honeycreepers.

The potential problem with the study's conclusions, as with everything concerning the po'ouli, is that it was based on so few examples. It's possible that the two young birds whose stomachs were examined on that particular day had chanced upon a snail bonanza and normally wouldn't eat as many. It may have been a good year for snails in Hanawi but not typical of most others. Though it seems certain that snails made up at least part of the average po'ouli's diet, it is difficult to be sure how much, based on just two birds.

Tonnie Casey's field notes from the 1970s provide a clue to the variety of the bird's diet. It took two years of watching the po'ouli eat grubs, berries, and insects before she noticed it eating a snail.

Thane Pratt, the U.S. Geological Survey biologist who shepherded po'ouli programs during the mid-1990s, questioned whether the birds' observed foraging behavior—prying up bark and moss on tree limbs—was indicative of a snail eater. Leaves, not limbs and bark, are prime snail habitat.

While there are questions about just how much the po'ouli depended on snails, the idea that the po'ouli ate insects too has never been debated. Even the stomachs examined in the 1980s contained insect parts and berry remnants, indicating that the po'oulis didn't live exclusively on snails.

But the questions over just how dependent the po'ouli was on snails highlights how difficult the bird was to study and how handicapped researchers were when making program decisions. Such information is critical in designing and prioritizing conservation measures. Researchers don't have to waste time counting native snails versus introduced garlic snails if a bird doesn't eat them at all, but this may be an important focus if a bird is wholly dependent on them.

But given that the po'ouli did disappear, the finding that it couldn't live where it did as a snail specialist may have hit the nail on the head. It would be no surprise, then, that a bird adapted to eating snails in warm, lowland forests would struggle when pushed uphill by disease to wet, cool rainforest, where it had to switch to insects to survive.

The question of the bird's diet illustrates a common problem when dealing with rare species: even when a researcher does make an observation, be it on diet, mating, or death, it's difficult to know whether that's what the subject usually does or just did in this one case. Science needs many observations for certainty, but observations are in short supply for rare species.

While chasing po'oulis through the forest in the early 1990s, Paul Baker observed a male po'ouli presenting nesting material to a female Maui parrotbill, causing some to wonder whether this meant that toward the end, the remaining po'oulis had lost what it meant to be a po'ouli.

That interpretation—and too much of what we know about the bird—is based on random observation rather than long-term scientific study. Maui Forest Bird Recovery Project coordinator Kirsty Swinnerton says that even the information gained through scientific study was based on a tiny remnant population. Almost by definition, that population was made up of unusual individuals. In short, we may never know what life was like for a typical po'ouli.

"These little anecdotes have been gathered over the years, and I'm not sure how to interpret them," Swinnerton says. "You're trying to deduce the ecology of a species from watching three individuals, and those three survived the longest for one reason or another. The three birds weren't typical po'ouli, because all the typical po'ouli died."

The problem is a common one when dealing with rare species. Conservation officials across the country are plagued by the necessity to make choices based on too little information. One review of how well the Endangered Species Act has worked in the past few decades said that ignorance hand-cuffs decision makers:

> The biggest gaps in our knowledge, of course, concern the biology of the species we are trying to protect. . . . To have confidence in decisions we must make, including listing decisions, jeopardy or no jeopardy determinations, recovery goals, and critical habitat designations, often requires years of data collection, modeling and analysis. Frequently, little or no research or data collection effort is expended on a species until after it is listed. Especially in the early years, therefore, both the wildlife agencies and the regulated community are working almost in the dark.

That's perhaps why so much was learned from that last, dead po'ouli. San Diego Zoo veterinarians found out that it was very old, giving us a better sense of how long po'ouli lived: somewhere between eight and twelve years. They also determined that the birds are susceptible to the fungal disease aspergillosis—no surprise—and that at least one of them had lived for some time after being infected with malaria.

They confirmed something else that the aviculturists had feared: that with a small bird about which little is known, things can go south with startling speed.

Other studies have been published since the po'ouli's disappearance. Jim Groombridge and several colleagues published data in 2006 on patterns of spatial use by the po'ouli, concluding that home range sizes fell somewhere between five and twenty-two acres. This corresponds with population density estimates in the 1970s and 1980s, when a population whose density could be estimated still existed.

Eric VanderWerf, together with Groombridge, Swinnerton, and Scott Fretz of the Hawaii Division of Forestry and Wildlife, published another paper that same year detailing the statistical methods that were used to sift through action options after the translocation failed. Those methods helped recovery officials decide to captively breed the birds and could provide guidance for others in a similar situation.

Yet another paper, published in 2005, examined the likely impact on po'ouli from aerial broadcast of rodenticide in Hanawi, providing more of the scientific underpinning that Earl Campbell had said was missing in order to truly address the problems of rats in native areas across the state. The study showed that the likelihood of po'ouli dying from eating snails that had in turn eaten poisoned rat bait was very low after one day of exposure. The risk, however, rose over time, and the authors concluded that by fourteen days, it may be significant. In areas with sensitive birds like the po'ouli, they suggested using a different poison with a lower danger of being passed along through the food chain.

Knowledge isn't the only thing that continues to be built in the wake of the po'ouli's recovery program. Hawaii's conservation infrastructure is still being strengthened. William Steiner, in his 2001 analysis of the cost in the 1990s of conserving Hawaiian birds, observed that it may be difficult to determine the success of applying research gains to conservation programs during that decade. That's because many of the period's activities involved building conservation infrastructure rather than taking species-specific action.

Land has been protected in reserves and refuges, captive-breeding facilities have been constructed and staffed, and fences, roads, and field stations have been constructed. Steiner quoted Thane Pratt as saying that Hawaii has been in an "investment phase" in its conservation programs, and that the current generation of managers, workers, and scientists has "inherited a very bad situation and has had to start from scratch to build conservation programs and do land acquisition and capital improvements."

The state government also has come a long way since 1973, with the Department of Land and Natural Resources and its Division of Forestry and Wildlife undergoing a transformation. From a traditional hook-and-bullet outfit that focused mainly on maintaining game species for the islands' hunters, it has grown, professionalized, and dramatically increased its focus on conservation of nongame species.

"I've known everyone in that agency for a long time and watched it change, for the better, over time," says University of Hawaii zoology department chair Sheila Conant.

Of course, that's not to say things are perfect there today. The traditional tension still exists between managing game—almost exclusively introduced species that have a negative impact on the native ecosystem—and nongame species.

With the po'ouli's home forest on state land, it might be said that conservation of the species became entangled in the institutional evolution as state game managers resisted being dragged into the modern age. Because of the institutional learning process, at least one observer of the recovery effort says that if the bird had lived a bit uphill, on National Park Service land in Haleakala National Park, the outcome may have been different. Cliff Smith, the University of Hawaii botany professor who headed the university-federal collaboration on po'ouli recovery says:

> Because of the likes of Brian Harry in the National Park Service taking on his superiors in San Francisco, the Park Service was ten to fifteen years ahead of everyone else in terms of conservation. Had the po'ouli been within their jurisdiction, we would possibly have a very different story. But that's how the cookie crumbles. It was not within their jurisdiction. And they were not allowed to work in areas outside their property. Had the Fish and Wildlife Service worked with the Park Service at the very beginning, it might have been—it *might* have been—a different story, but it was probably too late.

Over the decades since 1973, conservation managers employed a variety of tools in their efforts to conserve the po'ouli: they watched and counted and fenced and poisoned. They banded and netted and translocated and eventually captured the bird.

Jim Jacobi, who was there at the beginning, reflects on the recovery effort's trajectory, saying that ultimately they had no way to address all of the problems that affected the po'ouli and continue to affect Hawaiian forest birds today: "The first approach was to deal with the landscape, to deal with the bigger issues, the ungulates, and it was right on. Then we ran out of tools, and that's the problem. We can deal with ungulates, but we can't deal with predators, we can't deal with mosquitoes."

A new tool for dealing with predators may be around the corner. Earl Campbell, now of the Fish and Wildlife Service, said in mid-2007 that after a decade of work, department staff finally submitted the paperwork to the state and the U.S. Environmental Protection Agency for aerial broadcast of the rat poison diphacinone in pig-free conservation areas. They hope to begin use on a small island off Niihau and Kauai, called Lehua islet, in an attempt to clear rats from the island entirely.

Tools to fight the islands' biggest scourge of avian life, malaria, remain scarce, however. The perception of Hanawi as a refuge for native Hawaiian birds assumes that the area is mosquito- and malaria-free, but the po'ouli's necropsy illustrates that this isn't the case. Though the area is considered to be above the normal range of mosquitoes, they apparently do visit the area at least occasionally.

Carter Atkinson, an avian malaria specialist with the U.S. Geological Survey, says that knowledge about avian malaria in the area is incomplete because not much fieldwork has been done on it. Still, what work has been done indicates that the area wasn't malaria-free in 1992. A survey conducted during February and July that year sampled 122 birds from six species in Hanawi. Researchers tested the birds' blood for the presence of malaria and found that almost 12 percent of apapanes were infected, as were 2 percent of amikihis, 3 percent of Maui creepers, and perhaps most alarmingly, 20 percent of the endangered crested honeycreepers. The results also indicated that the forest was in the midst of a malaria outbreak in July, as prevalence of the disease had jumped to 9.8 percent, up from 2.9 percent in February.

The idea of malaria moving upslope is worrisome. The mountains inhabited by susceptible native birds only go so high, and if the mosquitoes move too far up, the birds will run out of forest.

That's why those working in Hawaiian conservation keep a nervous eye on the latest news about global warming. With each degree rise, the amount of turf the mosquitoes can claim as their own increases.

A study of the impact of a two-degree Celsius warming over the next hundred years presents a scary scenario for Hawaiian birds. The computer model showed the mosquito-free forest in Hanawi dropping by half. As bad as that seems, Hanawi was one of the bright spots. The same projection indicated that two other forests important to native birds would have their mosquito-free areas virtually disappear.

Changes may already be under way. A 2001–02 study of malaria in the Hakalau Forest National Wildlife Refuge, at 6,200 feet up the slopes of Mauna Kea, revealed that its prevalence had more than doubled over the previous ten years, to 5.4 percent.

But the news on the malaria front isn't all bad. After more than a century of struggling to survive with the scourge, some native Hawaiian birds seem to be making it. Despite prior studies that determined that a single bite from a malaria-infected mosquito could be deadly, surveys in 2003, 2004, and 2005 documented populations of Hawaii amakihi and apapane at low altitudes in malaria-infested forests on the Big Island of Hawaii. The 2003 and 2004 surveys found both species in areas where neither turned up during searches a decade earlier. Together, the two made up 13 percent of all birds observed, though the amakihi, much more broadly distributed, seems to be leading the way.

The 2005 biologists discovered that the bird made up between 24.5 and 51.9 percent of the local community. Moreover, after netting the birds and sampling their blood, researchers learned that between 55 and 83 percent were infected with malaria but, like the po'ouli, had developed the chronic form of the disease.

Further studies showed that malaria-infected amakihi at Hawaii Volcanoes National Park not only were living with malaria, but were raising families at a rate fast enough that the population could be growing on its own, rather than merely swelling through immigration from other populations.

Other species of native Hawaiian birds have also shown resistance to malaria, though the presence of a tolerant i'iwi or Hawaii akepa is not as significant as the entire population of malaria-resistant amakihi that seems to be taking root along the coast.

Though a great deal of progress has been made in Hawaiian bird conservation, much remains to be done. One 2001 assessment pointed out that little work has been conducted on the impact of competition between the native and alien bird species that now share the forests. Alien birds compete with native birds for food and nest sites. According to the assessment's author, they may have as great of an impact as predators such as rats, feral cats, and mongooses.

Lessons learned over the past decades—from the po'ouli and other Hawaiian birds—are helping some species with which the po'ouli shared the forest and often flocked. As the po'ouli program ground to a halt, the Maui Forest Bird Recovery Project shifted its attention to the Maui parrotbill. Recovery workers reasoned that while working with the parrotbill, they could keep their eyes peeled for po'oulis, in case the birds made a reappearance. In the meantime, they could do some good for the po'ouli's avian cousin.

The parrotbill is an insect eater with a sharply overhung upper beak used to tear up moss and bark and pry open cavities in wood to get at insects. Nicknamed the Maui can opener, parrotbills live in six-acre territories and are limited to the same part of Maui as the po'ouli was. Monogamous and with juveniles dependent on their parents for relatively long periods of time, parrotbills frequently occur in family groups. Considered endangered by the U.S. government and critically endangered by the World Conservation Union, the parrotbill population was estimated at about five hundred in 1980.

"The nice thing about the parrotbill is the population is at a size where it's very recoverable," Swinnerton says.

The Maui Forest Bird Recovery Project currently is banding and counting parrotbills. A captive-breeding program is already under way, employing the same double-clutching techniques as in recovery programs for the Mauritius kestrel, black robin, and several other Hawaiian birds. The results using this technique can be dramatic, particularly with a bird like the parrotbill, which lays only one egg each season, potentially doubling the production of new birds.

"Here is a population they are keeping track of, doing transects, counts, and point counts," Lieberman says of the parrotbill effort. "If it starts to fail, at least we'll know when the population starts to fail."

In the meantime, new parrotbills are being raised in the breeding center. The first parrotbill egg was brought in to the Maui Bird Conservation Center in 1997. That egg hatched, and the bird, a male, was raised. Two more eggs were gathered in 1999, both female. In 2000, the first breeding took place. By December 2006, the center had twelve captive parrotbills and hoped to get the captive population up to five breeding pairs.

Although those at the center now have a lot of experience with birds like these, breeding parrotbills in captivity is proving to be a challenge. "It's a tough bird to breed," Lieberman says. "There are some very easy to breed, like the puaiohi. Predictability of reproduction is always the key. The parrotbill is not very predictable."

Swinnerton agrees: "They have complex social behavior. In the wild, chicks remain with the parents and continue to be fed by them for five to eight months, a long juvenile dependency. They're quite intelligent birds, live in a complex environment, and have special feeding habits. They're probably one of the hardest species we've got."

The center is considering bringing in juvenile parrotbills in hopes that their wilderness rearing will make them better breeders in captivity, and the po'ouli capture efforts have given the staff confidence in the ability to capture juveniles and bring them in unharmed, she says.

The ultimate goal of the parrotbill breeding program is reintroduction to the wild, but not to the same forests from which the birds were taken. Parrotbills were once known to favor drier forests dominated by koa trees, though recent research shows the birds favor highly diverse forests. Establishing two separate populations of the birds will also be a hedge against a catastrophe that may strike one of them, such as a hurricane or disease outbreak.

The center plans to reintroduce the birds to a patch of forest on the leeward side of Maui, Swinnerton says. "It's dry koa-ohia forest, very different, but historically parrotbills were recorded on that side of the island. So we suspect that habitat may be more their preferred kind than this very wet forest. Clearly what we're seeing by studying the birds here is that many of the nests fail in the heavy rainstorms."

The forest, Kahikinui, covers about twelve hundred acres above five thousand feet on Haleakala's south slope. Fencing has started, and there are several protected gulches with intact pieces of the original koa forest that can provide a starting point for the work ahead.

"We were surprised how many native species are there, especially in the protected patches of forest," Swinnerton says. "It has huge potential for restoration."

As more native forests have been protected and restored in recent decades, the overall prospects for native birds have improved. Forest bird data collected over thirty years shows that in forests that are protected, bird numbers today are either stable or increasing, according to Thane Pratt. "It's the first real demonstration that we can do something on the ground for Hawaiian honeycreepers and other forest birds," he says.

Though the state's birdlife has undergone tremendous losses, Pratt says the perception that all Hawaiian birds are basket cases is wrong. He sees amakihi and apapane regularly visiting the azalea bushes outside his office. Jacobi, who works near Pratt, says that many alien plants are in Hawaii to stay, so the sight of a native bird sitting in an azalea bush is good news, showing that the birds are learning to use their new environment.

"There's a lot that can be done for Hawaiian birds," Pratt says. "It's a matter of really knuckling down and doing it."

18

A FOREST BIRD'S
ECHO

QUITE A FEW PEOPLE HAVEN'T GIVEN UP ON THE PO'OULI YET.

When asked whether they believe the bird is now extinct, the firm answer of many is maybe. Few argue that the last known population is gone, though some grumble that the bird is so hard to find that even that isn't a certainty. Given the age of the last three birds, however, there seems little doubt what the intervening years without a sighting means.

But what of unknown others?

The forests that the po'ouli called home have been extensively searched. Hundreds upon hundreds of hours have been spent looking, to no avail. Those who worked with the bird to the end acknowledge that it's certainly possible that a handful still exist, tucked away in some hidden corner. But if that is the case, they say, the birds are functionally extinct, no longer playing their role in the forests' ecosystems. And if the cause of the po'ouli's decline remains unaddressed, it may be just a matter of time until any living birds are gone as well.

Still, some aren't so sure. Stephen Mountainspring, who worked in Hanawi in the 1980s, points out that other Hawaiian birds have disappeared, to resurface years—even decades—later. The po'ouli is just about as inconspicuous as a bird can be. Not only is it brown and black in a dark forest, but its call—one of the signs to an observer that a bird is nearby—is quiet and rarely given. In his opinion, science does not have enough knowledge to know for certain whether it's extinct.

Michelle Reynolds, who headed the Hawaii Rare Bird Search, which found the last known po'ouli population, is another believer that the bird may hang on somewhere. She was amazed after they found the po'ouli family that they couldn't relocate it in the days following. They were in the same part of the forest, and they *knew* the birds were there somewhere. Reynolds says:

> We thought that there were more birds out there, considering how difficult they were to detect and the search effort required and areas we had not been able to cover. We figured there's got to be at least ten to fifteen out here. That was in 1994–95. We thought there were a lot of areas that needed additional searching to be sure the birds weren't there.

But whether there were fifteen or three, she says, the species was close to the brink of extinction. "If there's one or two out there undiscovered, it doesn't really matter, because they're functionally extinct."

That very possibility, however, highlights the importance of continuing to preserve the native Hawaiian ecosystems across the islands. If po'oulis are still out there, she says, it would be a great thing if habitat preservation efforts were helping them.

Those who continue to work in Hanawi acknowledge that the tangled surroundings could hold a few birds, but with the known ones gone, they feel their absence.

"The forest has lost something," said Eric VanderWerf of the Fish and Wildlife Service (FWS) during a 2006 trip to Hanawi. The expedition was his first back to the forest since the captive bird died. Those involved with the po'ouli had always felt an undercurrent of excitement that they might see one, he said. "That's gone now."

Maui Forest Bird Recovery Project Coordinator Kirsty Swinnerton also feels the loss, as she recalls her first po'ouli sighting. "I have fixed images of exactly what it looked like when I first saw it, coming down that hill trail. Something's disappeared from the forest. Something's gone, and it's never going to come back again."

When asked how the po'ouli story could have turned out differently, most of those involved did not want to assign blame, particularly on those who labored to save the bird near the end.

Cameron Kepler, the FWS biologist on Maui during the 1970s and 1980s, says he can't imagine how difficult it must have been trying to work with just three birds that were hard to find even when their numbers were greater. "In our day, at least there were more. They must have gone weeks without seeing or hearing anything. It's a sinking feeling when you're dealing with a bird that's that much on the edge."

If there is a lesson to be learned, most say that it's "don't wait." Conservation efforts take time to go from planning to population increases, so it's important to get started as soon as possible. The building of Hanawi's fence consumed more than a decade, and though it apparently worked wonders on the forest, it didn't reverse the po'ouli's decline.

"It wasn't too little too late, but too late," says Jim Groombridge, who headed the Maui Forest Bird Recovery Project during the 2002 translocation. "I don't think we did too little. We did everything we possibly could."

Groombridge agrees with virtually everyone else that it would have been best to get started as soon as the bird was discovered, and he thinks several opportunities to get ahead of the game were missed over the years. For example, though the sighting of the nest in 1986 was a wonderful chance to observe po'ouli nesting, some eggs or young could have been taken to start a breeding program at that time.

Thane Pratt of the U.S. Geological Survey says that if captive-breeding facilities were running in the 1970s, several bird species that have since disappeared might have been saved. But such facilities weren't built and put in place until the 1980s, at which point the species had only one or two individuals left or were extinct.

Kepler agrees that it would have been preferable to have started earlier. "It was just too late," he says, but the government was not well enough informed, focused, prepared, or even willing to begin captive breeding at that time. The climate, both biological and political, was not right until the mid-1980s, after the forest bird survey and monograph were completed.

Even near the end, some say, the outcome might have been different if the final, more intensive management actions were taken sooner.

"The reluctance to undertake more invasive management actions may stem partly from a fear of risk and partly from fear of blame in case of failure," VanderWerf and colleagues wrote in a 2006 review of po'ouli decision making. "Lack of universal support for risky actions can increase the fear of blame, resulting in no action, which ultimately may incur the most risk of all."

J. Michael Scott, who led the Hawaiian Forest Bird Survey and today is a prominent national expert on species conservation, agrees. Explaining why po'ouli captive propagation wasn't undertaken earlier, he says simply, "Because people don't like to fail."

A review of on-the-ground conservation efforts written in 2006 for an examination of the Endangered Species Act's thirtieth anniversary observed that recovery programs are sometimes held up by the slow pace of administrative actions: "In Hawaii, where conservation issues are nearly overwhelming and in need of quick action, recovery teams took over ten years to update and draft two recovery plan revisions ('alala, the Hawaiian crow, and Hawaiian forest birds) that are only now being reviewed by the public."

Paul Baker, who captured and banded the first live po'ouli, says it was the need for consensus among the many different parties involved that gummed up the process:

> I think one of the problems up there was the number of players involved in the game. It took way too long to make a consensus. When I caught the first one, if we had something in place that said, "As each one is caught, it will be brought in," we could have. Then there might have been three in captivity.

Baker thinks the time to have begun captive breeding was in the mid-1990s, after the last population was discovered and before it too began dying. "At that time, we still presumed there were five. That was the time to throw the eggs into one basket, if you're going to do it." There might have been two birds of one sex and three of the other, giving a far better chance for the species' recovery.

Some involved with the po'ouli question whether the bird was ever really recoverable, however. John Kjargaard, the leader of the initial Hana Rainforest Project expedition, thinks that with such a small range, the species was virtually extinct even then, and that the chance of its surviving was minuscule. And University of Hawaii botany professor Cliff Smith says that most now would agree that they didn't really have a chance with the bird, except maybe at the very beginning.

For such a small bird, the effort to save it had a large impact on the lives of many involved. Whatever the other problems with the recovery effort, a lack of passion didn't seem one of them. People cared a lot. And they were willing to fight over it.

"The po'ouli kind of consumed people," Alan Lieberman observes. "A lot of people just gave up on life, basically, when that bird died. A lot of people had their souls wrapped up in it, and they didn't recover." He admits that he was exhausted by the raw emotion of it all. "It's just a shame that the last one died, and a bigger shame the species died with it," he says. "Nobody should see the last of a species die."

News of the last po'ouli's death brought tears to several of those who knew it, including Baker, who says that hearing about it brought back a lot of memories, some good, some not so good. He remembered the hard work and all the unpleasant politics involved. And the loss saddened him. "We've lost something we didn't know a lot about," he says.

Veterinarians Bruce Rideout and Beth Bicknese, who were an intimate part of the bird's end, say they were shaken by their brush with extinction. Says Rideout, who has a picture of the po'ouli hanging at home:

I think about it a lot. All you have to do is look away for a period of time, and when you look back, a species like this is right at the brink of extinction. That's how fast things are changing. There's only a few of us that have seen this bird close up and appreciate its beauty and the role it played in the environment—this magnificent bird with its incredible lifestyle. There's a bit of sadness there that we lost a treasure and there's not a lot of people who knew we had it to begin with.

Bicknese calls her involvement in the experience an honor, adding, however, that it's the kind of honor she hopes doesn't come along again. "Being involved in one extinction is enough for any one vet. Hopefully the rest of my endangered animal work here will have a better outcome than this."

No one was closer to the death of the last known po'ouli than Rich Switzer, who was managing the Maui Bird Conservation Center at the time. Switzer says he was scarred by the experience. He dedicated his life to conserving endangered species but now has had a hand in losing one. In the weeks after the bird's death, he endured ribbing that he'd always be known as the guy who killed the po'ouli. He knows they were meant good-naturedly, but he had a tough time seeing the humor, after spending so much time worrying about the bird. In retrospect, he says, he now feels a tremendous sense of honor, in a humbling way, to have worked with the po'ouli and have been there to witness an extinction taking place.

Some of the others who worked with the po'ouli before the end say that the experience affected their lives. The frustration that she couldn't do more sent Reynolds back to graduate school to earn a doctorate. "I think about it all the time," she says. "It's a great, great tragedy, and it definitely influenced the path my career took. This is part of the United States, and a bird went extinct and it didn't get any attention. There's lots of other species that we can do something about, but extinction isn't something that's happening in the future, it's happening right now."

Kepler, who left Hawaii in 1987 to work on Kirtland's warbler recovery in Michigan, says it was a relief to watch the warbler's numbers climb from 167 breeding pairs to 1,400. "After Hawaii, it was wonderful to work on a bird that actually responded to management." Besides the po'ouli, he had also worked with the Kauai 'o'o. "On my last trip in," he says, "I heard the male singing off in the mist . . . that disembodied voice floating. Then it's gone. It's crushing."

Tonnie Casey, the po'ouli's codescriber and one of the first people ever to see the bird, left Hawaii for Missouri in 2005 after decades of fighting conservation battles on the islands. She needed a change of pace and left, taking her small herd of horses with her. "I feel a bit like I deserted the po'ouli cause, though, so I'll try to get back to something close to it," she says. "The last bit was very frustrating for me, to get people to do something to conserve the species." She reflects on the species' demise: "It's a really harsh thing. I wasn't ever thinking about them not being there."

Those who continue to fight extinction on the Hawaiian Islands admit that their optimism and pessimism sometimes battle for supremacy.

"I am not optimistic that we can halt or even correct the decline and extinction of many of our remaining endemic forest birds. However, I do think that we know better what to do, and we know we have to act quickly," says University of Hawaii zoology department chair Sheila Conant. "Hawaii is my home. I love the plants and animals. I love the birds. There are still a lot of birds out there. I should stop every now and then and just enjoy these things I've been trying to conserve."

Those working on the islands keep up their optimism by looking at the victories and continuing to move ahead, Kepler says. Instead of letting their sadness over the po'ouli immobilize them, they dedicate themselves to helping other species such as the endangered crested honeycreeper, which shares the forests of Hanawi with the Maui parrotbill. They hope that the birds' greater numbers, coupled with habitat management, will help it—like the apapane and the amakihi—one day develop resistance to disease and have a more secure future. One goal is to save a remnant of the original ecosystem, Kepler says. "It was a wonderful one, with all kinds of flightless geese and flightless ibises and rails running around. It must have just been awesome." And good things are happening too. "Instead of being depressed about the status of crows and po'ouli, you have to look at the successes and glory in the silversword comeback."

Part of the optimism that some feel comes because of the lessons learned through the po'ouli and other Hawaiian bird programs that can be used to save others.

"I think we're making good advances," Jim Groombridge says. "Any mistakes along the way were being made as we moved forward. It's a wonderful place to test our ability to deal with extinctions and endangered species. I think we can apply what we've learned."

Perhaps optimism should be one of the job requirements, because it doesn't look to be getting easier any time soon. Intractable problems of malaria and rat infestations remain, not to mention unknown impacts of alien snails and insects. Conservation workers also toil under the constant threat of devastating new invasions, such as that of the brown tree snake in Guam, which decimated that island's bird population. In some ways, conservation in the state is a never-ending rear-guard action, defending the native against the foreign with the aim of giving Hawaiian species as much time as possible to adjust to a new blended reality.

Jim Jacobi, who's seen his share of extinctions, says the real shame will come if the lessons hard learned aren't applied and relatively common Hawaiian species disappear. Though people can look at pictures and hear what the birds were like, they'll never be able to experience the ones that have gone extinct. "It kind of chokes me up even now, quite honestly," he says. "I don't want to get into a situation where my grandkids say, 'You actually saw an 'i'iwi?'"

Despite its bitter ending, Jacobi's experience with the beginning of the po'ouli's story has fueled him with optimism and a belief that something unexpected may always lie ahead.

"Keep your eyes and ears open," he says. "I tend to be one of the optimists who feel we may still see another."

ENDNOTES

CHAPTER 1

3   They had returned to the forest: News release, Sept. 10, 2004, "Po'ouli Brought to Breeding Center in 'Last Ditch' Effort to Save Species," U.S. Fish and Wildlife Service, Hawaii Department of Land and Natural Resources, Zoological Society of San Diego.

3   A small brown and gray forest bird: Ibid.

3   The last known po'ouli breeding: Draft, "Po'ouli Five Year Recovery Work Plan," Po'ouli Working Group and Hawaiian Forest Bird Recovery Team.
    Alan Lieberman et al., "Capture and Captive Management of the Po'ouli (*Melamprosops phaeosoma*)," Hawaii Conservation Conference, 2005.

6   "When we see po'ouli": Kirsty Swinnerton, e-mail to Marilet Zablan, Sept. 13, 2004.

9   In 2002, birds thought to be: Trent Malcolm, e-mail to Amber James, Mar. 26, 2003.

9   When queried about the inconsistent: A. James, e-mail to T. Malcolm, Apr. 3, 2003.

10   It made such a stir: A. Lieberman, e-mail to Scott Fretz, Paul Conry, M. Zablan, Gina Schultz, and Eric VanderWerf, Sept. 10, 2004.

11   Lieberman began to play defense: A. Lieberman, e-mail to S. Fretz and E. VanderWerf, Sept. 9, 2004.

11   In a press release issued: News release, "'Last Ditch' Effort."

11   Its initial howdy cage: A. Lieberman, e-mail to S. Fretz and M. Zablan, Sept. 10, 2004.

12   When they noticed it wasn't visiting: Lieberman, "Captive Management."

12   For the next several weeks: Hawaii Endangered Bird Conservation Program, "Report #50 FWS-FY'04: Weekly Activities Report for the week ending 19 September 2004."

12   It completed its thirty-day quarantine: HEBCP, "Report #1 FWS-FY'05: Weekly Activities Report for the week ending 10 October 2004."

12   Blood was drawn for sexing: HEBCP, "Report #52 FWS-FY'04: Weekly Activities Report for the week ending 3 October 2004."

12   "Our hopes are for a long life": A. Lieberman, weblog to San Diego Zoo, "The Rarest Bird in the World," Oct. 2, 2004.

13   When that work was done: K. Swinnerton, e-mail to M. Zablan, Sept. 13, 2004.

14   "We have continued to look": K. Swinnerton, e-mail to A. Lieberman, Oct. 1, 2004.

15   With field crews searching: HEBCP, "Report #4 FWS-FY'05: Weekly Activities Report for the week ending 31 October 2004."

15   They immediately moved: HEBCP, "Report #5 FWS-FY'05: Weekly Activities Report for the week ending 7 November 2004."

16   The staff took a blood sample: HEBCP, "Report #6, FWS-FY '06: Weekly Activities Report for the week ending 14 November 2004."

CHAPTER 2

19   Their bird—thought for years: Leona Chemnick, memo to A. Lieberman, "Gender Determination in Po'ouli," Nov. 15, 2004.

22   "I would suspect that po'ouli": E. VanderWerf, e-mail to A. Lieberman, Nov. 18, 2004.

23   If that was the case: A. Lieberman, e-mail to E. VanderWerf, Nov. 18, 2004.

23   The fact that the bird: Carter Atkinson, e-mail to A. Lieberman, Nov. 19, 2004.

CHAPTER 3

30   Taking advantage of a National: John Kjargaard, ed., "Scientific Report of the Waihoi Valley Project," University of Hawaii, 1972.
     David R. Zimmerman, "Hawaii's New Honeycreeper," *National Parks and Conservation Magazine* (January 1976): 16–17.

31   A few islands away: U.S. Department of Commerce, "Highest Average Annual Precipitation Extremes," National Climatic Data Center. Online at www.ncdc.noaa.gov.

31   Davis set off first: Kjargaard, "Waihoi Valley," 1972.

34   Casey noted that the trees: Tonnie Casey, "Preliminary Report on the Bird Life in Waihoi Valley" in "Scientific Report of the Waihoi Valley Project," University of Hawaii, 1972.

34   By the trip's end: Casey, "Bird Life in Waihoi Valley."

35   One extraordinary day: Harry Whitten, "Our Environment: World's Wettest Spot?" *Honolulu Star-Bulletin* (December 8, 1973).

38   The weather refused: J. Kjargaard, e-mail to author, Oct. 25, 2006.

38   They kept a round-the-clock: Alvin Yoshinaga, e-mail to author, Oct. 2, 2006.

42   They found fifteen-foot-tall: Whitten, "World's Wettest Spot?"

42   They observed at least four: USFWS, "Threatened and Endangered Animals in the Hawaiian Islands." Online at www.fws.gov.
     H. Whitten, "Our Environment: Rewarding Hana Expedition," *Honolulu Star-Bulletin* (September 15, 1973).

CHAPTER 4

45   The bird flew off: Zimmerman, "New Honeycreeper," 16–17.

46   The birds appeared to be: Marguerite Rho, "Po'ouli Bird Calls Maui Home," *Maui Today* (January 1975): 6–7.

46   "It seemed to know exactly": Ibid.

47   They were quieter: "In Rain Forest: Unique Bird is Found on Maui," *The Maui News* (December 29, 1973): A1.

47   One, Andrew Berger: Jim Jacobi, interview with author, Aug. 18, 2006.

48   They planned to send two: T. Casey, letter to Dean Amadon, Sept. 5, 1973.

48   The last new bird discovery: H. Whitten, "New Species of Bird Found on Haleakala," *Honolulu Star-Bulletin* (December 28, 1973).

49   In a note attached: D. Amadon, note to Les Short and Walter Bock, Sept. 25, 1973.

49   "The bird is remarkable": D. Amadon, letter to T. Casey, Nov. 2, 1973.

49   Casey wrote back: T. Casey, letter to D. Amadon, Nov. 16, 1973.

49   Amadon called the find: D. Amadon, letter to T. Casey, Nov. 2, 1973.

50   "The discovery is quite": "New Species of Bird, First in a Decade," *Science News* 105 (1974): 22.

50   Despite his initial skepticism: Andrew Berger, letter to W. Bock, Dec. 5, 1973.

50   She went on to detail: T. Casey, letter to D. Amadon, Oct. 9, 1973.

50   An article in the *Honolulu*: H. Whitten, "New Species."

50   The discovery is an exciting: "New Honeycreeper Bird is Found in Hawaiian Forest," *The New York Times* (January 6, 1974): 55.

CHAPTER 5

55   Then come Kauai: Alan C. Ziegler, *Hawaiian Natural History, Ecology, and Evolution* (Honolulu: University of Hawai'i Press, 2002).

55   Formed by the same Hawaiian: Ibid.

55   And curving to the north: Ziegler, *Hawaiian Natural History*.

55   Despite the distance: Ibid.

56   Although Maui is just: Ibid.

56   The coral reef at Midway: Ibid.

56   There were no other: Ibid.

58   The only existing native: Ibid.

59   Even on smooth: Donald R. Drake, "Seed Dispersal of *Metrosideros Polymorpha (Myrtaceae)*: A Pioneer Tree of Hawaiian Lava Flows," *American Journal of Botany* 79, no. 11 (1992): 1224–1228.

59   On 'a'a lava: D. R. Drake and Dieter Mueller-Dombois, "Population Development of Rain Forest Trees on a Chronosequence of Hawaiian Lava Flows," *Ecology* 74, no. 4 (1993): 1012–1019.

59   Studies have shown: Drake, "Seed Dispersal," 1224–1228.

59   Still, the study indicated: Ibid., 1227.

59   Their nets revealed: Ziegler, *Hawaiian Natural History*.

60   Snails, on the other hand: Ibid.

60   With so many species: Ibid.

60   Much of that diversity: Ibid.

60   Whereas similar snails: Ibid.

CHAPTER 6

63   Scientists believe those finchlike: Ziegler, *Hawaiian Natural History.* H. Douglas Pratt, *The Hawaiian Honeycreepers* (Oxford: Oxford University Press, 2005).

64   At that time, the two: Ibid

64   Eventually, those wind-borne finches: Fifty-one honeycreeper species were detailed in H. D. Pratt's *Hawaiian Honeycreepers.* Another four fossil honeycreepers have recently been discovered. Sheila Conant, e-mail to author, Oct. 3, 2007.
T. Pratt, note to author, Sept. 17, 2007.

64   The group's diversity would: Ziegler, *Hawaiian Natural History.* Pratt, *Hawaiian Honeycreepers.*

64   Some began to take advantage: Ibid.

64   Those birds' bills eventually: Ziegler, *Hawaiian Natural History.*

64   Others evolved long: Pratt, *Hawaiian Honeycreepers.*

66   He wrote in 1992: H. D. Pratt, "Is the Poo-uli a Hawaiian Honeycreeper (*Drepanidinae*)?" *The Condor* 94 (1992): 173.

66   He pointed out that: Ibid.

66   "The Poo-uli does not": Ibid.

66   An examination of mitochondrial: Robert C. Fleischer et al., "Phylogenetic Placement of the Po'ouli, *Melamprosops phaeosoma,* Based on Mitochondrial DNA Sequence and Osteological Characters," *Studies in Avian Biology 22* (Lawrence, KS: Allen Press, Inc., 2001).

66   The po'ouli, they explained: Ibid.

67   "The Po'ouli has had a long": Ibid., 103.

67   One-third of the known: Pratt, *Hawaiian Honeycreepers.*

67   Of the remaining eight: The Kauai creeper and 'akeke'e suffered population crashes. S. Conant, e-mail to author, Oct. 3, 2007.

68   Despite modern conservation: Pratt, *Hawaiian Honeycreepers.*

69   The nene program: Paul C. Banko et al., "Conservation Status and Recovery Strategies for Endemic Hawaiian Birds," *Studies in Avian Biology 22* (Lawrence, KS: Allen Press, Inc., 2001).

69   Hawaiian honeycreepers involved: Cyndi Kuehler et al., "Restoration Techniques for Hawaiian Forest Birds: Collection of Eggs, Artificial Incubation and Hand-rearing of Chicks, and Release to the Wild," *Studies in Avian Biology 22* (Lawrence, KS: Allen Press, Inc., 2001).

69   Dependent on the seeds: P. Banko et al., "Palila *(Loxioides bailleui).*" Online at bna.birds.cornell.edu.

70   It was down to sixteen hundred: J. O. Juvik and S. P. Juvik, "Mauna Kea and the Myth of Multiple Use: Endangered Species and Mountain Management in Hawaii," *Mountain Research and Development* 4, no. 3 (1984): 191–202.

70   The mamane on which: Ibid., 195–196.

70   The state drafted: Ibid., 198.

70   The court found the state: Ibid., 199.

70   Some say the case: Ibid., 201.

70   Though the palila prefer: Banko, "Palila."

70   Unlike the case of: Ibid.

CHAPTER 7

74 By 1986, much: Stephen Mountainspring et al., "Ecology, Behavior, and Conservation of the Poo-uli (*Melamprosops phaeosoma*)," *Wilson Bulletin* 102, no. 1 (1990): 109–122.

74 From initial estimates: Paul E. Baker, "Status and Distribution of the Po'ouli in the Hanawi Natural Area Reserve Between December 1995 and June 1997," *Studies in Avian Biology* 22 (Lawrence, KS: Allen Press, Inc., 2001).

74 Though no estimates exist: Andrew Engilis Jr., "Field Notes on Native Forest Birds in the Hanawi Natural Area Reserve, Maui" *Elepaio* 50, no. 8 (1990): 67–72.

74 Pigs, rats, and bureaucratic: Edward O. Wilson, *The Future of Life* (New York: Alfred A. Knopf, 2002).

74 But fossil finds indicate: J. Michael Scott et al., "Forest Bird Communities of the Hawaiian Islands: Their Dynamics, Ecology, and Conservation," *Studies in Avian Biology* 9 (Lawrence, KS: Allen Press, Inc., 1986). Mountainspring, "Conservation of the Poo-uli," 109–122.

77 On April Fool's Day: Cameron B. Kepler et al., "Nesting Behavior of the Poo-uli," *Wilson Bulletin* 108, no. 4 (1996): 620–638.

79 That soggy field team's: Mountainspring, "Conservation of the Poo-uli," 109–122.

81 In the water: Richard E. Warner, "The Role of Introduced Diseases in the Extinction of the Endemic Hawaiian Avifauna," *The Condor* 70 (1968): 101–120.

82 "Dr. Judd was called": Ibid., 104.

82 One study in 1959: Ibid., 114.

83 Farther south, in the Incan: Jared Diamond, "The Arrow of Disease," *Discover* 13, no. 10 (1992): 64–73.

83 Others think it arrived: Charles van Riper III, Sandra G. van Riper, and Wallace R. Hansen, "Epizootiology and Effect of Avian Pox on Hawaiian Forest Birds," *The Auk* 119, no. 4 (2002): 930.

83 Recent research shows: Deoki N. Tripathy et al., "Characterization of Poxviruses from Forest Birds in Hawaii," *Journal of Wildlife Diseases* 36, no. 2 (2000): 225.

84 R. C. L. Perkins in 1903: Warner, "Introduced Diseases," 106.

84 As one researcher, Richard Warner: Ibid., 106.

85 Even more suspicious: Ibid., 102.

85 The birds gradually weakened: Ibid., 108.

86 In 1902, an observer: Ibid., 106.

86 "I am convinced that the mass": Ibid., 107.

87 An examination of the birds': Ibid., 110.

87 After nine days: Ibid., 112.

88 Two other native bird: Susan I. Jarvi et al., "Immunogenetics and Resistance to Avian Malaria in Hawaiian Honeycreepers (*Drepanidinae*)," *Studies in Avian Biology* 22 (Lawrence, KS: Allen Press, Inc., 2001).

89 This elevation coincided: Warner, "Introduced Diseases," 115.

89 Their most hopeful finding: C. van Riper III et al., "The Epizootiology and Ecological Significance of Malaria in Hawaiian Land Birds," *Ecological Monographs* 56, no. 4 (1986): 327–344.

CHAPTER 8

92 The fossil evidence: Storrs L. Olson and Helen F. James, "Fossil Birds from the Hawaiian Islands: Evidence for Wholesale Extinction by Man Before Western Contact," *Science* 217 (1982): 633–635.

93 "Unquestionably, its humorous": Paul H. Baldwin, "The Fate of the Laysan Rail," *Audubon Magazine* 47 (1945): 343–348.

93 In June 1944: Ibid.

94 "But two short years ago": I. A. E. Atkinson, "A Reassessment of Factors, Particularly *Rattus Rattus L.,* that Influenced the Decline of Endemic Forest Birds in the Hawaiian Islands," *Pacific Science* 32, no. 2 (1977): 109–133.

94 The decline was so mysterious: Ibid.

95 On Maui, the seminal event: Ibid.

95 Observers at the time: Ibid., 125.

96 "Why the Ou should have": Ibid., 124.

96 Studies in the Hanawi: R. T. Sugihara, "Abundance and Diets of Rats in Two Native Hawaiian Forests," *Pacific Science* 51, no. 22 (1997): 189–198.

97 In those studies researchers: Ibid., 194.

97 Though the examination: P. H. Baldwin and T. Casey, "A Preliminary List of Foods of the Po'o-uli," *Elepaio* 43, no. 7 (1983): 53–56.

97 "The agencies now threatening": Atkinson, "Endemic Forest Birds," 125.

98 "We suspect that only": Michael G. Hadfield, Stephen E. Miller, and Anne H. Carwile, "The Decimation of Endemic Hawaiian Tree Snails by Alien Predators," *American Zoologist* (1993): 610–622.

98 With a vast array of colors: Robert H. Cowie, "Patterns of Introduction of Non-indigenous Non-marine Snails and Slugs in the Hawaiian Islands," *Biodiversity and Conservation* 7 (1998): 349–368.

98 And in freshwater streams: Ibid.

99 Looking to add some extra: Albert R. Mead, *The Giant African Snail: A Problem in Economic Malacology* (Chicago, University of Chicago Press, 1961).

99 Another group of the same: Ibid.

99 At least some from: N. L. H. Krauss, "Investigations on Biological Control of Giant African (*Achatina fulica*) and other Land Snails," *Nautilus* 78, no. 1 (1964): 21–27.

99 One snail expert: Cowie, "Patterns of Introduction," 349–368.

100 Ironically, the giant African: Ibid., 362.

101 The garlic snail is thought: Ibid., 357.

101 But by the time it was: C. M. J. Cooke and H. B. Baker, "*Oxychilus Allarium* (Miller) in Hawaii," *Nautilus* 61, no. 1 (1947): 36.

101 "Endemic snails remained": M. Severns, "Another Threat to Hawaii's Endemics," *Hawaiian Shell News* 32, no. 12 (1984): 1, 9.

102 A 1990 report: Mountainspring, "Conservation of the Poo-uli," 109–122.

103 They reported a 473 percent: Ibid., 118.

103 Perhaps more importantly: S. Mountainspring, "An Ecological Model of the Effects of Exotic Factors on Limiting Hawaiian Honeycreeper Populations," *Ohio Journal of Science* 86, no. 3 (1986): 95–100.

104   Cook released the first: C. P. Stone, "Feral Pig (*Sus scrofa*) Research and Management in Hawaii," *Biology of Suidae* (Edmonton, Canada: IRGM, 1985).

104   When the pigs were eliminated: Ivan P.Vtorov, "Feral Pig Removal: Effects on Soil Microarthropods in a Hawaiian Rain Forest," *Journal of Wildlife Management* 57, no. 4 (1993): 875–880.

CHAPTER 9

105   "The Poʻo Uli has the most": Winston E. Banko, "Part 1. Population Histories—Species Accounts: Forest Birds: ʻAmakihi, Creeper, ʻAkepa & Poʻo Uli," *Avian History Reports (AHR) A Historical Synthesis of Recent Endemic Hawaiian Birds (1979–1990)* 8 (1984): 255.

106   Banko had missed: S. Conant, "Recent Observations of Endangered Birds in Hawaii's National Parks," *Elepaio* 41, no. 7 (1981): 55–61.

107   So little was known: C. B. Kepler, telephone interview with author, Feb. 20, 2007.

107   In the months after: "New Honeycreeper," 55.

108   In January 1974: T. Casey, letter to D. Amadon, Jan. 18, 1974.

108   Members of the Hana: Yoshinaga, e-mail, Oct. 2, 2006.

108   In November, Casey's: A. Berger, letter to D. Amadon, Jan. 14, 1974.

108   Jacobi led a trip: T. Casey, letter to D. Amadon, Mar. 14, 1974.

108   Casey led trips in April: Yoshinaga, e-mail, Oct. 2, 2006.

108   "This last trip was": T. Casey, letter to D. Amadon, Sept. 3, 1974.

108   Berger described his: A. Berger, letter to W. Bock, Dec. 5, 1973.

109   Casey and Jacobi toiled: T. Casey and J. Jacobi, "A New Genus and Species of Bird from the Island of Maui, Hawaii (*Passeriformes: Drepanididae*), *Occasional Papers of the Bernice P. Bishop Museum* 24, no. 12 (1974): 215–226.

109   "*Melamprosops* appears to feed": Ibid., 222–223.

110   The article recommended: Ibid., 224.

110   Five months later: Lynn A. Greenwalt, "Listing of Endangered and Threatened Species," *USFWS Federal Register* 40 (1975): 44149–44151.

110   In listing the bird: Ibid.

110   In 1978, Walter Bock: W. Bock, "Tongue Morphology and Affinities of the Hawaiian Honeycreeper *Melamprosops phaeosoma*," Ibis 120, no. 4 (1978): 467–478.

111   His friend had wanted: David Woodside, telephone interview with author, Mar. 21, 2007.

113   About a third of the territory: Scott, "Forest Bird Communities," 5.

113   The survey was larger: Ibid., 33.

114   "Despite earlier studies": Ibid., 4.

115   Carrying all their gear: Ibid., 37.

115   "It's like there was": S. Mountainspring, telephone interview with author, Apr. 9, 2007.

116   Work on Maui was conducted: Scott, "Forest Bird Communities," 37.

116   Observers clambering around: USFWS, "Maui-Molokai Forest Birds Recovery Plan," *USFWS* 110 (1984): 16.
        Scott, "Forest Bird Communities," 68.

116   "We got to Maui": C. B. Kepler, telephone interview with author, Feb. 15, 2007.

116   Because of the low number: Scott, "Forest Bird Communities," 183.

116   Together, the estimates: C. B. Kepler, memo to Peter Stine, Apr. 1, 1985. Mountainspring, "Conservation of the Poo-uli," 109–122.

116   Densities for the bird: Ibid.

116   Over time, Mountainspring says: Mountainspring, interview, Apr. 9, 2007.

117   And the pigs' wallowing: Casey, "New Genus," 183.

118   The plan said that: USFWS, "Maui-Molokai," 5.

118   "It is clear that": Ibid., 44.

118   Once the fences were up: Ibid., 35.

CHAPTER 10

122   Within seventy-two years: James K. Baker and Donald W. Reeser, *Goat Management Problems in Hawaii Volcanoes National Park: A History Analysis and Management Plan* (Washington D.C.: National Park Service, 1972).

122   "In less than 200 years": Ibid.

122   At Hawaii Volcanoes, goat: D. W. Reeser, "Establishment of the Resources Management Division, Hawaii Volcanoes National Park" (paper presented at the Partners in Stewardship Seventh Conference on Research and Resource Management in Parks and on Public Lands, 1992).

123   "Drives and hunts were": Ibid.

123   They ate saplings: Baker, *Goat Management*.

123   As in some horror movie: Ibid.

124   The most famous exclosure: Ibid.

125   Once the goat browsing: Ibid.

125   When Morris left: Reeser, "Hawaii Volcanoes."

125   Sport hunting was not allowed: Ibid.

125   Finally National Park Service: Ibid.

125   Instead of fulfilling: D. W. Reeser, telephone interview with author, Mar. 19, 2007.

126   "You were either going": Ibid.

126   Then, in an effort: Reeser, "Hawaii Volcanoes."

127   When they set about clearing: Ibid.

CHAPTER 11

131   Pig damage in the forest: Kepler, memo to Stine, Apr. 1, 1985.

133   On October 31: Deputy Project Leader, FWS, Honolulu, meeting minutes, Oct. 31, 1985.

134   Lee also revealed another: Ernest Kosaka, telephone record, Jan. 8, 1986.

134   Lee chastised Cameron Kepler: E. Kosaka, telephone record, Jan. 7, 1986.

136   The state had no money: Allan Marmelstein, memo to Assistant Regional Director for Federal Assistance, Portland, Apr. 24, 1985.

137   Kepler was leaving: Hugo Huntsinger, memo to USFWS Pacific Area Direction, Sept. 2, 1986.

145   "Our belief is that fence": Cliff Smith, "Status Report on Hanawi NAR Fencing Programme Maui," Cooperative National Parks Resources Unit, University of Hawaii (1993): 6.

CHAPTER 12

147   The sighting report noted: Engilis, "Native Forest Birds," 71.

148   Rather than rejoicing: Ibid.

148   In 1991 no birds: Baker, "Distribution of the Poʻouli," 145.

148   Smith had spent years: Robert Smith, e-mail to author, Sept. 25, 2007.

148   Together, those factors: Karen Rosa, telephone interview with author, Oct. 2, 2007.

148   The Honolulu office: Ibid.

149   "As recently as three weeks": Ronald L. Walker, "Implementation of the Endangered Species Act for Native Hawaiian Wildlife and Plants" (Hearing before the Ad Hoc Subcommittee on Consumer and Environmental Affairs, U. S. Committee on Governmental Affairs, One Hundred Second Congress, 1992).

150   When other members: Rebecca L. Camm, e-mail to author, Jun. 20, 2007.

150   Birds with vanishingly small: Draft, "Breeding Behavior and Population Ecology of 'Akohekoe and Maui Parrotbill in Rainforests on the Windward Slope of Haleakala Volcano, Maui," USFWS (Aug. 30, 1993): 3.

151   "Betsy Gagné, Tonnie Casey": K. Rosa, telephone record, Sept. 13, 1993.

151   "Unsuccessful efforts to locate": William Evanson, "Status Report on RCUH Project #8497 Feral Pig Removal, Hanawi Natural Area Reserve, Maui," Department of Land and Natural Resources, Division of Forestry and Wildlife (1994): 4.

151   The research project focused: Baker, "Distribution of the Poʻouli," 144.

152   Some of the lost birds: J. K. Lepson and S. M. Johnston, "Greater ʻAkiaola (*Hemignathus*) and Lesser ʻAkiaola (*Hemignathus obscurus*)," *The Birds of North America* No. 512 (2000).

153   The greater ʻakiaola: Michelle H. Reynolds and Thomas J. Snetsinger, "The Hawaii Rare Bird Search 1994–1996," *Studies in Avian Biology 22* (Lawrence, KS: Allen Press, Inc., 2001).

157   All together, the Rare Bird: Ibid., 140.

157   Adding the poʻouli: T. Pratt, "Poʻo-uli Contingency Plan," *National Biological Survey* (Sept. 8, 1995).

158   He was concerned enough: T. Pratt, "Poʻo-uli and the Birding Community," memo to Hawaii Forest Bird Recovery Team, Sept. 16, 1994.

158   Within a month, Fish: K. Rosa, "Poʻouli and Nukupuʻu," memo to J. M. Scott and Scott Derrickson, Oct. 26, 1994.

158   "Now that these extremely": K. Rosa, "A New Chance to Save Maui's Rarest of the Rare," note to Mark White, Nov. 25, 1994.

159   The following summer: T. Pratt, letter to Maui Forest Bird Cooperator, Aug. 16, 1995.

160   Over the next nineteen: Baker, "Distribution of the Poʻouli," 147.

160   In October, Baker reported: T. Pratt, letter to Maui Forest Bird Cooperator, Oct. 31, 1996.

160   Home Range 4 was: Baker, "Distribution of the Po'ouli," 148.
161   "On 15 January 1997": P. Baker, "A Description of the First Live Po'ouli Captured," *Wilson Bulletin* 110, no. 3 (1998): 307–310.
162   "Given a fairly sedentary": Baker, "Distribution of the Po'ouli," 149.
162   In 1996, Hanawi's: Ibid., 145.
163   A 1985–86 study: Meeting minutes for "Maui Forest Bird Project," Sept. 1, 1995.
164   The two told him: W. Evanson and Fern Duvall, "Update on Rodent Management at Hanawi NAR Based on Meeting with Dr. Paul Baker about Current Field Conditions," memo to Paul Conroy, Oct. 7, 1996.
165   In response, Baker scaled: Ibid.
165   "Some individuals are concerned": R. Smith, letter to Michael Buck, Oct. 21, 1996.
166   Though most believed that aerial: Earl Campbell, telephone interview with author, Jun. 20, 2007.

CHAPTER 13
170   He'd also worked with: BirdLife International, "*Leucospar rothschildi*," *2006 IUCN Red List of Threatened Species* (2006).
171   He wanted to use supplemental: Mark Collins, memo to Maui Forest Bird Recovery Partners, Jul. 23, 1997.
173   By January 1998: Po'ouli Partnership meeting, minutes, Feb. 18, 1998.
173   They had to step up: Ibid.
173   With no sign of another: News release, Apr. 30, 1998, "Conservation Biologists Determine Sex of Endangered Bird: It's a Boy!" Hawaii DLNR.
174   "For the Po'ouli": Ibid.
174   Though Buck's letter: M. Buck, letter to K. Rosa, Apr. 16, 1998.
175   More personally, he then: Po'ouli Recovery informational meeting, minutes, Apr. 27, 1998.
175   Because of its uniqueness: Ibid.
176   They also agreed to look: M. Buck, letter to po'ouli recovery meeting participants, May 18, 1998.
180   "The Peregrine Fund": R. Smith, e-mail to author, Sept. 25, 2007.
180   Lieberman responded to such: Patricia Tummons, "Peregrine Fund Says it Won't Accept Po'ouli at its Facilities," *Environment Hawaii* 9, no. 5 (1998).
180   With The Peregrine Fund unwilling: Ibid.
183   With the variable weather: Jim J. Groombridge et al., "Evaluating Stress in a Hawaiian Honeycreeper, *Paroreomyza montana*, Following Translocation," *Journal of Field Ornithology* 75, no. 2 (2004): 183–187.
184   Researchers examined the blood: Ibid., 185–186.
184   Eleven of the eighteen: Ibid., 185.
184   Creepers and po'ouli: Groombridge, "Evaluating Stress," 186.
184   And the researchers hoped: Groombridge, "Attempt to Recover," 365–375.
184   Eighteen birds had been: J. Groombridge et al., "An Attempt to Recover the Po'ouli by Translocation and an Appraisal of Recovery Strategy for Bird Species of Extreme Rarity," *Biological Conservation* 118, no. 3 (2004): 365–375.

184 They secured permits: E. VanderWerf et al., "Update on Recovery Efforts for the Po'ouli," *Elepaio* 63, no. 4 (2003): 27.

185 This would allow: Groombridge, "Attempt to Recover," 365–375.

185 They had a veterinarian: David N. Phalen and J. Groombridge, "Field Research in Hanawi: A Story about Working with the World's Most Endangered Bird," *Journal of Avian Medicine and Surgery* 17, no. 1 (2003): 39–42.

185 They had anesthesia: Groombridge, "Attempt to Recover," 365–375.

185 If the worst happened: Ibid.

185 They spotted him repeatedly: Ibid.

186 "The next day began": Phalen, "Field Research in Hanawi," 41.

187 She was spotted twenty-one: Groombridge, "Attempt to Recover," 365–375.

187 On June 25, 2002: VanderWerf, "Recovery Efforts," 27.

187 With some reluctance: Ibid., 28.

187 In January 2003: Ibid.

CHAPTER 14

189 The dried skin still bore: Mary Anne Andrei, "The Accidental Conservationist: William T. Hornaday, the Smithsonian Bison Expeditions and the US National Zoo," *Endeavour,* 29, no. 3 (2005): 109–113.

190 He wanted to create: Ibid., 100.

190 By the end of the year: Ibid., 111.

190 That endeavor in turn: Ibid., 112–113.

190 If possible extinctions: Jonathan E. M. Baillie, Craig Hilton-Taylor, and Simon N. Stuart, *2004 IUCN Red List of Threatened Species: A Global Species Assessment* (Cambridge, UK: IUCN Publications Services Unit, 2004).

191 The last two decades: Ibid.

191 Known only by their scientific: The World Conservation Union, *2006 IUCN Red List of Threatened Species,* 2006.

191 Some scientists say: Michael J. Novacek and Elsa E. Cleland, "The Current Biodiversity Extinction Event: Scenarios for Mitigation and Recovery," *Proceedings of the National Academy of Sciences* 98, no. 10 (2001): 5466–5470.

191 The World Conservation Union: The World Conservation Union, *2006 IUCN Red List of Threatened Species*, 2006.

192 The toad hasn't been: Baillie, 2004 *IUCN Red List*.

192 As many as 122: The World Conservation Union, "Global Amphibian Assessment," IUCN fact sheet, 2004.

192 Rays eat clams: Ransom A. Myers et al., "Cascading Effects of the Loss of Apex Predatory Sharks from a Coastal Ocean," *Science* 315 (2007): 1846–1850.

193 The beginnings of such: Marsha Walton, "Audubon: Common Backyard Birds Becoming Less Common." Online at www.cnn.com.

194 The species bred well: Carsten Rahbek, "Captive Breeding—A Useful Tool in the Preservation of Biodiversity?" *Biodiversity and Conservation* 2 (1993): 426–437.

194   Today there are fifteen hundred: Phoenix Zoo, "Arabian Oryx." Online at
      www.phoenixzoo.org.

194   The oryx is the first: Rahbek, "Captive Breeding," 428.

194   At about the time: Tom J. Cade and Carl G. Jones, "Progress in Restora-
      tion of the Mauritius Kestrel," *Conservation Biology* 7, no. 1 (1993):
      169–175.

194   By 1974, the Mauritius: Ibid., 170.

195   The artificially hatched: C. G. Jones et al., "The Restoration of the Mauri-
      tius *Falco punctatus* Population," Ibis 137 (1993): S173–S180.

195   Luckily, pesticide bans: Cade, "Progress in Restoration," 171.

195   Thirteen captive pairs: Ibid., 173.

195   It was discontinued: Jones, "Mauritius Kestrel," S176.

195   In the United States, captive: USFWS, *Report to Congress on the Recovery of
      Threatened and Endangered Species Fiscal Years 2003–2004* (Washington,
      D.C.: USFWS, 2004).

195   It marked the first: Erik J. Tweed et al., "Breeding Biology and Success of
      a Reintroduced Population of the Critically Endangered Puaiohi
      (*Myadestes palmeri*)," *The Auk* 123, no. 3 (2006): 753–763.

196   Either way, the need: Michael Soulé et al., "The Millenium Ark: How
      Long a Voyage, How Many Staterooms, How Many Passengers?" *Zoo Biol-
      ogy* 5 (1986): 101–113.

197   Instead, he wrote: Andrew Balmford, Georgina M. Mace, and N. Leader-
      Williams, "Designing the Ark: Setting Priorities for Captive Breeding,"
      Conservation Biology 10, no. 3 (1996): 719–727.

197   "It is hard to imagine": Rahbek, "Captive Breeding," 433.

197   But compared with: N. Leader-Williams, "Black Rhinos and African Ele-
      phants: Lessons for Conservation Funding," *Oryx* 24, no. 1 (1990): 23–29.

198   The Chatham Island: Baillie, *2004 IUCN Red List*, 133.

198   Among its five remaining: Department of Conservation, "DOC's Work
      with the Black Robin." Online at www.doc.govt.nz.

199   "Even where nature reserves": William G. Conway, "The Practical
      Difficulties and Financial Implications of Endangered Species Breeding
      Programmes," *International Zoo Yearbook* 24/25 (1986): 210–219.

199   Recovery goals, starting: Alan Rabinowitz, "Helping a Species Go Extinct:
      The Sumatran Rhino in Borneo," *Conservation Biology* 9, no. 3 (1995):
      482–488.

200   Even habitat management: Ibid., 486.

200   "Emphasis in time": Ibid.

200   An examination of captive: Noel Snyder et al., "Limitations of Captive
      Breeding in Endangered Species Recovery," *Conservation Biology* 10, no. 2
      (1996): 338–348.

200   "Captive breeding can divert": Ibid., 344.

201   One study of Endangered: Timothy H. Tear et al., "Recovery Plans and
      the Endangered Species Act: Are Criticisms Supported by Data?" *Conser-
      vation Biology* 9 (1995): 182–195.

202   They did far worse: Lynn M. Woodworth et al., "Rapid Genetic Deterio-
      ration in Captive Populations: Causes and Conservation Implications,"
      Conservation Genetics 3 (2002): 277–288.

202   Even that was tempered: Ibid., 286.
203   The implication, the authors: M. Elsbeth McPhee, "Generations in Captivity Increases Behavioral Variance: Considerations for Captive Breeding and Reintroduction Programs," *Biological Conservation* 115 (2003): 71–77.
203   Officials finally recaptured: P. Banko et al., "Hawaiian Crow (*Corvus hawaiiensis*)," *The Birds of North America* (2002): 648.
203   The last two wild crows: BirdLife International, "*Corvus hawaiiensis*," *2006 IUCN Red List of Threatened Species* (2006).
203   The breeding has been: Jeffrey M. Black et al., "Survival, Movements, and Breeding of Released Hawaiian Geese: An Assessment of the Reintroduction Program," *Journal of Wildlife Management* 61, no. 4 (1997): 1161–1173.
203   It has kept the nene: Ibid., 1161.
204   As of 1997: P. Banko et al., "Hawaiian Goose (Nene) (*Branta sandvicensis*)," *The Birds of North America* (1999): 434.

CHAPTER 15
205   Clearing the forests: David E. Blockstein, "Passenger Pigeon (*Ectopistes migratorius*)," *Birds of North America* (2002): 611.
205   The unceasing harassment: Ibid.
206   The ferocity and single-mindedness: National Museum of Natural History, "The Passenger Pigeon," Smithsonian Institution.
206   An effort was made: Ibid.
206   From the once enormous: Ibid.
207   Congress outlawed hunting: The Brookings Institution, "Government's Greatest Achievements of the Past Half Century: Protect Endangered Species," The Brookings Institution (2000).
207   In 1967, then U.S. Secretary: The Associated Press, "78 Species Listed Near Extinction / Udall Issues Inventory with Appeal to Save Them," *The New York Times* (Mar. 12, 1967): 46.
207   In 1969, the act: Dale D. Goble, "Evolution of At-Risk Species Protection," *The Endangered Species Act at Thirty: Vol. 2: Conserving Biodiversity in Human-Dominated Landscapes* (Washington, D.C.: Island Press, 2006).
207   President Richard Nixon: Richard W. Pombo, "The ESA at 30: A Mandate for Modernization," report to the House Committee on Resources (2004).
207   Since that time, the landmark: Daniel J. Rohlf, "Six Biological Reasons Why the Endangered Species Act Doesn't Work—And What to Do About It," *Conservation Biology* 5 (1991): 273–282.
       David S. Wilcove, Margaret McMillan, and Keith C. Winston, "What Exactly Is an Endangered Species? An Analysis of the U.S. Endangered Species List: 1985–1991," *Conservation Biology* 7 (1993): 87–93.
       C.V. Wilcox and B. D. Eldered, "The Endangered Species Act Petitioning Process: Successes and Failures," *Society and Natural Resources* 16, no. 6 (2003) 551–559.
207   A 2006 estimate said: USFWS Threatened and Endangered Species System, "Delisted Species." Online at ecos.fws.gov.
       J. M. Scott et al., "By the Numbers," *The Endangered Species Act at Thirty: Vol. 1: Renewing the Conservation Promise* (Washington, D.C.: Island Press, 2005).

208   As of September 30, 2000: Ibid.
208   Included in that group: USFWS, "Revised Recovery Plan for Hawaiian Forest Birds: Region 1, Portland, Oregon (2006): 622.
209   The Center for Biological: Kieran Suckling, Rhiwena Slack, and Brian Nowicki, "Extinction and the Endangered Species Act," Center for Biological Diversity (2004): 2–10.
209   "These species were not": Ibid., 6.
209   After ten years of inaction: D. Noah Greenwald et al., "The Listing Record," *The Endangered Species Act at Thirty: Vol. 1: Renewing the Conservation Promise* (Washington, D.C.: Island Press, 2005).
209   From Udall's original: USFWS, "General Statistics for Endangered Species." Online at ecos.fws.gov.
209   In 1975, two years: Greenwald, "Listing Record."
210   In the 1970s, the FWS: Ibid.
       Holly Doremus, "Science and Controversy," *The Endangered Species Act at Thirty: Vol. 2: Conserving Biodiversity in Human-Dominated Landscapes* (Washington, D.C.: Island Press, 2006).
       J. M. Scott, D. Goble, and Frank W. Davis, "Introduction," *The Endangered Species Act at Thirty: Vol. 1: Renewing the Conservation Promise* (Washington, D.C.: Island Press, 2005).
210   "Congress has spoken": Greenwald, "Listing Record."
210   The amendments made the listing: Scott, "Introduction."
210   The lawmakers also began: Ibid.
210   It has also become: Tim W. Clark and Richard L. Wallance, "Keys to Effective Conservation," *The Endangered Species Act at Thirty: Vol. 1: Renewing the Conservation Promise* (Washington, D.C.: Island Press, 2005).
211   Republican president Ronald Reagan: Greenwald, "Listing Record."
211   Though some consider: Ibid.
211   In 1993, one startling: Timothy H. Tear et al., "Status and Prospects for Success of the Endangered Species Act: A Look at Recovery Plans," *Science* 262 (1993): 976–977.
211   The findings prompted: Ibid., 976.
211   In the 1990s, authors: Rohlf, "Biological Reasons," 275.
211   They also found shaky: T. Tear et al., "Recovery Plans and the Endangered Species Act: Are Criticisms Supported by Data?" *Conservation Biology* 9 (1995): 182–195.
211   More recent studies: J. Alan Clark et al., "Improving U.S. Endangered Species Act Recovery Plans: Key Findings and Recommendations of the SCB Recovery Plan Project," *Conservation Biology* 16 (2002): 1510–1519. U.S. General Accounting Office, "Fish and Wildlife Service Uses Best Available Science to Make Listing Decisions, but Additional Guidance Needed for Critical Habitat Designations," report to Congressional Requesters (2003): 3.
212   "By mandating that scientific": J. R. DeShazo and Jody Freeman, "Congressional Politics," *The Endangered Species Act at Thirty: Vol. 1: Renewing the Conservation Promise* (Washington, D.C.: Island Press, 2005).
212   "Our results are striking": Ibid.

213 "The best-case scenario": Ibid.

213 Spending decisions are more: Ibid.

213 "As it turns out": Ibid.

214 A 2005 survey: Union of Concerned Scientists, "U.S. Fish and Wildlife Service Survey Summary." Online at www.ucsusa.org.

214 "The costs of making decisions": Richard L. Wallace, "Social Influences on Conservation: Lessons from U.S. Recovery Programs for Marine Mammals," *Conservation Biology* 17 (2003): 104–115.

215 In 1983, the service: Marco Restani and John M. Marzluff, "Funding Extinction? Biological Needs and Political Realities in the Allocation of Resources to Endangered Species Recovery," *Bioscience* 52 (2002): 169–177.

215 A 2002 study looking: Ibid.

215 Funding also reflected: Ibid., 174.

216 "Expenditures often fail": Ibid., 172.

216 The results showed that: Julie K. Miller et al., "The Endangered Species Act: Dollars and Sense?" *Bioscience* 52, no. 2 (2002): 163–168.

217 Researchers examined the influence: Restani, "Funding Extinction?" 169–177.

217 In 2003, the Department: News release, May 28, 2003, "Endangered Species Act 'Broken'—Flood of Litigation Over Critical Habitat Hinders Species Conservation." Online at www.doi.gov.

217 In fiscal 2004: USFWS, "Federal and State Endangered and Threatened Species Expenditures, Fiscal Year 2004," USFWS 219 (2004): 7.

218 The Stellar sea lion: Ibid., 6.

218 Of these, the woodpecker: Ibid., 6.

218 The po'ouli that year: Ibid., 61.

218 A press release issued: News release, "Department of Land and Natural Resources 2007–2009 Biennium Budget Request," Hawaii DLNR. Online at www.hawaii.gov.

219 A 1998 survey by the International: Deborah Richie and Jennifer Holmes, *State Wildlife Diversity Program Funding: A 1998 Survey* (Washington, D.C: International Association of Fish and Wildlife Agencies, 1998).

220 A study published in 2006: Lawrence Niles and Kimberly Korth, "State Wildlife Diversity Programs," *The Endangered Species Act at Thirty: Vol. 1: Renewing the Conservation Promise* (Washington, D.C.: Island Press, 2005).

220 Ronald L. Walker: Walker, "Hawaiian Wildlife," 18.

221 The state sent the money: Ibid., 30.

221 The author said the amount: William W. M. Steiner, "Evaluating the Cost of Saving Native Hawaiian Birds," *Studies in Avian Biology 22* (Lawrence, KS: Allen Press, Inc., 2001).

221 State funding was inadequate: Ibid.

222 The law undoubtedly has: Steve L. Yaffee, "Collaborative Decision Making," *The Endangered Species Act at Thirty: Vol. 1: Renewing the Conservation Promise* (Washington, D.C.: Island Press, 2005).

222 Thirty years is barely: Doremus, "Lessons," 195.

222 "Most species do not": Ibid., 197.

CHAPTER 16

225 "This is to inform": A. Lieberman, e-mail to Beth Bicknese, Nov. 27, 2004.

225 The tissue samples arrived: Marlys Houk, e-mail to A. Lieberman, E. VanderWerf, Jay Nelson, M. Zablan, P. Conry, S. Fretz and G. Schultz, Nov. 28, 2004.

226 By shortly after noon: A. Lieberman, e-mail to po'ouli group, Nov. 12, 2004.

226 While Ryder's crew: Bruce Rideout, e-mail to A. Lieberman, Nov. 28, 2004.

227 In his November 30 report: B. Rideout, "Final Necropsy for Po'ouli," report, Nov. 30, 2004.

227 "Although most native Hawaiian": Ibid.

228 The examination also showed: Ibid.

228 Rideout reported that the body: Ibid.

228 In essence, the last po'ouli: Ibid.

228 What the aging process: Lieberman, "Captive Management."

230 "We are always sad": News release, Nov. 30, 2004, "Po'ouli Death Leaves Species Future Uncertain," USFWS, Hawaii DLNR, ZSSD.

230 "Our goal of saving": Ibid.

230 "Although we have not": Ibid.

231 They returned to the forest: Ibid.

231 By this time, the Home: K. Swinnerton, e-mail to A. Lieberman, Nov. 26, 2004.

231 The Home Range 3 bird: K. Swinnerton, e-mail to A. Lieberman, Oct. 1, 2004.

CHAPTER 17

236 This is largely because: W. P. Porter et al., "Po'ouli Landscape Bioinformatics Models Predict Energetics, Behavior, Diets, and Distribution on Maui," *Integrative and Comparative Biology* 46, no. 6 (2006): 1143–1158.

236 Researchers stopped the analysis: Ibid.

239 "The biggest gaps": Doremus, "Lessons," 205.

240 This corresponds with population: J. Groombridge et al., "Patterns of Spatial Use and Movement of the Po'ouli—A Critically Endangered Hawaiian Honeycreeper," *Biodiversity and Conservation* 15 (2006): 3357–3368.

240 Those methods helped recovery: E. VanderWerf et al., "Decision Analysis Guide to Recovery of the Po'ouli, a Critically Endangered Hawaiian Honeycreeper," *Biological Conservation* 129 (2006): 383–392.

240 The risk, however, rose: John J. Johnston et al., "Probabilistic Risk Assessment for Snails, Slugs, and Endangered Honeycreepers in Diphacinone Rodenticide Baited Areas on Hawaii, USA," *Environmental Toxicology and Chemistry* 24, no. 6 (2005): 1557–1567.

240 In areas with sensitive birds: Ibid., 1566.

241 Steiner quoted Thane Pratt: Steiner, "Cost of Saving," 379.

243 Researchers tested the birds': R. A. Feldman, L. A. Freed, and R. L. Cann, "A PCR Test for Avian Malaria in Hawaiian Birds," *Molecular Ecology* 4, no. 6 (1995): 663–668.

244   The same projection indicated: Tracy L. Benning et al., "Interactions of Climate Change with Biological Invasions and Land Use in the Hawaiian Islands: Modeling the Fate of Endemic Birds Using a Geographic Information System," *Proceedings of the National Academy of Sciences* 99, no. 22 (2002): 14246–14249.

244   A 2001–02 study: L. A. Freed et al., "Increase in Avian Malaria at Upper Elevation in Hawaii," *The Condor* 107 (2005): 753–764.

244   Despite prior studies: Caleb S. Spiegel et al., "Distribution and Abundance of Forest Birds in Low-altitude Habitat on Hawai'i Island: Evidence of Range Expansion of Native Species," *Bird Conservation International* 16 (2006): 175–185.
    Bethany L. Woodworth et al., "Host Population Persistence in the Face of Introduced Vector-Borne Diseases: Hawaii Amakihi and Avian Malaria," *Proceedings of the National Academy of Sciences* 102, no. 5 (2005): 1531–156.

244   Together, the two made: Spiegel, "Forest Birds," 175–185.

245   Further studies showed: A. Marm Kilpatrick, "Effects of Chronic Avian Malaria (*Plasmodium relictum*) Infection on Reproductive Success of Hawaii Amakihi (*Hemignathus virens*)," The Auk 123, no. 3 (2006): 764–774.

245   Other species of native: Freed, "Avian Malaria," 759.

245   According to the assessment's: Steiner, "Cost of Saving," 383.

245   Monogamous and with juveniles: Maui Parrotbill Working Group and Hawaiian Forest Bird Recovery Team, "Maui Parrotbill Five Year Recovery Work Plan." Online at www.dofaw.net.

246   Considered endangered by the U.S: Ibid.

247   The forest, Kahikinui: Ibid.

CHAPTER 18

252   "The reluctance to undertake": VanderWerf, "Analysis Guide," 291.

253   "In Hawaii, where conservation": William Burnham et al., "Hands-on Restoration," *The Endangered Species Act at Thirty: Vol. 1: Renewing the Conservation Promise* (Washington, D.C.: Island Press, 2005).

INDEX